Naturally
Ontario

Naturally Ontario

Exploring the Wealth *of* Ontario's **Wild** Places

Betty Zyvatkauskas

RANDOM HOUSE OF CANADA

Canadian Cataloguing in Publication Data

Zyvatkauskas, Betty
    Naturally Ontario: exploring the wealth of Ontario's wild places

Includes index.
ISBN 0-679-30921-7

1. Wilderness area — Ontario — Guidebooks. 2. Ontario — Guidebooks. I. Title.

FC3057.Z985 1999   917.1304'4   C97-932290-1
F1057.7.Z985 1999

Printed and bound in the United States of America

10 9 8 7 6 5 4 3 2 1

TABLE OF CONTENTS

Acknowledgments IX
Introduction 1

FINE FEATHERS

November Gull Gatherings at Niagara Falls 5
Catering to Hummingbirds at Landon Bay 9
Kayaking with Loons on a Kawartha Lake 13
White Pelicans at Lake of the Woods 17
Hawk Migrations at Port Stanley and Holiday Beach 21
Banding Warblers at Thunder Bay 25
Winter Birds at Lynde Shores and the Kortright Centre 29
Turkey Vultures at Crawford Lake 33
A Century Day at Point Pelee 36

FIELDS AND FLOWERS

Finding Fungi on a Mycological Foray 41
Spring Ephemerals in Toronto 45
Tall Grass Prairie at Ojibway Park 50
Orchids of Bruce Peninsula National Park 55
Insect-Eating Plants in Ontario's Wetlands 58

AT THE BEACH

Sand Dunes and Snappers in Prince Edward County 63
A Rare Savannah at Pinery Provincial Park 67
Spring Migrations at Long Point 70
Waterfowl Weekend at Presqu'ile 73

NIGHT PROWLERS

Howling at Wolves in Algonquin 79
Prowling for Owls in Guelph 82
Little Brown Bats at the Bonnechere Caves 86
Listening to Spring Peepers at the Kortright Centre 90

ROCKY REMINDERS

Finding Trilobites at Craigleith, Georgian Bay 95
Rock Hounding Near Bancroft 97
Stories in Stone at Petroglyphs Provincial Park 101
Discovering Devonian Fossils at Rock Glen and Rock Point 104
Exploring the Drumlins of Peterborough County 108
Hiking the Niagara Escarpment 111

SMALL BUT SIGNIFICANT

Blackflies and Blueberries on the Canadian Shield 117
Lichens Colour the Landscape 120
The Five-Lined Skink, Ontario's Only Lizard 123
Migrating Monarchs at Presqu'ile 126
Seeking Salamanders in the Dundas Valley 129

ON THE WATERFRONT

Smallmouth Bass in Baptiste Lake   135

Frogs, Fowl and Dragonflies at Conroy's Marsh   138

Island Hopping at St. Lawrence Islands National Park   141

Exploring the Grand River   146

Return of the Swans to Wye Marsh   149

URBAN WILDERNESS

Rambling Through Toronto's Rouge Valley   155

Back to Nature in Toronto's Don Valley   158

Coyotes on the Toronto Waterfront   162

Return to Paradise in Hamilton   165

Second Marsh and McLaughlin Bay in Oshawa   168

Feeding Chipmunks in Toronto's Edward's Gardens   172

MAJOR MAMMALS

Looking for Moose in Algonquin Park   177

Watching White-Tailed Deer in Ontario's Deer Yards   181

Spring Porcupine Sightings   185

Black Bears and the Aspen Valley Wildlife Sanctuary   188

A Beaver Changes the Algonquin Landscape   193

Watching Wildlife at Sleeping Giant Park   196

Observing Wolves in Haliburton Forest   200

GREAT FORESTS

The Old-Growth Forests of Temagami and Shaw Woods　207

Backus Woods, A Carolinian Forest　212

At the Edge of the Boreal Forest in Mississagi Provincial Park　215

Autumn Colours at Silent Lake　218

Discovering Niagara's Hidden Glen　222

Exploring the Oak Ridges Moraine in Durham Forest　225

REMOTE ADVENTURES

Taking the Train to James Bay　231

Rossport and Slate Islands in Lake Superior　236

First Nations Culture at Camp Jeegibik and Golden Lake　239

The Boreal Forest of Wabikimi　243

Ontario's Long-Distance Hiking Trails　249

Nature Watcher's Calendar　253

Resources　256

Bibliography and Recommended Reading　260

Index　266

ACKNOWLEDGMENTS

The research and design of this book was made possible with generous assistance and advice from many agencies, including the Ministry of Natural Resources, Ontario Tourism, Parks Ontario and The Conservation Lands of Ontario. Casts of animal tracks were provided by the Royal Ontario Museum. The photograph of the tree on the front cover is from the collection of The Toronto and Region Conservation Authority.

I am grateful to Alan Foster at The Toronto Region Conservation Authority for sharing his knowledge and enthusiasm on a wide range of subjects. Special thanks to Sonia Zyvatkauskas for her research.

INTRODUCTION

Fascination with our natural world comes easily to young children. Whether watching the iridescent slime trail of a garden slug or catching tadpoles in a stream, they are deeply, intensely involved. Those adults who can maintain that relationship with nature, despite the pressures of urban life, the cynicism of postmodern times and easy comforts of industrialization, are keeping alive a creative, joyful part of themselves. The urge to be in nature is primal. Nature puts our human strivings in perspective and soothes the frustrations of modern living.

This book comes from a place that is not necessarily scientific in its observations of nature. Although scientific knowledge often enhances our appreciation of the natural world, it is meaningless unless we have an eye for its beauty, a sense of awe for its grandeur and a sense of wonder at its meticulous details. These essays have grown out of my enjoyment and observations of the wildlife and wild places I have encountered on my travels around Ontario.

Whether birding, rock-hounding or looking for wildflowers, observing one facet of nature tends to lead to another. Walking through a grassland in search of wild indigo, you can't help noticing the vast array of butterflies and other insects that feed on the flowers. Search for Devonian fossils at a southern Ontario conservation area and you will start to notice the Carolinian forest. To make the most of any experience outdoors, it is essential to live in the moment, to appreciate the whole of your surroundings and to value each discovery, whether it be a moose or a dragonfly.

Ontario is a vast province encompassing five forest zones, from the lush Carolinian forest of Point Pelee to the tundra of the Hudson Bay lowlands. In this province you can find both prickly pear cactus and polar bears, prairie pelicans and Atlantic gulls. The diversity begs exploration. Rather than attempting to chronicle and catalogue the vast array of wildlife in the province, as has already been so aptly done in several fine reference works and field guides, I have endeavoured to share my personal discoveries, my favourite places and most fascinating finds. What follows is both a personal observation and a user-friendly guide to finding and enjoying Ontario's natural beauty.

Wildlife is not always predictable. Seasonal fluctuations, changes in weather patterns and time of day are among the factors that come into play. A few basic guidelines will improve your viewing success and help protect the wildlife you are watching:

- Wildlife tends to be most active at dusk and dawn. The early birder gets the sighting.
- Stay on paths, boardwalks or viewing towers to avoid habitat destruction.
- Don't stress wildlife. Avoid nesting areas. Refrain from excessive use of taped bird and animal calls. Don't feed animals.
- Equip yourself with practical gear including sturdy footwear, lightweight binoculars and a well-illustrated field guide.

Some cautions should be noted. This book includes recipes that use wild plants. I have tested them all, but just as allergic reactions may be brought on by a host of ordinary foods, they might also be brought on by something new. Never assume that seeing a bird or animal eating a wild plant proves that it is safe for you to consume. Many creatures are specially adapted to feed on plants that are toxic to others. One further caveat: programs, prices and schedules do change, so if you plan to visit any of the places mentioned in this book, be sure to telephone in advance.

FINE FEATHERS

November Gull Gatherings at Niagara Falls

November ought to be a quiet month for Niagara Falls, with the tour boats drydocked for the winter, the gardens faded in the frost and brooding, grey skies driving tourists away. But November also brings a grand spectacle to the Niagara River: tens of thousands of gulls circling above the spume, squawking multitudinous complaints.

It's not just the sheer quantity of gulls that makes this spectacle so fascinating, but their diversity—as many as thirteen different species from across the continent gather at Niagara, a greater variety than is found anywhere else in the world. Four species nest on the Great Lakes: herring, ring-billed, great black-backed and little gulls. Others come from much greater distances. Bonaparte's gulls fly south from the boreal forests where they nest in the shaggy spruces of the northwoods. Franklin's gulls travel east from their summering grounds in the prairie sloughs. The black-legged kittiwake arrives from the opposite direction, the rocky shores of the North Atlantic.

Some of these birds are only passing through and will winter on the Gulf of Mexico or the Atlantic. A few are simply confused, having drifted from their migratory course. But several will spend the winter here, finding ample food in Niagara's open waters.

Though commonly used, the term "seagull" is not a scientifically accurate moniker. Many gulls frequent fresh waters as well as salty seas, so the correct term, which encompasses all species of this waterfowl, is simply "gull."

Gull watchers have speculated that gulls gather at this central point in the continent because the rushing waters of the Niagara River remain open year-round, providing ready access to fish. Anyone who has watched urban ring-billed gulls pluck scraps out of garbage cans in public parks knows what scavengers these gulls can be. Chances are they are drawn to the numerous fish killed both by the falls and the massive hydroelectric generating stations on both sides of the river.

BONAPARTE'S GULL
The small, elegant gull with its distinctive black head was named after ornithologist Charles Lucien Jules Laurent Bonaparte, nephew of the French emperor, Napoleon. A distinguished zoologist, he taught at the Academy of Natural Sciences in Philadelphia in the 1820s.

The variety of foods on gull menus is often astonishing. While the black-headed gull is often sighted walking on the ground in search of earthworms, insects and trash, the little gull flies just above the water's surface looking for small fish. Besides eating fish and mussels, herring gulls will gorge on garbage, rodents and even baby birds. Great black-backed gulls are ferocious feeders known to snatch a tern or similar small seabird during an airborne attack and break its neck with a vigorous shake. Fish seems to be the food they all have in common.

First-time gull watchers may find it difficult to discern the differences between species, but there are a few simple identification tips. Ring-bills, the urban gulls with attitude, can be identified by the black ring adults have at the tip of their beak. Most of the black-hooded gulls tend to be Bonaparte's gulls. The large, grey-backed herring gulls have pinkish legs and a pink spot near the tip of their beaks. Gulls with brown feathers are generally the immature of various species. Some, such as the great black-backed and the glaucous, do not grow their adult plumage until they are four years old.

On a good November day hordes of birders stake out spots near the falls where they set up their tripods and telescopes. Most welcome a chance to chat about their finds. But even if you never become accomplished at sorting out the species, the sight of thousands of white gulls flying over this powerful, grey river is stirring.

In *Winter Studies in Canada* Anna Brownell Jameson gives an amusing account of her first visit to Niagara Falls in the 1830s. As she was contemplating her view of the cataract from the balcony of the Clifton Hill Hotel, she was approached by "a little Yankee boy" who noticed her fascination with the birds "hovering and sporting amid the spray."

> "Now, do you know what them 'ere birds are, out yonder?"
> "Those birds?" said I. "Why, what are they?"
> "Why, them's EAGLES!"
> "Eagles?" It was impossible to help laughing.
> "Yes," said the urchin sturdily; "and I guess you have none of them in the old country?"
> "Not many eagles, my boy; but plenty of gulls!" and I gave him a pretty considerable pinch by the ear.
> "Ay!" said he, laughing; "well now, you be dreadful smart—smarter than many folks that come here!"

First-Hand Experience

One of the most popular spots for gull watching is the Niagara Parkway, directly above the Niagara Falls. To reach the parkway, take the Highway 55 exit from the Queen Elizabeth Way, and follow it into Niagara-on-the-Lake. From there you can drive (or bike along paved trails) south on the parkway, through Niagara Falls and all the way to Fort Erie, stopping for great riverside views—and even some winery samplings—along the way. Gulls typically begin to congregate here late in October and may stay into early December.

If you are going birding, once you have a good guidebook your second purchase is usually a pair of binoculars. Choose a magnification power of 7 to 10. The 7 shows a wider area. The 10 has a bigger image, but holding the focus can be a problem. Look for a lens diameter that is roughly four times larger than the magnifying power (e.g., 10x40). Binoculars should be light enough to carry all afternoon.

In November there is usually ample parking at Table Rock and at the Niagara Parks Greenhouse. When you get too cold to watch the gulls, try moving indoors to the Niagara Parks Butterfly Conservatory, just south of Queenston. Thousands of butterflies fly freely among the gardens and waterfalls in this lush and humid greenhouse. Wear a brightly coloured shirt, and the butterflies will be tempted to land on you. The Butterfly Conservatory is open daily year round (except Christmas Day). Admission is $7 for adults, $3.50 for children, and children under five are admitted free. Timed ticket reservations are suggested for peak summer months. For more information and reservations call (905) 358-0025.

For more information on Niagara Falls attractions contact the Niagara Parks Commission at (905) 356-2241 or the Niagara Falls Canada Visitor and Convention Bureau at (905) 356-6061.

A good field guide is indispensable and greatly increases your enjoyment. One of the most popular is *A Field Guide to the Birds* by Roger Tory Peterson. I also like the *Stokes Field Guide to Birds* for its interesting descriptions of bird behaviours and its great colour photographs.

Catering to Hummingbirds at Landon Bay

With the buzz of its wings, surprising dives and irides-cent colours, the ruby-throated hummingbird com-mands attention. Hummers display their flying finesse across the southern half of Ontario, from Cornwall to Kenora. Little birds with lots of aggression, hummers will defend a favourite food source with the mid-air manoeuvres of a fighter plane, diving suddenly towards an offending intruder. They seldom shy away from larger rivals and will even swoop past a man's head to warn him away from a feeder. With their super-speedy metabo-lisms—a hummingbird's heart beats 1,260 times a minute—they constantly search for high-energy food, especially sweet nectar.

At Landon Bay, east of Gananoque, wildlife biologist and gardener David Vincent leads guided walks through The Gardens, a 71-hectare park known for its diverse wildlife and the community gardens planted by service groups and dedicated individuals. Sandy Zulak's Hum-mingbird Garden contains ten different shrubs that bloom in sequence to provide hummers with an ongo-ing source of food throughout the summer. Potentilla, beauty bush, rose of Sharon, honeysuckle and spirea each take their turn offering food and shelter. Forsythia proves particularly valuable to birds and insects because

During a 5-metre dive a male hummingbird's wings beat up to two hundred times a sec-ond.

it blooms early in the spring when little nectar is available. Hummers extend their tongues to lick up a flower's sweet liquid at thirteen licks a second.

"Hummingbirds will also 'hawk' insects," explains David. "Particularly during spring when they are raising young and need the extra protein. Hummers will sit in a shrub patiently watching for insects, then dart out when the bugs are spotted."

Fruit flies are a particular favourite with hummers, so David has designed a low-maintenance fruit-fly farm to attract them. An old glass jar contains rotting fruit in which fruit flies lay their eggs. Small holes in the jar's lid allow the newly hatched flies to escape into the hummingbird garden. David also provides the birds with sections of soft oranges mounted on a post. These juicy tidbits also prove effective in luring orioles.

Of the sixteen species of hummingbirds that breed in North America, only the ruby-throated is found in Ontario. It's a mere 9.5 centimetres long, with a green head and back, white undersides and, if male, the distinctive red patch under its beak.

These tiny creatures make incredibly long journeys between their Ontario nesting sites and their wintering grounds in Central America and Mexico. They return to Ontario early each spring, often weeks before any nectar-producing flowers are in bloom. Faced with a flowerless landscape, they feed instead on the sap oozing from trees drilled by yellow-bellied sapsuckers. Small insects stuck in the sap provide extra protein.

The female steals silk from spider webs to bind her nest, which is covered with lichens or bud scales on the outside. Inside it is lined with the soft down of pussy willows to protect her two white eggs, each less than 1 centimetre long. The tiny young hatch within sixteen days, although cool weather and a shortage of food may delay

HOMEMADE
HUMMER FOOD
A solution of four parts water to one part sugar, boiled until the sugar dissolves, is a good substitute for nectar. Food colouring is not necessary and may even be harmful. Hummers will be attracted to the bright red and yellow plastic parts of the feeding container.

hatching for an additional two weeks. The babies emerge from their shells completely featherless, so the downy pussy-willow lining plays a major role in keeping them warm.

Hummingbirds are most commonly sighted when feeding at flowers. While it has often been held that they choose only red tubular flowers, they will, in fact, try many different nectar-producing blooms. Flowers that are known to attract hummingbirds are bee balm, purple bergamot, cardinal flower, wild columbine, fireweed, Canada lily, Indian paintbrush, smooth phlox and trumpet honeysuckle. I have watched them hovering over honeysuckle in a Toronto backyard, darting between wild columbines in cottage country and enjoying nectar from the orange blooms of spotted jewelweed on Manitoulin Island. I've even seen one confused hummer probing the red circular base of a thermometer.

To keep pesky wasps away from humming-bird feeders, dab a little vegetable oil around the opening. This makes the plastic surface too slippery for the wasps to land on. Hummers, however, don't need to perch to feed.

First-Hand Experience

The Gardens at Landon Bay are located 8 kilometres east of Gananoque on the Thousand Islands Parkway. Guided walks along The Gardens' 3 kilometres of wood-chip trails cost $4 and provide an extraordinary insight into nature-friendly gardening techniques. Osprey nest on a platform in the swamp, snapping turtles nest on the lawns, and even the rare black rat snake (Ontario's longest) is sometimes sighted along the Woodland Trail, which leads to a clifftop view of the Thousand Islands. For information call (613) 382-5048 or (613) 382-2719. Family camping is available.

During September passages of migrating humming-birds have been observed at Holiday Beach Conservation Area in Essex County, 10 kilometres southeast of

Amherstburg (see page 24). As many as two hundred ruby-throated hummingbirds have been seen on a single September day. Call the Essex Region Conservation Authority at (519) 736-3772 or (519) 776-5209.

If you plan to buy a hummingbird feeder, choose something that's easy to clean, since frequent cleaning prevents the growth of mould and dangerous bacteria. You should be prepared to change the food daily during hot summer weather. A simple glass-bottle style feeder with coloured plastic openings through which the bird can sip works well.

Kayaking with Loons on a Kawartha Lake

The quintessential sound of a northern summer—the eerie wail of a loon on a misty lake—strikes a primal chord in all of us.

Within a few days of the ice breaking on a Canadian Shield lake, the loons return to their favourite bays. They are among the earliest of spring's migrants, hurrying northward to secure the best waters, calling to establish their territories or to summon a mate.

Paddling a sleek and silent sea kayak is one of the best ways to observe loons and other waterfowl without disturbing them. At Kawartha Kayaking on Stony Lake, Wil Tranter guides small groups of novices past some of the lake's eleven hundred islands. You might see a mother loon with babies nestled on her back, a great blue heron fishing along the shore or an osprey soaring overhead. Kayaks are easily manoeuvred through the narrowest of channels overhung with vegetation or through the shallow waters of the weedy bays preferred by nesting loons.

Space is all important to loons since a single pair requires in excess of 360 kilograms of food in one six-month season to feed themselves and raise a single chick. A pair of breeding loons normally requires an entire lake or, at the very least, a substantial bay on a large lake.

To build its nest, the loon shapes a low mound of dead vegetation on a sheltered shore, never more than a metre from the water, so it can easily flop out of its

Maximum flight speed for a migrating loon is estimated to be 100 kilometres per hour.

nest directly into the lake. Loons have great difficulty manoeuvring on land. With legs placed far back on their body, balance is difficult. They only manage to hobble around by using their wings for support, as though they were leaning on crutches.

In the water they come into their own and can out-manoeuvre most fish. By rolling their weight and tucking their tails, they can pivot in a way that enables them to catch zigzag swimmers like perch. Because they can stay underwater for as long as three minutes at a time, they can easily chase down the swift bass.

The common loon is a hefty duck that weighs as much as 7 kilograms. Perhaps as an adaptation to diving, the loon's bones are solid, instead of hollow like most birds. The added weight means loons need a long runway and much thrashing and flapping for takeoff, but once they make it into the air they fly with great strength, which they need for their migration to Atlantic shores.

Attentive parents, loons spend nearly a month incubating their clutch of two eggs. Once the young hatch, they are soon in the water. A sight dear to all cottagers and campers is a downy black loonling riding on the back of a parent to stay warm and safe from snapping turtles, pike and other predators.

Later in the summer the loon parents show their social side, joining young adults for ritualized loon "dances" in which several birds gather on a large lake, flapping and calling to one another.

The common loon can be found on most Canadian Shield lakes from ice-out to freeze-up. In Algonquin Park they have been known to arrive as early as April 10 and stay as late as December 15, although a November departure is more the norm.

When Elizabeth Simcoe, wife of Upper Canada's first governor, first heard a loon call she likened it to "a

> One of the biggest threats to Ontario's loons comes from anglers who are inadvertently poisoning the birds. According to Environment Canada, roughly 500 tonnes of lead sinkers and jigs are lost annually in Canadian waters. Just one sinker the size of a pea is enough to poison a bird.

man hollowing in a tone of distress." Others have described it as "the wail of the wilderness." The calls vary according to their purpose. The long loon wails so often heard during the stillness of the early morning and evening are the sounds of a pair staying in touch with each other. Undulating calls, sometimes referred to as yodelling, are the loon's way of advertising its territory. The birds are generally silent during winter months when they migrate south. Their distinctive checkered markings become a grey blur in the winter, and even the loon's haunting red eyes turn grey.

Besides the common loon, easily identified by its white speckles against iridescent black and its red eyes, Ontario is home to two smaller species, the red-throated loon and the arctic loon, both of which nest in the far north near Hudson Bay.

First-Hand Experience

Kawartha Kayaking is based on Stony Lake, near Lakefield, and is open from mid-June to mid-September. In Toronto call (416) 229-0494. During summer months call (705) 877-2735. Day trips cost roughly $75 to $90, depending on the day of the week. Guests start their adventure with a lesson on basic paddling strokes while exploring the shoreline. Later they have time for a swim and barbecue lunch.

Loons can be found in most of the provincial parks along the Canadian Shield, from Frontenac (north of Kingston) in the east to the remote Quetico, west of Thunder Bay. To get a free copy of *Nearby and Natural*, the guide to Ontario's provincial parks published by Ontario Parks, call 1-800-ONTARIO.

You don't have to go north to see loons during
spring migration. From late March through April, birdwatchers along the Great Lakes may see them touching
down near the shore in various places. Try Long Point
(Lake Erie) or the Scarborough Bluffs (Lake Ontario).

White Pelicans at Lake of the Woods

It is a view reminiscent of the Gulf of Mexico: white sandy beaches, impossibly blue waters and white pelicans soaring above. But this is a scene from the far western corner of Ontario, on the sprawling shores of Lake of the Woods, near Kenora.

American white pelicans are prairie birds that were first noticed in Ontario in the late 1930s when eight pairs started nesting on Dream Island in Lake of the Woods, making them the easternmost colony in North America. Since then the colony has prospered, and today thousands of white pelicans inhabit the area in and around Lake of the Woods, where they breed in protected sanctuaries on the offshore islands.

Often cast as comical creatures, with their big bills and fish-toting pouches, pelicans are among the most spectacular birds in the sky, putting on lively displays of diving and soaring over their breeding grounds. These huge birds have a wingspan greater than a bald eagle's and are adept at flying in formation, a skill that proves particularly useful in co-operative fishing. A group of pelicans will alight on the water in a line or half-circle, then drive the fish into shallow waters where they scoop them up in their long, orange beaks and swallow them immediately.

Pelicans use the gular pouches on the lower parts of their beaks to collect regurgitated fish to feed their

White pelicans are among the largest birds on the North American continent, measuring 155 centimetres from the tip of the beak to the end of the tail. By comparison, a bald eagle measures 75 to 108 centimetres. The pelican's wingspan is at least 30 centimetres wider than the bald eagle's.

young. During the Middle Ages this process of regurgi-
tation was interpreted as the pelican feeding its lifeblood
to its children, making the bird a symbol of Christ.

Other prairie birds, including the yellow-headed
blackbird and the western meadowlark, can be found in
Ojibway Heritage Park on Lake of the Woods, along with
southern species such as scarlet tanagers and Baltimore
orioles. Situated near the borders of Ontario, Manitoba
and Minnesota, this is an area where northern, southern
and prairie environments converge. Here you will find
evergreens typical of northern boreal forests (spruce,
Jack pine) growing near deciduous trees more often
found in Southern Ontario's Carolinian forests (ash,
basswood). This is the only corner of Ontario where you
might see western animals like Franklin's ground squirrel and the white-tailed jackrabbit. The southern ambi-
ence is enhanced by sandy beaches and warm shallow
bays favoured by sunbathers and swimmers.

Park manager Jason White offers this tip for finding
pelicans, "They are pretty smart birds ... pelicans are
hip to a free meal and will follow a fishing boat. See if
you can find a fisherman, or find out when the commercial fishing boats will be leaving from Big Grassy
Reserve. The birds will follow the fishing boat."

First-Hand Experience

Pelicans can be observed in and around Lake of the
Woods, from Rainy River in the south to Kenora in the
north. During the spring they are often sighted along
the Rainy River and in the town of Fort Frances on
Rainy Lake, where they feed at the rapids. They nest on
the Three Sisters Islands, north of Rainy River and
accessible only by boat.

Lake of the Woods is vast, shallow and often rough. Experienced boaters should be equipped with a good set of charts. Local guides can be hired. Al Meline of Nestor Falls will take birdwatchers on a six- to eight-hour boat trip to see the pelicans roosting on bald rocky islands, as well as cormorants, loons, Arctic terns and assorted gulls. The day trip costs $200 per person, with a minimum of three people. Call (807) 484-2483 or toll-free 1-800-561-3166. Meline is also a fishing guide, and pelicans often visit his landing for scraps after fish cleaning. His Web site is: www.presence.mb.ca/melines.

Scott Hamilton of Jack-Fish Hammy's Guide Service is based in Fort Frances. He specializes in the Rainy Lake area, known for its pelicans, bald eagles, osprey and peregrine falcons. He charges $275 for a full day of sightseeing for two people and $75 per person for a half day. For information call (807) 274-2503.

Bobby Harrington of Bobby's Guide Service in Kenora offers boat tours to see pelicans and other wildlife for $30 per hour for two people. Her specialty is a three-hour tour with a stop on one of the islands for a lavish fish-fry lunch at $140 for two people. For more information call (807) 468-FISH.

For tourist information on the Kenora area, including boat rentals, accommodation and guide services, call the Sunset Country Travel Association at 1-800-665-7567.

Formerly known as Lake of the Woods Provincial Park, Ojibway Heritage Park is undergoing a transition and is scheduled to be operated by the Big Grassy First Nation in 1999. The park offers nearly one hundred campsites at two campgrounds as well as excellent day-use facilities including a sandy beach. From the park's shoreline you may see pelicans, gulls and large flocks of cormorants. The park is located on Highway 621, roughly 40 kilometres north of Highway 11. A cultural heritage program is being planned that will include guided powerboat tours to ancient rock-painting sites, traditional crafts, powwows and an Ojibway village where visitors can spend the night in a teepee. For more information contact the park at (807) 488-5531, or the Big Grassy First Nation at 1-888-309-8883 or (807) 488-1046.

Hawk Migrations at Port Stanley and Holiday Beach

Broad-winged hawks soar on the thermals, cruising in a long southward migration. Reluctant to cross the water, they linger high above the shoreline, their numbers swelling with new arrivals. Although there are many places where hawks can be observed on their autumn migration, Hawk Cliff on the north shore of Lake Erie is definitely one of the best. On the right sort of September day, hawks are here in the thousands. Mid-September usually brings the right conditions: a high-pressure system from the north, bright blue skies and fluffy cumulus clouds after a period of rain.

As birdwatching goes, this is pretty easy. You just step out of your car on a sunny autumn afternoon at a grassy spot atop the 40-metre-high cliffs of clay and sand. Here the shoreline arcs, and thermal winds formed by sun-warmed air make for easy gliding.

Broad-winged hawks belong to a family known as the buteos, characterized by their thickset appearance and rounded tails. Most feed on rodents, rabbits, reptiles and grasshoppers. Some biologists believe that during migration the broad-winged hawks either fast or eat only at a limited number of places—a remarkable feat, since they travel all the way to Central and South America. In September the days are still warm enough

Falconers have long trained raptors such as peregrines to hunt for smaller birds. Today professional birdkeepers use raptors in education and agriculture. Hawks stationed in a berry field scare away hordes of blackbirds and sparrows that may severely damage the ripening crop. In August, raptors from the Golden Creek Bird Farm and School of Falcons are sometimes stationed in the blueberry fields of Wilmot Orchards north of Bowmanville.

and the thermal winds are strong enough that the birds can do a lot of coasting.

By mid-morning, when the sun-warmed thermals have developed a good upward push, the broad-winged hawks can often be seen arriving in "kettles," or small groups. As the day wears on, their numbers increase until hundreds or thousands of hawks circle in the sky. They watch their fellow migrants to find the next thermal and continue coasting toward their winter destination.

You can recognize broad-winged hawks by their chunky look and the evenly spaced bands of black and white on the underside of their tails. Although their vast numbers make their migration one of the most dramatic spectacles, many other interesting migrants pass over the cliff. It is possible to see kestrels and sharp-shinned hawks throughout September. Peregrines appear slightly later in the month. October typically brings red-shouldered hawks, goshawks and rough-legged hawks. A few red-tailed hawks may even stay the winter, wandering no further south than Pennsylvania in search of prey.

Because Hawk Cliff sees such vast numbers of raptors, it has become the annual site of a bird-banding project that enables researchers to monitor the birds' numbers and migration patterns. Visitors are welcome during the second and third weekends in September, when they can chat with knowledgeable birders such as professional naturalist Bruce Duncan. After two decades of bird banding at Hawk Cliff, he has observed changing numbers in various species. Sharp-shinned hawks and kestrels both seem to be declining in numbers. On the other hand, he has observed an increase of golden eagles, bald eagles, peregrines and osprey, probably as a result of banning DDT.

As the hawks follow the thermals in search of the shortest crossing over Lake Erie, they are funnelled westward until they reach the Detroit River, which offers a much shorter crossing. Many of these birds find their way to Holiday Beach Conservation Area, one of the prime fall birding sites in North America. Situated on Lake Erie near Amherstburg, east of the Detroit River, Holiday Beach sees more than one hundred thousand raptors a season. As many as sixty-five thousand broad-winged hawks have passed through here on a single day. A 10-metre tower overlooking Big Creek Marsh is a favourite spot for birders to set up their telescopes. In addition to the hawks, large numbers of ruby-throated hummingbirds, blue jays and American goldfinches pass through on their fall migrations. Other winged migrants here include bats and dragonflies. The 221-hectare park offers many opportunities for family fun in a natural setting, including half a kilometre of sandy beach, a stocked trout pond and barbecues where you can cook your catch.

Falcons swoop down on their prey at speeds in excess of 200 kilometres an hour.

First-Hand Experience

Hawk Cliff is located east of Port Stanley, directly south of St. Thomas. From Highway 401 take Highway 4 south to Port Stanley. Turn east (left) on Lake Road to the cliff. Birdwatchers may use the municipal road allowance for their observations, but the property on both sides of the road is private. For information call Kettle Creek Conservation Authority at (519) 631-1270. Bring a lawn chair, picnic and binoculars—you should be prepared to spend some time waiting and watching. There are no visitor facilities at Hawk Cliff, but the town of Port Stanley is a delightful fishing port popular with tourists. The Kettle Creek Inn serves fresh local perch.

Holiday Beach Conservation Area is located on Lake Erie, between Amherstburg and Harrow, on Essex County Road 50. It offers overnight camping, picnic shelters, a nature trail and a public beach. The annual Hawk Festival, which has informative birdwatching events, usually begins the first weekend after Labour Day and continues into October. For updates during September and October you can call the Essex Region Conservation Authority Hawk Watch Hotline at (519) 736-3772 or the Windsor, Essex County and Pelee Island Convention and Visitors Bureau at 1-800-265-3633 or (519) 255-6530.

At Golden Creek Bird Farm near Muskoka's Sparrow Lake, staff raise and train raptors used in bird control at airports, marinas and farms. The hawks frighten smaller birds away, preventing them from being sucked into jet engines or eating fruit. On the farm tour visitors see bald eagles, golden eagles, peregrines, gyrfalcons, prairie falcons, red-tailed hawks and Harris hawks, as well as many others. Falconry demonstrations are held twice a day on summer weekends. Courses in falconry are also taught here. Golden Creek Bird Farm is located on South Sparrow Lake Road (Concession 12), north of Orillia, via Highway 11. Telephone (705) 689-9121 or (705) 689-9550. To learn when the hawks will be at Wilmot Orchards call (905) 987-5279.

Banding Warblers at Thunder Bay

The early morning dew glistens on the leaves as our team of dedicated bird lovers trudges through the bush on our fifth round past the mist nets. High atop the dramatic, flat-topped mesa hills north of Thunder Bay the air is crisp and abuzz with insects. A raptor circles high overhead, but our party of biologists and amateur birdwatchers is more concerned with the bird in hand.

We carefully pluck a chestnut-sided warbler from the invisible pockets of the fine mist net, then gently place it in a cloth bag. Walking quickly to minimize the time the bird is held, we carry it back to the temporary work station that has been set up on the trunk of a car and record its species and measurements. We band it and release it within minutes.

Teams of independent biologists are studying the effects of forest cutting on the songbird population and submitting their results to the Canadian Wildlife Federation. Through Blue Loon Adventures of Thunder Bay, amateur birdwatchers may join one of these studies at the Fallingsnow Ecosystem Project. Biologist John Woodcock welcomes Blue Loon's ecotourists to join him as he treks through the thick tangle of aspen, honeysuckle and wild rose that grow up in the decade following a cut, removing birds that lie caught in the nets. It is a rare opportunity for birdwatchers to actually handle the creatures they normally view only through

Delicate hummingbird legs present a problem for bird banders. One resourceful researcher improvised tiny bands from individual links of a gold chain.

binoculars. Sometimes the results are surprising. Following John's instructions I held a white-throated sparrow that was ready for release.

"Hold it in your palm, so that it is lying on its back, then gently open your fingers."

To my horror, the sparrow did not move. I thought it was dead.

"Don't worry," said John. "It's just found itself in a position it has never been in before. Birds always stay on their feet, so when you hold it like that, it doesn't know how to react."

Once gently turned back on its feet, the sparrow flew off.

Many of the morning's finds are warblers. These brightly coloured birds, the jewels of the north woods, can both delight and frustrate birdwatchers who seek to add these lovely creatures to their lists. Their confusing array of colours and markings that change with season and age make identification difficult.

Smaller than sparrows, wood warblers are exclusive to the New World and most abundant in the mixed woods of the northeastern part of the continent. Most winter in warmer climes, as evidenced by their names—palm, Tennessee, magnolia. In Ontario they first appear late in the spring on their northern migration, passing through Point Pelee and other spots along the Great Lakes. But it is when they reach the north, where the mixed forests give way to the boreal, that the northern-breeding warblers come into their own. These birds save their songs for their nesting habitat, and each species has its own special niche.

The magnolia warbler favours spruce, while the Blackburnian warbler forages and nests in hemlock groves. Cape May warblers thrive during spruce budworm outbreaks, which provide them with ample food.

The chestnut-sided warbler prefers the dense shrubbery of young aspen and willow that often results from
clear-cutting forests. Lumbering in Algonquin Park has
made the chestnut-sided the most prolific warbler in the
park, although the bird was considered rare in the time
of the great ornithologist John James Audubon in the
early nineteenth century.

The results of songbird population studies show
that warblers can often benefit from the diversity of
habitat resulting from properly managed cutting. Like
moose, they seem to have found a way of thriving in
some of humankind's most invasive and potentially
destructive activities, which is not to say that they are
not vulnerable to man's incursions. In his great survey
of American birds Audubon painted two warblers that
have never been seen again, possibly as a result of the
same activity that created such a favourable habitat for
the chestnut-sided.

In spring the chestnut-sided warbler sings up to four thousand times a day to attract a mate.

First-Hand Experience

Blue Loon's birding adventures vary in length from a
morning to nearly a week. Clients can opt to stay in
town or at the Blue Loon Research Station and tent
base camp adjacent the bird-banding site. All accommodations and food are provided. Activities vary depending on the interests of the guests, but typically
include a day each of small mammal studies and bird
banding at the research site, a wetland canoe tour and
hikes to explore the local flora, fauna and geology.
Evenings are spent stargazing or calling for owls and
wolves. Blue Loon's team of biologists have a remarkable knowledge of the area and can share some rare
sights with birders, including a fascinating visit to the

world's largest nesting colony of red-necked grebes.
Tanya Wheeler-Smith and Laura McLennan have studied these seldom-seen waterfowl in great depth. They
will bring interested birders to their study site on
Whitefish Lake, where they canoe through the wild rice
marshes where the grebes build floating nests on matted weeds.

Other outings include a day trip to Sleeping Giant
Provincial Park to observe warblers, and a day trip to
the three-hundred-year-old white pine stand in Greenwood Forest.

To take part in a bird-banding project in warbler
nesting grounds, contact Blue Loon Adventures, Thunder Bay, at 1-888-846-0066 or (807) 964-2823, or visit
their Web site at http://www.foxnet.net/~blueloon/.

Day trips cost $125 per person and include lunch.
For an overnight stay of two days and two nights at the
base camp, with various activities, expect to spend about
$350 per person.

Winter Birds at Lynde Shores and the Kortright Centre

The nearly 200-hectare Lynde Shores in Whitby is a wonderful place to watch birds year-round, thanks to its varied habitats—woods, marsh and creek. But winter brings the special delights of the bird-feeder trail where more than twenty bird feeders offer excellent opportunities to observe winter birds at close range. Roughly half a kilometre long, the walking trail winds through an old farm woodlot where native species of hawthorn provide shelter, berries and a good source of overwintering insects for hungry birds.

The trail's most frequent visitor is the black-capped chickadee. Winter seems to bring out the boldness in these little birds as they gorge on sunflower seeds in the feeders and even take peanuts from an outstretched human hand.

Found across all but the most northerly parts of the province, black-capped chickadees add a spark of life to a white winter landscape. Cross-country skiers soon come to recognize these plump little members of the titmouse family dipping and darting among the snowy branches of pine trees. They take their name from their distinctive call, a perky sounding "chicka-dee-dee-dee." Black caps and bibs and white cheeks make them easy to identify.

Make a winter treat for birds by smearing peanut butter onto pine cones, rolling the cones in birdseed and then tying them to tree branches with pieces of yarn.

Only 13 centimetres long, chickadees are acrobatic little birds whose antics never fail to amuse. They can manoeuvre upside down, clinging to twigs in search of insects, seeds and berries. When lucky enough to find a feeder full of sunflower seeds these dexterous birds will hold a seed in their feet while cracking it open with their beak.

During winter months black-capped chickadees flock together in groups of six to ten birds. However, larger flocks are occasionally seen moving south in autumn months when there are food shortages.

While the cute and colourful birds of winter often get the most attention, common crows also number among over-wintering birds. A flock of roughly eighty thousand roosts near the town of Essex, east of Windsor. During January and February they can often be seen arriving at the local woods around dusk to roost.

Birds at Lynde Shores are accustomed to being hand-fed, so visitors who bring along a bag of energy-laden black oil sunflower seeds will likely find a flock of birds willing to accept them. Besides the cheeky chickadees, downy woodpeckers and white-breasted nuthatches have also been known to take seeds from humans here. The nuthatches are especially fun to observe as they move headfirst down the trunk of a tree. Their unique upside-down approach gives them the benefit of a different perspective, allowing them to find hidden insects that may have been missed by other birds on the way up.

In cold weather small birds require more food fuel but the shorter days leave them less time to find it, so their search for seeds seems almost compulsive. Anyone who has ever filled a bird feeder knows how quickly the seed can disappear. A single evening grosbeak has been known to eat nearly one hundred sunflower seeds within five minutes.

While sunflower seeds feed the winter songbirds, they in turn feed large raptors such as the great horned owl, which may be observed hunting in the area during winter months.

Another favourite spot for winter birdwatching is the Kortright Centre for Conservation near Kleinburg.

Dozens of different styles of bird feeders are stationed over a 1-kilometre trail suitable for walking or skiing. Informative programs help explain the importance of menu-planning and feeder design.

Favoured for their high calorie content, black oil sunflower seeds appeal to a wide range of birds, including blue jays. Insect-eating woodpeckers prefer rich blocks of suet in wire cages, which they can cling to from a vertical position in much the same way they manoeuvre along tree trunks. Ground-dwelling birds, such as mourning doves, contentedly coo over cracked corn placed on a low wooden shelf just high enough to keep the snow off.

Birds find seed by sight, so it is important that it be visible. And they need a comfortable perch. Metal can freeze their feet and should be covered with plastic. Placing the feeders near appropriate shelter is also important. Birds will often seek cover in nearby evergreens, where they can nibble in relative security.

Keeping squirrels off bird feeders is always a challenge, and I have seen some ingenious ideas at the Kortright Centre, such as stringing old vinyl records above hanging feeders.

After walking the snow trails, you can warm up in the Kortright's café where mirrored glass allows a one-way view of birds as they eat from feeders attached to the window. The birds are close enough that you can observe each feather in detail.

As spring approaches, listen for black-capped chickadee mating songs, which coincide with the start of the sugaring-off season. Flocks disperse as mating couples set about building nests in dead tree cavities or even birdhouses. Blue jays will form courtship flocks, with males bobbing up and down to attract a female's attention. One of the most fascinating spring behaviours is

Birds of a feather don't necessarily flock together. An escaped parakeet is more likely to feed, bathe and roost with a flock of house sparrows than any other species.

the male cardinal seemingly kissing his mate—in fact he is feeding her by placing a seed in her beak. But beak-to-beak feeding is strictly for springtime. At the winter bird feeder the male serves himself first.

Bird-feeder watchers may contribute to scientific research through studies such as Project Feederwatch, which was started by the Long Point Bird Observatory (see page 72), and joined by Cornell University. Participants are asked to count and identify the birds at their home feeders for a two-day period every two weeks from November to March. They submit their data via the Internet or by mail, and it is compiled and analyzed to reveal patterns in winter bird populations.

First-Hand Experience

Lynde Shores Conservation Area is located in Whitby on Victoria Street West, south of Highway 401, via Brock Street. Look for the trail map at the information kiosk in the parking lot. Parking costs 50 cents for thirty minutes or $2 a day. There are no washroom facilities. For information contact the Central Lake Ontario Conservation Authority at 100 Whiting Avenue, Oshawa L1H 3T3, or telephone (905) 579-0411.

The Kortright Centre for Conservation is located on Pine Valley Drive, south of Major Mackenzie Drive and west of Highway 400. Admission costs $5 for adults and $3 for children. For information call (416) 661-6600 or (905) 832-2289.

Participating in Project Feederwatch costs $20. Participants receive an information kit, bird-feeder recipes, three issues of the newsletter and a report on the year's findings. For more information check out the Bird Studies Canada Web site at www.bsc-eoc.org.

Turkey Vultures at Crawford Lake

I had always thought of vultures as southern birds with bad attitude, tough guys who hang out on cacti waiting for the next drought-stricken, sun-baked carcass to fall. What a surprise it was then to find them soaring over the lush farmland of southern Ontario. I was hiking a section of the Bruce Trail through Crawford Lake Conservation Area, near Milton, where a rocky outcrop offered a panoramic view of the countryside below. While resting at the lookout, I became aware of large bird shadows circling the ground. They soared in slow, continuous movements, seldom beating their wings.

They were turkey vultures riding the summer afternoon thermal winds generated near the cliffs of the Niagara Escarpment, in a section known as the Nassagaweya Canyon. Of the seven species of vultures found worldwide, only the turkey vulture is found in Ontario. Although their presence often seems menacing, these massive birds with their 2-metre wingspan provide a valuable service by cleaning up roadkill and other carcasses. Like carrion eaters the world over, they play an often reviled, but nonetheless essential role in the food chain: janitors.

No doubt their bizarre appearance adds to their unfortunate reputation. But their bright red, bald heads are actually a hygienic adaptation, preventing bits of rotting flesh from adhering to their feathers. Having no

Could vultures be the latest lawn ornament? Based on new genetic and anatomical information, the American Ornithologists' Union recently reclassified the turkey vulture, moving it from the family of falconidae (which includes hawks, osprey and falcons) to the ciconiidae (which include storks and flamingos).

syrinx or vocal organ, they are virtually silent birds. Their utterings—only grunts and hisses—are usually reserved for quarrels over food. Like most scavengers they are opportunists. Surveys of their droppings have revealed as much as 25 percent vegetable matter, most of which was grass.

Once found only in the United States, the turkey vulture is expanding its range northward. Like coyotes, they are able to adapt to growing urbanization. More highways mean more roadkill, and the vulture's ecological niche increases. Some migrate north each spring to nesting areas in Ontario—seldom farther than the north shore of Georgian Bay. Vultures are social birds and spend their nights in communal roosts. Nests are typically spartan affairs atop dead trees or cliff ledges.

Besides its scenic escarpment views and soaring vultures, Crawford Lake is known for its rare meromictic lake and its reconstructed Iroquoian village. The existence of the village was revealed through the lake's unusual structure. Meromictic lakes are very deep, but have a small surface, so sediments, such as dead leaves and pollen, settle in layers on the cold lake bottom. These layers, called varves, can be read like tree rings to reveal the botanical history of the area surrounding the lake. When corn pollen was found in the layers corresponding to the time between 1434 and 1459, scientists suspected Woodland Indians had farmed the area. Local finds of prehistoric tools confirmed their suspicions, and an archeological dig began in the 1970s. The dig revealed a village of eleven Woodland Indian longhouses.

Several of those 8-metre high, bark-covered longhouses have been reconstructed, complete with sleeping platforms covered with cedar boughs and furs, smoky fires and tools for grinding corn and gathering food. Sunday afternoon programs demonstrate Woodland

Indian life of the period, from three-sisters-style agriculture (growing corn, beans and squash together), to the production of maple syrup. Both the village and trail leading around Crawford Lake are wheelchair accessible.

First-Hand Experience

Crawford Lake Conservation Area is located on Steeles Avenue south of Milton. To see the turkey vultures follow either the Woodland or Escarpment Trail, each about a thirty-minute walk one way. From Crawford Lake the Nassagaweya Trail leads to Rattlesnake Point for another excellent view. The Crawford Lake Conservation Centre boasts an interesting display on the birds, which includes a stuffed turkey vulture for up-close inspection. Crawford Lake is open weekends year-round, and daily from May to October. Admission is $4 for adults, $3.25 for seniors and youth, $2.75 for children and free for preschoolers. For information call (905) 854-0234.

A Century Day at Point Pelee

Point Pelee is one of the smallest of our national parks, but also one of the most famous. On the same latitude as northern California, Pelee is home to plants and animals seldom seen anywhere else in Canada, from cacti to Kentucky coffee trees. But Pelee is most famous for its birds; 360 species have been sighted here.

May is the big birding month at Pelee, and the best time of year for birders to attempt Century Day, when they try to identify one hundred species in a single day. To accommodate birders, the park opens at 5 a.m., and at 6 a.m. a propane-powered train takes them from the visitor centre to the south end of the park, a 2-kilometre trip with a stop halfway at the Woodland Nature Trail. With binoculars and birding checklists in hand avian fans follow the 12 kilometres of seasonal birding trails (only open during spring migration), as well as the 12 kilometres of permanent gravel or boardwalk trails.

Spring migration begins as early as February with the first horned larks. In March hundreds of tundra swans float amidst broken sheets of ice. In April they are joined by massive rafts of ducks and honking geese. By the second week in May every inch of Pelee seems alive with birdsong. The park is one of the best places to see Connecticut warblers, and the prothonotary warbler, brilliant yellow with blue-grey wings, makes a rare and remarkable sighting.

Eastern and western migratory flyways overlap at Point Pelee, so whether warblers fly north through Texas or Florida they have a good chance of touching down here. The peninsula is far enough north to be on the migratory route of Cape May warblers flying to their nesting grounds in northern spruce forests, but also far enough south to be within range of southern species such as the tiny cerulean warbler.

While birds seem to be the main event at Point Pelee, the array of plant life is not to be overlooked. An estimated 750 plant species have been reported here. These include the prickly pear cactus, which grows in grassland and savannah areas, and Carolinian species such as tulip trees, sassafras, chinquapin oak and paw-paw, whose fruits are enjoyed by many small mammals.

Seldom seen in other parts of the province, the hack-berry, buckeye and giant swallowtail butterflies are all found here. During the peak butterfly months of July and August, when you may see three dozen species, the public is invited to join in Pelee's annual butterfly count.

Marshes cover two-thirds of the park and can be explored via a 1.4-kilometre boardwalk. Blanding's turtles, rare in other parts of Ontario, are common here. Other turtles include snapping, musk, spotted, map and painted. Point Pelee has its own variation of the eastern garter snake. It's solid black with no stripes. Other seldom seen reptiles include the eastern fox snake and five-lined skink. Many of the park's live reptiles, amphibians and insects are caught by naturalists to be displayed during fifteen-minute talks called "Creature Features," held daily at 1:30 and 4:30 p.m at the visitor centre.

A one-and-a-half-hour ferry trip from Leamington to Pelee Island leads to more birding at the southernmost place in Canada, Fish Point Provincial Nature

Wine meets warblers on Pelee Island, where pretty yellow prothonotary warblers grace the labels of Pelee Island Winery's Blanc de Blanc. During the summer months Pelee Island Winery Pavilion welcomes visitors for vineyard tours and tastings. Call (519) 724-2469.

Reserve. Prothonotary, hooded and mourning warblers are often sighted in the wet woodlands, while Carolina wrens and yellow-breasted chats hide in the thickets.

First-Hand Experience

Point Pelee is located 10 kilometres south of Leamington via Essex Road 33. Bike trails make for easy exploration. You can rent both bikes and canoes at park concessions. Daily passes cost $3.25 for adults, $2.40 for seniors, $1.60 for students and $8.55 for families. For information call (519) 322-2365. There is no camping in the park (expect for organized groups), but Wheatley Provincial Park, 20 kilometres to the east on Highway 3, offers 220 campsites as well as 2 kilometres of sandy beach on Lake Erie. For more information call (519) 825-4659. There are several private tent and trailer parks close to Point Pelee and park staff will happily give you their names and telephone numbers.

During spring the ferry to Pelee Island departs from Leamington; in August it departs from Kingsville. Reservations are essential if you plan to take your car. One-way fares are $16.50 per vehicle, $7.50 per adult and $3.75 per child. A cheaper alternative is to bring a bicycle for $3.75. Some means of transportation is essential because the best birding areas are spread across the island. For ferry schedules and reservations call (519) 724-2115. Accommodations are booked at least a year in advance on the island, so your best bet is to plan a day trip. For information on Pelee Island wildlife and history visit the Heritage Centre near the ferry dock or call (519) 724-2291.

FIELDS AND FLOWERS

Finding Fungi on a Mycological Foray

Autumn brings the delights of mycologists' dreams: plump puffballs, great clusters of honey mushrooms and best of all, the tasty boletes. For those trained in fungi identification, the autumn woods hold a treasure trove of edibles.

While many European cultures enter into mushroom collecting with great gusto, Anglo-Canadian culture, by contrast, seems somewhat reticent, even fungi-phobic. Of course the fear of poisoning oneself by frying up a panful of incorrectly identified toadstools is a legitimate one, but on guided outings, such as the mushroom forays led by the Mycological Society of Toronto, you can learn how to separate the palatable from the poisonous while discovering the strange underworld of fungi.

The mushrooms that you see sprouting on lawns and in woods are only the fruiting bodies of the organism—the apples on the tree, as it were. Mushrooms spread spores so that new colonies of fungi may be established. But the mushroom itself is a product of a colony below the soil or hidden inside decaying wood or other organic material. This part of the fungus is a network of threads that form a web called the "mycelium."

The mycelium can live and grow for many years virtually undetected until the right combinations of moisture and temperature stimulate it to fruit—that is, produce mushrooms.

One of the easiest edible fungi to identify is the giant puffball, *Calvatia Gigantea*. Because of its enormous size—easily as big as a football when fully grown—it is not likely to be confused with any poisonous species. These puffballs are best eaten when young and the flesh inside still white. The flesh yellows as the puffball ages. Slice them into steaks and sautée gently in butter till browned.

Not all mushrooms look like the cap-and-stem affairs of supermarkets and fairy tales. They can be shaped like balls or brackets, cups, corals or clubs, even trumpets or stars. Although many have rows of spore-producing gills radiating from the centre stem, others produce their spores on spines or pores. Mushrooms come in myriad shapes and colours, with subtle variations that play an important role in identification.

That's where the collected wisdom and years of experience of the club members come in. Scientists, artists, cooks and lovers of the outdoors all join the Mycological Society of Toronto to develop their knowledge of fungi on spring and autumn forays to various local woods and fields. First-time fungi finders are welcome to join an outing before taking out membership. Equipped with identification guides, baskets and small knives, the mushroom seekers meet at a prearranged parking lot to learn the precise location of the day's foray, which is generally kept secret until the morning of the event in order to prevent pillaging by unscrupulous mushroom hunters.

Calvatia gigantea lives up to its name. It is not unusual to find one of these puffballs weighing 4 kilograms, and some even as much as 20 kilograms.

On an early September afternoon in King Township woods, I was unprepared for the wealth that awaited. The outing began with a spectacular find of oyster mushrooms growing on the trunk of a large dead beech tree. While the mushroom hunters cut down the delectable oysters, our guide explained that these were one of the few types of carnivorous fungi, which supplements their woody diets with the occasional earwig or small worm.

A mass of honey mushrooms provided the next round of excitement for those with culinary intentions, but I was fascinated to learn that honey mushrooms growing on hemlock trees become luminous at night. For cooks, the greatest fall find is the king bolete or

Boletus edulis. It is often found growing with Norway spruce, and one of the best ways to find good specimens is to look for raised bulges in the carpet of dead leaves, where the newly grown mushrooms have pushed upwards. Mushroom collectors refer to these bulges as "shrump."

Before the morning was out we had collected a selection of white and beige coral fungus; tiny, bright orange cups of orange-peel fungus; beautifully striped brackets of turkey tail; assorted russolas in hues of yellow, violet and white; and two great puffballs the size of human heads, which were sliced up and shared among the group for fried feasts.

The ancillary finds, like the red-back salamander under the rotting log or the hummingbird buzzing between jewelweed flowers, were a bonus. Perhaps the most attractive part of any mushroom hunt is the way it forces you to notice the details of forest and field: the brilliant red berries of a wilted Jack-in-the-pulpit, the skin-smooth texture of beech bark and the woody smells of autumn.

First-Hand Experience

Membership in the Mycological Society of Toronto costs $25 and includes participation in spring, summer and autumn mushroom forays, which are informal outings geared to the study of wild mushrooms in fields and woodland on the outskirts of Toronto. Anyone who would like to experience a foray may participate once as a guest. After that you are requested to take a membership. Members may attend meetings in October, November, January, February and April to hear guest speakers lecture on mycology. Members are also eligible

"After a while she remembered that she still held the pieces of mushroom in her hands, and she set to work very carefully, nibbling first at one and then at the other, and growing sometimes taller and sometimes shorter, until she had succeeded in bringing herself down to her usual height."

— LEWIS CARROLL,
Alice in Wonderland

to participate in the Cain Foray, three days of mushroom collecting and cooking at a Haliburton lodge. For information on the Mycological Society of Toronto call their information line at (416) 443-8644 or HI-FUNGI.

Spring Ephemerals in Toronto

As soon as the bright April sun warms the soil, spring ephemerals shoot into action. These are plants in a hurry. They have only a few short weeks to produce their blooms before the deciduous trees come into leaf and shade the woodland floor. Once the area is shaded, the wildflowers will not get sufficient energy to produce blooms and set seed.

Though their season is short, their beauty delights. Even their names are colourful: bloodroot, trout lily, coltsfoot and yellow lady's slipper. They are easily found in well-wooded conservation areas, maple sugar bushes and even some urban ravines.

The West Don River Valley, as it meanders south from Glendon College in Toronto, offers varied habitats for a wide range of wildflowers. The river flows through a flood plain where rich soils and forested slopes provide an ideal habitat for bloodroot, trillium, hepatica, spring beauty and wild ginger.

A real harbinger of spring, the subtle coltsfoot is often found on muddy river banks in the flood plain. While March winds are still whipping the last spring sleet, these little blooms affirm the seemingly impossible arrival of spring. Coltsfoot's yellow tufts of bloom are often mistaken for little dandelions, but the reddish scales on the stalk and the large rounded leaves that only reveal themselves much later are the telltale signs of the

"A lily of a day
Is fairer far in May
Although it fall
and die that night;
It was the plant and
flower of light."

— BEN JONSON,
*To the Immortal
Memory and Friendship
of That Noble Pair,
Sir Lucius Cary and
Sir H. Morison*

first wildflower of spring. Pioneers prized the first plants
to emerge each spring, often using them as tonics. The
leaves of coltsfoot were used in making coughdrops.

Abundant on the West Don's wooded slopes, the
trout lily takes its name from the dappled markings on
its leaves, said to resemble the speckled markings of the
brook trout. A single, tiny, yellow bloom nods downward from a delicate stem, as though too shy to look
directly at the sunlight.

While last summer's grass still lies brown and flat-
tened, the bright white blooms of bloodroot can be seen
emerging on a May morning. Though the park is used by
thousands of dog walkers, joggers and nature lovers,
bloodroot seems to thrive no more than a step or two
away from the path. This very fragile flower takes its
name from the roots, which "bleed" dark orange or red
juice when broken. Bloodroot juice has a reputation as
an insect repellent. Nineteenth-century settler Catharine
Parr Traill described the many uses of this fascinating
plant in *The Backwoods of Canada*.

> As soon as the sun of April has warmed the earth
> and loosened it from its frozen bonds, you may dis-
> tinguish a number of purely white buds, elevated on
> a naked foot-stalk, and partially enfolded in a hand-
> some fine-shaped leaf, of a pale bluish green, curi-
> ously veined on the under side with pale orange. The
> leaf springs singly from a thick juicy fibrous root,
> which on being broken, emits a quantity of liquor
> from its pores of a bright orange scarlet colour: this
> juice is used by the Indians as a dye, and also in the
> cure of rheumatic and cutaneous complaints.

Another early bloomer is the spring beauty. Its pink
and white blooms, no bigger than a man's thumbnail,

are often found on south- or southwest-facing slopes, emerging through a litter of dead leaves.

Marsh marigolds flourish in the Don's swampy lowlands. Bright yellow flowers, like overgrown buttercups, rise above clumps of green, heart-shaped leaves in the still, black waters of marshy woodlands. Bearing no relation to actual marigolds, the marsh marigold's leaves, stems and flowers contain a toxin.

White trilliums, possibly the showiest of spring flowers, cover west-facing slopes with large, three-petalled blooms when the first green haze appears on the maple trees above them. Ontario's provincial flower, the trillium is ubiquitous in well-managed woodlots and parks across southern Ontario. There are thirty varieties of trilliums in North America. In the Don Valley, as in most of southern Ontario, the large-flowered trillium is most commonly seen. Its blooms start out a pristine white, then turn pinkish as they age. These age-coloured trilliums are not to be mistaken for the purple trillium, also found in Ontario, which attracts pollinating flies with an odour like that of rotting carrion. Native people have used trillium roots in various medicinal preparations, but because the plant requires at least six years of growth before blooming, picking it or disturbing it in any way is ill advised. It is not illegal to pick trilliums outside provincial parks, just inconsiderate.

In May and June common blue violets bloom in bottomlands. Not all violets are violet. Their five-petalled flowers may be white, as in the Canada violet and northern white. The round-leaved yellow violet sports the colour of its name, while the delicate birdfoot violet is purple-mauve. European perfume makers have cultivated violets for centuries to extract their fragrance. Their sweet taste and lovely colour have also been prized by confectioners who have a long tradition of sugaring

"A very beautiful plant of the lily tribe abounds both in our woods and clearings; for want of a better name, I call it the Douro Lily, though it is widely spread over a great portion of the continent."

— Catharine Parr Traill on finding trilliums, *The Backwoods of Canada*

the blossoms. Violet leaves and petals may be added to salads and are particularly rich in vitamin C.

First-Hand Experience

Sunnybrook, Serena Gundy and Wilket Creek Parks all connect along the west branch of the Don River. From the north you can access the valley via the Glendon College campus at Bayview and Lawrence and follow it south. The Toronto Field Naturalists' *Survey Study Number Eight* of the West Don River Valley offers a good description of the valley and the plants and animals found there. It costs $4 and is available from the Toronto Field Naturalists, whose number is (416) 968-6255.

Throughout the year the Toronto Field Naturalists offer outings to study flora and fauna across the city, from wildflowers in the spring to migrating birds in the fall. Membership costs $30 per family and includes the monthly *Toronto Field Naturalist* newsletter which describes upcoming outings. Roughly fifteen to twenty guided expeditions are offered each month. All are accessible from a point on Toronto's public transit system and most are two or three hours long. Typical spring outings may include an evening ramble through Serena Gundy Park to look for trilliums and learn some of the folklore that surrounds them, or a day on the Toronto Islands looking for migrating birds.

To help identification there are numerous excellent field guides. I prefer the *National Audubon Society Field Guide to North American Wildflowers* for its full-colour photographs. For first-time flower seekers there is no substitute for instruction in the field. Excellent spring wildflower hikes are offered at both the Kortright Centre for Conservation whose number is (905) 832-2289 (see page 32) and the Mountsberg Wildlife Centre near Milton whose number is (905) 854-2276 (see page 89). On these walks, naturalists show visitors how to identify many of the common spring ephemerals.

Tall Grass Prairie at Ojibway Park

Beautiful but misunderstood, goldenrod is often falsely accused of aggravating hay fever. The real culprit is ragweed pollen, which happens to appear just when the more flamboyant goldenrod bursts into bloom. A member of the sunflower family, tall goldenrod, the species found on the Ojibway Prairie, grows up to 2 metres tall.

It's an unlikely image for Ontario—a prairie of tall grasses waving in the wind—but open areas of big bluestem grass and colourful wildflowers are indigenous to parts of southwestern Ontario. They are the northern tip of a vast grassland that once extended into the midwestern United States.

Before European settlement, grasslands were the largest vegetation forms in North America. Today less than 5 percent of the original tall grass prairie remains. Of all the prairie environments—tall, short and mixed grasses—the tall grass covered some of the best arable land on the continent. Most were ploughed under. The tall grass prairie now exists only in scattered fragments.

In and near the city of Windsor, a precious patch of this rare habitat has been preserved. Jurisdiction over the more than 200-hectare prairie is split between three municipal parks: Ojibway, Black Oak Heritage and Tall Grass Prairie Heritage; and two special areas: Ojibway Prairie Provincial Nature Reserve and Spring Garden Area of Natural and Scientific Interest.

Protected since 1958, Ojibway Park is the oldest and best known of the three municipal parks and offers visitors the rare opportunity to wade through towering grasses and flower-filled fields.

Compared to the Kentucky bluegrass of so many well-sprinkled suburban lawns, the vision of the wild plumes of big bluestem standing 3 metres tall is spectacular. Named for its colour, big bluestem is the predominant grass at Ojibway, though it is joined by prairie cordgrass, Indian grass, Canada wild rye and switchgrass.

While the blooms begin as early as May with yellow star grass and blue-eyed grass, the best part of the spectacle occurs late in the summer. From late July to mid-August this prairie is awash with colour and the air is scented with mountain mint. Grasses and flowers that often tower over a man's head come into bloom, so you lose yourself in a sea of flowers. The tall grass prairie boasts numerous wildflowers: pink spikes of blazing star, delicate white blooms of flowering spurge, magenta tufts of ironweed, white plumes of Culver's root, and masses of yellow goldenrod and sunflowers. Here you can see more rare plants per hectare than at any other preserve in the province—of the more than 700 plant species found in the area, 110 are rarely found in Ontario.

Above the masses of flowers on the late-summer prairie hovers a bounty of butterflies. It is possible to spot as many as forty or forty-five species in a single day. Among them are the provincially rare southern cloudy wing and wild indigo dusky wing. Prairie-dwelling papapeima moths also frequent this unusual corner of the province.

Intermingled with portions of the prairie is the savannah, a place where forests ease into the grassland. Occasional pin oaks rise above the grass, creating an area favourable to ferns and foxgloves. The variety of the habitat makes for great birdwatching. Indigo buntings and field sparrows frequent the park. Yellow-breasted chats favour the thickets, while red-headed woodpeckers and orchard orioles prefer the savannah areas. In the surrounding woods look for tufted titmice.

Rare natural habitats need protection both for their beauty and their valuable genetic material. Domestic grains have their origins in wild grasses such as Canada wild rye. By protecting the diversity of grasses, researchers have a genetic bank with which to strengthen crops.

This rare remnant of prairie landscape results largely from a soil structure that is inhospitable to most trees: 2 metres of sand over 20 metres of clay. The impermeable clay keeps the spring ground too wet for most tree roots, while the sand is so dry during summer months that drought conditions prevail. Fire plays a key role in maintaining the tall grass prairie by burning off the litter of dead plants. The exposed soil is then able to warm more quickly, providing optimum conditions for long-lived native perennials, and preventing invasive weeds (such as dandelions) and trees from establishing a toehold. Dormant seeds of native flowers and grasses germinate without competition from invaders that would otherwise shade them out.

Centuries ago, lightning strikes or native people started the fires that renewed the prairie grassland. A Moravian missionary from New York City, Benjamin Mortimer, travelled through Upper Canada in 1798 and described such a burn.

> … we saw, and passed over, immense tracts of land, which had lately been set fire to by Indian hunters, and were in part still burning. In some places the sun was obscured, and the musquitoes were expelled, by the clouds of smoke ascending from the wide-extended conflagration. By this means the country is made more open to hunt in, and produces greater abundance of grass for the deer to feed on.

Today fires are carefully planned every two to three years, usually around mid-April. During these controlled burns fire squads may drop chemical fire starters from helicopters while ground crews watch to keep the blaze under control. This burning prevents tree saplings

Experiments in commercial goldenrod crops were undertaken in the United States when inventor Thomas Alva Edison was looking for alternative sources of rubber for tires. The discovery of inexpensive synthetic materials quashed the goldenrod project.

from taking over the prairie and ensures that the grasses prevail.

Controlled burns have also been used to restore some savannah areas in Toronto's High Park. Park staff knew there were remnants of the savannah near the playing fields at the west end of the park. The Group of Seven painter, J.E. Macdonald, had painted a typical savannah scene of flowering lupines in the park earlier in the century. Over time, though, the original habitat was degraded by invasive species.

Carol Walker Gayle, an urban forestry planner with the City of Toronto, explained, "Natural management, such as grass fires, grazing deer and elk, would produce scattered trees and shrubs, allowing plenty of sunlight to reach drought-tolerant, sun-loving native grasses. But as the city grew to encompass the park the natural cycle was disrupted." Not only were the grazing animals gone and the fires prevented, but numerous horticultural escapees such as Tartarian honeysuckle and Norway maples were squeezing out the indigenous plants. The stately oaks—some as old as 250 years—were starting to die, but no younger ones were taking their place because they could not germinate under the dense shade of the Norway maples and thick lawns of Kentucky bluegrass. After the burns, native plants such as sedges, blueberries, sweet fern, lupines and woodland sunflowers started to re-emerge.

First-Hand Experience

Ojibway Park boasts a nature centre with informative displays to help visitors understand the wildlife and ecology of the eastern tall grass prairie. The centre is open daily, year round. Trails—including one paved path suitable for wheelchairs and strollers—wind through the park. A picnic shelter and two picnic areas with charcoal grills allow visitors to have lunch al fresco.

Ojibway Nature Centre is located in Ojibway Park at 5200 Matchette Road, Windsor. From the E.C. Row Expressway, exit south on Matchette Road and drive 1 kilometre to the park. Telephone (519) 966-5852.

High Park in Toronto is easily accessible by public transit using the High Park subway station on Bloor Street. A burn site can be found off West Road, north of Grenadier Pond near the sports fields. For information on guided walking tours in High Park call the High Park Citizens' Advisory Committee at (416) 392-1748.

Orchids of Bruce Peninsula National Park

You don't have to go to a tropical rain forest to find orchids. Ontario boasts dozens of species from the flamboyant blooms of yellow lady's slipper to the subtle green Alaska orchid. One of the best areas to see these amazing flowers is the Bruce Peninsula, which boasts more than forty-four species of orchids. The best of the best is Dorcas Bay, a 134-hectare section of Bruce Peninsula National Park.

The park is divided into two areas: one on the east side of Highway 6, facing Georgian Bay, and the other on the west side of Highway 6, facing Lake Huron. The Lake Huron side of the park, known as Singing Sands or Dorcas Bay, is beloved by vacationing families for its gentle beach with long stretches of shallow water and splendid Lake Huron sunsets. But before the water warms up for swimming, the orchid hunters arrive in droves to explore the remarkable variety of flora. The varied landscape offers a wide range of opportunity for different species. Sand dunes, fens, coniferous woods, open clearings and slabs of flat dolomite limestone each offer a specialized habitat.

Orchid-hunting season at Dorcas Bay begins mid- to late May with pink calypso orchids and striped coralroot, which can be identified by its long clusters of purple and white striped flowers. This unusual orchid is saprophytic. Lacking chlorophyll, it draws its

Another rare find in the park is the eastern massasauga rattlesnake. This poisonous snake is unlikely to bite if left unmolested. To avoid nasty surprises don't reach into any dark, rocky crevices. Watch where you put your hands and feet.

nourishment from organic material through its many-branched roots.

Some orchids are obvious: the yellow lady's slipper can easily be spotted in large clumps along the roadside. Other orchids are so subtle that you could easily trample a rare specimen by walking carelessly. The tiny, fragile ramshead lady's slipper is fervently sought by nature photographers. Some of these plant paparazzi are so competitive that to prevent rivals from getting a good shot, they have stooped to such unscrupulous moves as destroying blooms after photographing them. Luckily the park is patrolled, and staff are trying to educate photographers in orchid-shooting etiquette. Dead vegetation should never be removed for the sake of a better shot—it may be what the orchid is drawing on for sustenance. Large light reflectors should be avoided because they may overheat delicate blooms.

In June your visit is rewarded by sightings of pink lady's slipper (also known as moccasin flower) whose puffy pink lip (or slipper) is veined with red, and showy lady's slipper, which lives up to its name, standing up to 90 centimetres tall and displaying flamboyant flowers of white and rose. In July prairie fringed orchids grow along the borders of inland lakes toward the south end of Bruce Peninsula National Park. Rattlesnake plantain, which is related to neither rattlesnakes nor the common garden weed plantain, sports tiny 6-millimetre white flowers on a long, thin stalk. Its white-veined leaves are so attractive that this plant has been poached for terraria.

Orchids may draw the tourists, but there are many other beauties to be found here. In spring you will find delicate columbines growing out of the limestone, and masses of blue dwarf lake iris, which grows only on the shores of Lake Huron. Not quite as showy as the orchids,

Helleborine is a European import that is commonly found around the park's campgrounds in the late summer. Look for tall spikes of greenish flowers tipped with purple.

but certainly just as interesting, are the carnivorous plants. The pitcher plant (see page 58) lures insects into its water-filled tubes, where they are dissolved by acids and gradually absorbed into the plant. Walk along the abandoned road into the woods, following the yellow blazes, and not only will you see a host of wildflowers, but also a hare or two. In spring you will be greeted by frog choruses and clouds of biting insects.

First-Hand Experience

Bruce Peninsula National Park is located south of Tobermory, off Highway 6. There are two sections in the park. On the east side of the highway is the Cypress Lake area with steep cliffs and rugged walks along Georgian Bay. To the west is the Singing Sands area with gentle Lake Huron beaches and Dorcas Bay. Camping is allowed in the Cypress Lake section and reservations are recommended. For information telephone Bruce Peninsula National Park at (519) 596-2233 or the Tobermory Chamber of Commerce at (519) 596-2452.

When accurate wildflower identification depends on the subtlest of details it is wise to refer to a guide that groups flowers by structure instead of colour. *Newcomb's Wildflower Guide* is often used by professional naturalists.

Insect-Eating Plants in Ontario's Wetlands

Pitcher plants often harbour microscopic non-prey animals within their death pools. Ontario's purple pitcher plant holds bacteria, protozoa and even small crustaceans in its trap fluid, which may play a role in helping the pitcher plant digest its insect meal. The liquid is also the exclusive home of a mosquito larva that feeds on matter found in its watery home.

Carnivorous plants capture the imagination because they seem like such a reversal of the natural order. Most plants are eaten—at least in some part—by animals, but carnivorous plants have become the predators. How does a rooted plant manage to capture and consume a moving insect? Often a plant's carnivorous ability is an adaptation to a harsh environment that allows it to get additional nutrients. Carnivorous plants occur around the world and several are found in Ontario.

I first discovered pitcher plants while looking for the more glamorous orchids, but this purplish plant with the strange shape proved the most fascinating find of the day. Thriving in bogs and wet areas, pitcher plants take their name from their waxy cups, which serve as pitfall traps for hungry insects. Nectar attracts insects to the tube-like "pitcher" at the base of the plant. In the same way that brightly coloured petals lure pollinating insects to other plants, purple pitcher plants advertise their sweet nectar with deeply coloured veins. Hapless bugs find their way to the sweet stuff just inside the mouth of the pitcher, then slip on the waxy lip and slide into the deadly liquid below. The pitcher's walls are covered with downward-pointing hairs to prevent escape. Those that fall into the death pool are slowly digested and their proteins absorbed into the plant, enabling it to thrive in a bog where few minerals exist.

The pitcher plant's overhanging hood prevents evaporation of the nectar on sunny days and saves it from being diluted with rainwater during wet weather. This striking plant is especially dramatic in bloom, when its round, purple flower hangs down from a stalk 20 to 60 centimetres tall.

The diminutive sundew uses the flypaper approach to catching insects. Its leaves—round or spoon-shaped, depending on the species—are covered with red hairs. At the tip of each hair is a gland that secretes a drop of fluid that sparkles in sunlight (hence the name). But the delicate droplets are not just water. They are sticky secretions that accumulate on an insect walking about the plant. The leaf slowly folds over the prey to digest it.

The round-leaf sundew is the most common variety and has tiny white flowers, sometimes tinged with pink, on a stalk no more than 22 centimetres high. They survive in bogs and poor soils in many parts of Ontario, including the Luther Marsh Wildlife Management Area, an impressive 5,261-hectare wetland noted for its numerous waterfowl.

Bladderworts, often found floating in marshes, employ tiny, bean-shaped bladders underwater to snare their prey. Each bladder has a trap door set by tiny hairs. Insect larvae, or even the odd tadpole, swimming past the bladder's sensitive hairs trigger the door to open. Prey is sucked in in a fraction of a second.

In 1874 Charles Darwin was the first naturalist to confirm that some plants capture and eat animals. His son Francis developed this observation and demonstrated that capturing prey enhances the growth of carnivorous plants.

First-Hand Experience

All these carnivorous plants can be found at various parks along the Bruce Peninsula, particularly in Bruce Peninsula National Park (see page 57).

Pitcher plants thrive in sphagnum bogs, such as the H.N. Crossley Nature Reserve, which is protected by the Federation of Ontario Naturalists. The reserve is located near Port Carling. For details call the federation at (416) 444-8419.

Another easily accessible place to see pitcher plants is on the Spruce Bog Boardwalk, just off Highway 60 opposite the visitor centre in Algonquin Park. The 1.5-kilometre loop passes two northern spruce bogs. For information call the park at (613) 637-2828.

One of southern Ontario's largest wetlands, Luther Marsh, is north of Highway 9 via Highway 25. Follow the signs. For details contact the Grand River Conservation Authority at (519) 621-2761 or the area superintendent at (519) 928-2832.

Twin-scaped bladderworts are among the bog-dwelling plants found at Mer Bleue Conservation Area near Ottawa, where a 1-kilometre floating boardwalk enables visitors to see a corner of the 2,500-hectare peatland with relative ease. Large purple-fringed orchids, river otters and Blanding's turtles are among the area's unusual flora and fauna. Mer Bleue is located east of Ottawa on Borthwick Ridge Road. For information call the National Capital Commission at (613) 239-5000.

AT THE BEACH

Sand Dunes and Snappers in Prince Edward County

A sun-bleached gopher skull protrudes from the hot sand. Only a few tufts of marram grass anchor the wind-rippled dunes. The area could be a movie set for a western desert, but this is Sandbanks Park, nestled in some of southern Ontario's richest farm country in Prince Edward County on the shore of Lake Ontario.

Poor farming practices caused these sand dunes to form when settlers brought their cattle to graze here two centuries ago. Herds of cattle soon damaged the sensitive topsoil and the underlying sand began to surface. In what must have seemed a surreal transformation, helpless farmers watched as the wind blew thousands of years' accumulated sand over their farmlands. Dunes grew to cover houses, barns and even fully grown trees. The fertile farms were soon buried and abandoned.

Left to take its course, nature slowly resettled the dunes. Marram grass was the first plant to colonize the arid dunes, followed by drought-tolerant prairie flowers such as hoary puccoon. Eventually the cottonwood poplars took hold.

Today visitors wander across these dunes where mature cottonwoods release their seeds in a soft white fluff that drifts on the warm wind like snow in June. Tangles of grapevines and poison ivy now grow intermingled with the pink blooms of wild roses.

With roughly four hundred thousand visitors a year, Sandbanks is an immensely popular park. Its campground is often full in summer months, but there are still quiet, pristine places to discover. I've found that most visitors gravitate to the more accessible beaches of the Outlet Sector. The massive three- and four-storey dunes of the West Lake Sector may be busy near the parking area at Dunes Beach, but if you are willing to walk these sandy hills you can find quiet hollows where all you can hear are the gulls and the wind in the grass. Climb a tall dune and on one side you will see the cold, choppy waters of Lake Ontario, on the other, the gentle beaches of West Lake. The dunes that separate the two bodies of water are known as baymouth dunes, and they are said to be the largest freshwater dune system in the world.

While the average adult snapper weighs about 7 kilograms, at least one record setter has tipped the scales at 22 kilograms.

Beaches like Sandbanks are not only popular with human visitors. Warm spring sunshine stirs snapping turtles to seek their place in the sand. By June most have come ashore to lay their eggs in sand or on loose gravel shores, but each year snapping turtles find more and more human competition for a spot on Ontario's lakesides. With increasing frequency the turtles turn to alternative nesting sites, and one that most readily meets their needs is the gravel shoulder of a country road near a swamp or lake.

I first stumbled on a snapper digging its nest when I was driving to Sandbanks Park on a warm, Victoria Day long weekend. On a gravel road shoulder just outside the park, a female snapper dug the hard-packed gravel with her powerful hind feet. So singular was her sense of purpose that she seemed indifferent to her audience of curious motorists who parked along the roadside, then approached to within 2 metres to observe her.

When the hole was roughly 15 centimetres deep she positioned herself over it to lay more than two dozen round, rubbery-shelled, white eggs no bigger than golf balls. That task completed, she covered over the nest with such care that it was impossible to detect where she had deposited the future generation.

That was the last she would ever have to do with her young, leaving the rest of the job to the summer sunshine, which warmed the eggs until they hatched in September. Most of the soft-shelled, young hatchlings would become autumn feasts for birds and fish, but a few would survive to bury themselves in the mud for their winter hibernation.

Since that May morning I have seen snappers nesting at the foot of the Scarborough Bluffs and along swampy sections of Highway 7 in eastern Ontario. Each time I can't resist the urge to watch. Turtles have been repeating this ritual for some 250 million years, making them one of the oldest creatures on the planet (by comparison, the dinosaurs became extinct 70 million years ago). Sadly, their habit of seeking sun-baked roadsides for nesting often turns them into road kill. One of the most effective ways of removing a snapper from the dangers of sun-warmed tarmac is to put a hefty stick in front of its face. When it chomps down, you'll probably be able to carry the stick, with turtle attached, at arm's length to a safer spot, giving it a chance to live out a natural life that may stretch into nine decades.

With its hooked beak and spiky tail, the snapper seems to summon all the ferocity of some ancient monster. In fact they are largely vegetarian creatures, existing on a diet of aquatic plants, except in the early days of spring when they feed on frogs, fish and the occasional duckling.

In 1995 the Toronto and Region Conservation Authority attached radio transmitters to the shells of half a dozen snapping turtles to identify hatching sites and population distribution. Nesting areas were identified along the Toronto Islands. At least one turtle was known to have swum 2 kilometres from the Leslie Street spit to the Toronto Islands.

The only turtle lacking the ability to fully retract into its shell, the snapper must rely on its powerful jaws and claws to redress its inadequate defence. Turtle watchers should beware of its sharp, hooked beak and tenacious jaws. With its long neck and startling speed, a snapper is not to be toyed with.

First-Hand Experience

Snapping turtles can be found throughout Ontario as far north as Lake Timiskaming. While they no doubt prefer quieter places, they've even been spotted on the Toronto waterfront.

Sandbanks Provincial Park is located in Prince Edward County, roughly 30 kilometres south of Belleville. For information contact Sandbanks Provincial Park at (613) 393-3319. For campsite reservations call (613) 969-8368.

You can explore Sandbanks' special environments on a self-guided walk along the 3-kilometre Cedar Sands Trail, with an explanatory brochure from the park's visitor centre. The centre also posts schedules of nature walks lead by park naturalists, such as an hour-long hike up and down the dunes to observe sand-loving flora.

A new amphitheatre, complete with sound and lighting systems, is scheduled to open in 1999 for evening performances relating to the park's heritage. A celebration that conveys a sense of the history of the park is the annual Lakeshore Lodge Weekend held each July, when visitors play park staff in a turn-of-the-century-style baseball game complete with costumes, corn-on-the-cob and country-fair-style amusements. For more information on scheduled events check the Friends of Sandbanks Web site at www.pec.on.ca/friends.

A Rare Savannah at Pinery Provincial Park

With its spectacular sand dunes and rare oak savannah, Pinery Provincial Park on the shore of Lake Huron lures both sun-seeking beachgoers and nature lovers. They come to explore one of the largest remaining oak savannahs in North America, a globally threatened habitat rarer than rain forests.

Red and white oaks are most easily distinguished by their leaves: round-lobed on white oaks and pointed on red.

This savannah evolved on the sandy shores of Lake Huron after the last ice age, when prevailing westerly winds scooped up the soft, white sand and dumped it at the shore. The shifting sands have grown over the millennia. The youngest dunes, those closest to the lake, are about a metre high, while further inland they rise to heights of 30 metres.

Shifting sands become anchored when marram grass, sea rocket and other drought-tolerant plants begin to grow on them. On the newer dunes you may find yellow blooms of hoary puccoon, a member of the forget-me-not family, which takes its name from the soft hairs that make its leaves look frosted. Sand cherry, little bluestem grass and balsam poplar all thrive in the dry conditions.

Farther inland, the older dunes support a landscape more typical of a prairie. This is the savannah, a small remnant of a habitat once found at the edges of grasslands across the North American plains. Agriculture and other human activity has reduced thousands of hectares of savannah to only a few. At Pinery Provincial Park red, white and black oak thrive alongside red and white pines. Where the woods give way to meadows, tall, graceful lupines bloom in early summer. As the season wanes the striking blue flowers of fringed gentians may be seen in the meadows, a sight that is becoming increasingly rare. More than seven hundred species of plants can be found in the Pinery.

The musical buzz of prairie warblers is one of the savannah's special sounds. Roughly three hundred bird species frequent the park. Five-lined skinks and rare hognose snakes are among the unusual reptiles found here.

Oaks produce acorns, an important food source for mammals such as white-tailed deer, squirrels, mice and even foxes. Pheasants, grouse, woodpeckers and blue jays are among the birds that make a meal of the acorn's rich nutmeat. Aboriginal people also ate acorns, although they removed the bitter tannins first by boiling, then roasting them.

Among the hosts of animals that dine on acorns are the secretive acorn weevils, insects belonging to the beetle order. The adult is seldom seen, but evidence of its existence is present in oak forests each autumn. When ripe acorns fall to the ground, examine them for round, pinhead-size holes. The female beetle drills them using an extended mouthpiece, or beak, as long as her entire body. After chewing through the tough shell she makes small chambers in the soft, white nutmeat and lays an egg in each chamber, then plugs the hole with a fecal pellet. Weevil larvae eat the acorn flesh and, after the acorn has fallen to the ground, escape by drilling their way out.

The Pinery's ten short nature trails (none of which is longer than 2 kilometres) offer a good sampling of the park's habitats. Start at the Cedar Trail near the

Seldom seen, but often heard, flying squirrels feed on the Pinery's ample acorns and nest in the mature oaks. Their chirping noises are often heard around 10 p.m. and 3 a.m.

visitor centre. It is one of three wheelchair accessible trails and covers the oak savannah, woods and shoreline. The rugged Nipissing Trail traverses the savannah as it rises up onto some of the oldest and highest dunes in the park. From the top you can see across the park all the way to Lake Huron. You can also see how a controlled burn in 1993 brought on savannah vegetation, such as New Jersey tea and fragrant sumac, thereby maintaining a habitat for such rare creatures as Olympia marble-winged butterflies. To see some magnificent tulip trees that are centuries old, explore the Carolinian Trail at the south end of the park. The banks of the Old Ausable Channel, which runs the length of the park, are great for sighting deer and beaver and can easily be explored in a rented canoe, kayak or paddleboat.

First-Hand Experience

Pinery Provincial Park is 6 kilometres south of Grand Bend on Lake Huron via Highway 21. Canoes, kayaks and paddleboats can be rented at the park store for forays along the Old Ausable Channel. Rental rates are roughly $12 per hour. Conducted walks during summer months are informative explorations of the park's flora and fauna, from warblers to wildflowers. The Pinery stays open during winter months when the dunes make for great tobogganing. Cross-country ski and snowshoe rentals are available for use on the trails. The Pinery boasts one thousand campsites, some of which are available in winter. For information call (519) 243-2220.

Spring Migrations at Long Point

While the province's roads are frequently dotted with deer-crossing signs, Highway 59, leading down the Long Point spit, is marked with turtle crossing signs alongside the marshes.

As though custom-built to aid the migrations of birds and butterflies, three dramatic sand spits extend from Lake Erie's north shore into the lake. Point Pelee, Rondeau and Long Point have been shaped over the millennia by sand washed from eroding shorelines. The longest of all these sandy peninsulas is Long Point, a haven for birds and the bird watchers who flock here to catch the spring and autumn migrations. Summer tourists also come for the beaches—4 kilometres of soft, white sand in Long Point Provincial Park.

On an April morning the trailer parks and tight rows of summer cottages surrounding the northern perimeter of Long Point Provincial Park still lie vacant. The morning air is pristine. Honking geese and sloshing waves are the loudest noises. Birds touch down in Long Point in prodigious numbers because it is the first land they encounter after an arduous crossing of Lake Erie on their northbound migration each spring. In fall the birds will stage here, feeding and gathering together, for the southbound journey.

Jutting 40 kilometres into Lake Erie, Long Point is the longest of the Erie spits and provides many different habitats in close proximity to each other: beaches and dunes, fields and grasslands, marshes and ponds, uplands forest and wet woods. This means that keen birders can add many species to their lists in a single visit, as well as have a variety of pleasant walks. More than 320 species of birds have been sighted at Long Point, including Ontario rarities such as the yellow-headed blackbird. The marshes attract dozens of species of waterfowl as they wait for northern lakes and prairie bogs to thaw. Tundra swans are among the earliest arrivals as they seek out watery gaps in between sheets of breaking lake ice. Shortly after them come a host of ducks: redheads, canvasbacks, blue-winged teal and more. Rarely seen species, such as sandhill cranes, and Arctic loons making their way north to Arctic nesting grounds, may also be glimpsed. Autumn brings migrating hawks who, reluctant to cross open water, try to stick to the shoreline as much as possible, following the spit far into the lake.

In keeping with its many habitats, Long Point boasts surprisingly varied plants. Here you can find the tulip trees and sassafras typical of southern Carolinian forests, as well as northern vegetation, like white cedar and tamarack, that thrives in the cool maritime climate moderated by Lake Erie waters.

Long Point is also home to one of the Long Point Bird Observatory's field stations. During spring and fall migrations visitors are encouraged to join staff and volunteer bird banders on their walks to roughly a dozen mist nets stationed in the wooded area. The staff gently trap migrating birds—typically passerines such as warblers, but also an occasional flicker or sandpiper. While holding the bird in one hand, they fasten an aluminum band onto its outstretched leg. By noticing the wear on its feathers and the colour of its plumage, banders estimate the bird's age and record the data to use in studies monitoring migration patterns.

A 2-kilometre loop of trails leads across the dykes at Big Creek Marsh National Wildlife Area, north of the observatory. These trails enable birders to cover

According to the International Crane Foundation, 6-million-year-old fossils of sandhill cranes in Nebraska prove they are the oldest bird species still living on earth. In Japan these graceful birds symbolize long life and happy marriage.

different marsh habitats and offer outstanding opportunities to watch waterfowl and—on a warm, sunny
day—turtles and marsh-dwelling snakes. An observation tower provides an expansive view of the marsh.

First-Hand Experience

Marsh whomper is a
name commonly used
for the eastern fox
snake sometimes
sighted in Lake Erie
marshes. These docile
snakes are not poiso-
nous, but they some-
times cause alarm with
their habit of mimick-
ing rattlesnakes by
shaking their tails.

Long Point Provincial Park is about 10 kilometres south
of Port Rowan via Highway 59. The park has 256 campsites, all within a five-minute walk to the beach. For
information call (519) 586-2133.

Long Point Bird Observatory's Old Cut Field
Station is located on Old Cut Boulevard, off Highway
59, just outside Long Point Provincial Park. Bird band-
ing takes place in spring (from early March to mid-
June) and fall (from early August to mid-November).
Call (519) 586-2885.

Big Creek Marsh National Wildlife Area is located
on Highway 59, 5 kilometres north of the Old Cut Field
Station. Some sections of the trail are closed during
migrations. For information call the Canadian Wildlife
Service at (519) 586-2703.

Waterfowl Weekend at Presqu'ile

As soon as the ice breaks up, our lakes are visited by inumberable flights of wild-fowl: some of the ducks are extremely beautiful in their plumage, and are very fine-flavoured. I love to watch these pretty creatures, floating so tranquilly on the water, or suddenly rising and skimming along the edge of the pine-fringed shores, to drop again on the surface, and then remain stationary, like a little fleet at anchor.

—— CATHARINE PARR TRAILL, *The Backwoods of Canada*

An infestation of foreign zebra mussels that has clogged water intake pipes and changed lake ecologies has been credited with increasing the numbers of overwintering ducks, particularly deep-diving ducks such as oldsquaws.

A wind that cuts like a cold knife is whipping off Lake Ontario, and there is still enough wet snow to keep your feet frigid. Welcome to spring at Presqu'ile Provincial Park. Despite the discomfort, the air is filled with optimism as hundreds of birdwatchers and spring seekers look for those first signs of the warming season: the returning waterfowl. Long before warm-weather warblers and other more delicate birds head north, an impressive array of ducks, geese and swans lead the migrations.

Typically the birds touch down on the north shores of the Great Lakes where they rest, feed and wait for the right weather conditions to continue their northward journey. Presqu'ile Provincial Park, on the north shore of Lake Ontario, near Brighton, is known for its out-standing waterfowl watching during this time of year.

A peninsula that points south into Lake Ontario, Presqu'ile provides an important stopover for as many as two hundred thousand waterfowl each spring. They come north from Chesapeake Bay, the Gulf of Mexico and other warmer waters, displaying their showiest plumage, ready to meet and mate. Their numbers are vast. It is not unusual to see rafts of two to three thousand ducks swimming together as they feed on aquatic plants and insects.

During the last weekend of March and the first weekend of April the park holds its annual Waterfowl Festival. Mobile viewing platforms dubbed "duck trucks" are stationed around the park. Volunteer naturalists join park staff in the duck search, with binoculars trained on oldsquaw, bufflehead, canvasback, scaup, redheads and goldeneyes. Telescopes are set up at key viewing locations to observe the widest range of habitats: open lake water, sheltered marshes and wave-washed beaches. On these special Waterfowl Festival weekends naturalists happily help visitors identify several often confusing species. From a distance canvasbacks and redheads look startlingly similar—until you learn to look for the downward sloping beak on the canvasback.

Male ducks outnumber females, so the gals make the choices. Males can often be seen in frantic courtship behaviour, while the female observes with a view to the best genetic material. She looks for the quality and colour of her mate's plumage as well as the vigour and endurance of his swimming and diving displays. Oldsquaw ducks are especially fun to watch as the noisy males show off their long tail feathers.

With its historic lighthouse, marsh boardwalk and 2 kilometres of beach, Presqu'ile is a great place for a

Presqu'ile's sandy spit provides a haven for migrating birds and butterflies, but it has been a hazard for ships. Early in the nineteenth century brush fires were often lit on the point to warn ships away. But the sinking of the schooner H.M.S. Speedy proved the need for a lighthouse. Today the 1840s lighthouse at Presqu'ile's Salt Point is one of the oldest on the Great Lakes.

waterfront walk at any time of year. Some parts of the beach are groomed for sun-seeking humans, but the most interesting sections are those left wild to provide feeding areas for shorebirds. Approximately 310 species of birds have been spotted at Presqu'ile.

After the outdoor waterfowl watching, visitors can warm up in the tea room operated by a local service club in one of the park's old houses. The Lighthouse Interpretive Centre displays artifacts relating to the marine heritage of the area and, during the Waterfowl Festival, bird-related displays.

First-Hand Experience

Presqu'ile Provincial Park is located south of Brighton, via Highway 30. For information call (613) 475-2204. One of the biggest provincial park events in Ontario, the Presqu'ile Waterfowl Festival usually takes place over the last weekend in March and the first in April. Be sure to dress warmly.

NIGHT PROWLERS

Howling at Wolves in Algonquin

It's a sound you don't soon forget—that first distant howl in the dark. Because the wolf has come to represent all that is wild, the idea of being able to elicit some sort of social response is tantalizing. So much so that since Algonquin Park staff started offering guided wolf howls in the late sixties, more than one hundred thousand people have turned out to the events held Thursday evenings from August to September.

The fascination with wolf-howl communication seems strangely at odds with the provincial hunting regulations that, with few exceptions, class wolves as fur-bearing animals that may be trapped year-round. The grey wolf, also known as the timber wolf, is the largest undomesticated member of the dog family. Once found throughout Canada, it has been forced out of southern Ontario by agricultural development. The highly adaptable wolf is probably capable of surviving in farmlands, but its predatory skills soon make it an enemy of farmers and game hunters.

Although organized wolf howls are now a widely popular program in Algonquin Park, they originally began as a practical method to locate wolves for researchers working on a wolf census. In the summer of 1959 researchers tried playing a taped record of wolf howls and got a reply from a wild pack on their first attempt, enabling them to locate the home areas of two

Large, black and ominous, the raven has often been seen in western culture as an omen of death. Perhaps this is because of the raven's clever surveillance of wolf packs in anticipation of scavenging a meal after a pack has fed. Biologists have been known to look for congregations of ravens as a way of finding a wolf pack's kill.

packs. From there it was a short step to abandoning the bulky recording equipment in favour of human "wolf howls." Wolves will respond to human imitations of their calls from 5 kilometres away and possibly as far as 10. But human hearing is not so acute. We only hear them 3.2 kilometres away at best.

Although the wolf's long, deep wails evoke fear and melancholy in most human hearts, for wolves they are merely a practical way of asserting their territory, guarding their kill and announcing the strength and size of their pack. Lone wolves seldom howl, probably for fear of betraying their vulnerability. The exception, though, comes in August, when pups not old enough to join the pack in a hunt are left behind to await their pack's return. These pups will howl back readily, perhaps because they are eager to hear their pack. That makes August the month for wolf howls in Algonquin, and a thousand or more people will turn out for a howl led by park staff. There is no limit to the number of people who may participate, so a line of cars stretching 15 kilometres is not unusual. The group heads out along Highway 60, following staff to a spot where wolves have been heard on the previous night. A calm, quiet night is best for howls, because the sounds of rain and wind can drown out voices. At the designated spot, cars are parked along the roadside and everyone gets out to quietly listen as park staff howl into the night. In 1997, two out of three of these sessions was greeted with a response from a wild pack.

A wolf can smell you up to 2.4 kilometres away.

First-Hand Experience

Wolf howls are held in Algonquin Park on Thursdays in August and September whenever a pack can be located.

The evening begins with a video and quick lesson in wolf biology, then participants drive to the site of the howl. For information call Algonquin Park at (613) 637-2828.

Wolf howls are also offered once a year at Bonnechere Provincial Park on Highway 62, near the east end of Algonquin Park. These tend to draw fewer visitors and seem more intimate. Bonnechere has a great campground with some riverside sites, as well as cabins that can be rented for $400 a week during summer months, or $65 to $75 during the rest of the year. The park has a sandy beach and playground as well as family programs on a range of subjects from archaeology to amphibians. For information call (613) 757-2103.

Prowling for Owls in Guelph

Caves inhabited by prehistoric man at Pessac-sur-Dordogne in France held thousands of snowy-owl claws. They may have been used as magic charms.

A snowy night in January is not the usual time for bird-watching, but in southern Ontario January is prime time for owl watching. This is the start of the nesting season for the great horned owl, a large and aggressive hunter.

One of the best ways to learn how to look for owls is to join an organized owl prowl such as those offered by the J.C. Taylor Nature Centre in the Arboretum at the University of Guelph. Located on campus, the 165-hectare arboretum boasts trim gardens and ornamental trees as well as some wonderfully wild old woods. After a preparatory talk indoors on owl behaviour and identification, participants head outside, crunching through the January snow by the light of the moon to listen for the resonant hooting of the great horned owls. Naturalist Chris Early hoots and calls, and usually the owls call back. "Most often we just hear them, but on a bright, moonlit night we've seen the silhouettes of screech owls as they land in trees near the path," Chris says.

More than twice the size of a screech owl, the great horned owl is often heard in the area. Found across the province, this powerful raptor kills small prey such as mice and squirrels, and hefty creatures like skunks, weasels, cats and other owls. The great horned owl even preys on porcupines. It avoids being stuck with quills by piercing the porcupine's eyes with its powerful talons, driving them right into the victim's brain.

With a wingspan of up to 1.5 metres, the great horned owl must be a scary sight to any creature under its shadow. Naturalist E. T. Seton called it "the winged tiger of the woods." It is so feared by other birds that during daylight hours a flock may try to charge it, relying on safety in numbers to drive it from their nesting or feeding area. The phlegmatic owl is not seriously threatened, but may temporarily fly off to avoid an irritating mob of cawing crows.

Perhaps to avoid the inconvenience of these noisy mobs, the great horned owl becomes secretive, hiding high in the thick green branches of conifers during the day. Even then it leaves telltale traces: droppings that look like white smear on the trunks of their favourite trees or regurgitated finger-length pellets of undigested fur, feathers and bone.

Because great horned owls take as much as six or seven months to raise their young, they need to get an early start on the nesting season. In January they begin hooting to proclaim their territories. In a season when most other large birds are still down south, owls can easily find an old hawk, heron or crow's nest to claim as their own, or use a cavity in a hollow tree. As early as February they may lay one to four white eggs.

Not all owls are nocturnal. Two visitors from the north, the snowy owl and the northern hawk owl, typically hunt by day. The northern owl scans fields and roadsides from a favourite perch, whereas the snowy owl seeks wide open spaces like its familiar tundra. Snowies are sometimes sighted at airports, beaches and marshes. In the Toronto area they have sometimes been spotted along the lakefront at Tommy Thompson Park. Seeing this magnificent white predator swoop down on a meal that may be as large as a Canada goose is one of the most exciting sights any birdwatcher can hope for.

"When blood is nipped, and ways be foul, Then nightly sings the staring owl."

—WILLIAM SHAKESPEARE, *Love's Labor's Lost*

Great grey owls are creatures of the northern boreal forest, but during a particularly brutal winter they may move south. Unlike the more aggressive great horned owls, the great grey owls rely almost entirely on small rodents. When lemming populations crash, or deep crusty snow makes for difficult hunting, great grey owls are driven south to seek small rodents in farmlands. The "great" part of their name comes from their impressive size—they are sometimes as much as 75 centimetres tall. Occasionally they are sighted standing eerily still on a roadside fence post or tree branch. Solemn, silent and still, they are listening for the movements of small rodents, which they can hear beneath as much as 30 centimetres of snow.

Ontario's smallest owl is the saw-whet, a diminutive 20 centimetres long. Found in coniferous woods throughout most of Ontario, this nocturnal bird has a reputation for being incredibly tame, even to the point of alighting on a birdwatcher's shoulder.

If you want to see more than a fleeting glimpse of an owl, visit a raptor rehabilitation centre such as Mountsberg Wildlife Centre. Located near Milton, Mountsberg is one of the largest bird-banding stations in Ontario. As many as ten thousand birds are banded there each year. Wounded birds of prey are brought to the avian hospital where they are treated and then prepared for their return to the wild.

Part of that treatment includes building their flying strength in the enclosed flyway, where 150 people can be seated to watch the birds during special presentations. Roughly fifteen to twenty species of hawks, falcons and owls may be seen here on a typical visit. Among the most commonly treated owls is the great horned owl. Screech, short-eared and long-eared owls are frequently seen as well. Snowy owls from the far

north, unaccustomed to traffic, are sometimes brought
in after roadside injuries.

First-Hand Experience

The J.C. Taylor Nature Centre at the University of
Guelph offers several excellent birdwatching programs
throughout the year to identify hawks, ducks and other
birds, including the popular winter-evening owl prowls.
Preregistration is required. Owl prowls cost $9 for
adults and $4.50 for children. For information call (519)
824-4120 ext. 2113; for registration call ext. 4110. The
Nature Centre is located in the Arboretum on the campus of the University of Guelph. From Highway 401,
exit north on Highway 6 to Stone Road where you turn
east to the university. On campus follow the East Ring
Road to Arboretum Road.

The Mountsberg Wildlife Centre, near Milton,
offers an educational look at dozens of owls and hawks
in its Raptor Rehabilitation Centre. During summer
months public presentations in the flyway are offered
twice daily, Wednesday through Sunday. At other times
of the year public programs take place on weekends and
holidays. For information call (905) 854-2276.

The fields and farmlands of Amherst Island in the
St. Lawrence River are also known as good places to
watch for wintering raptors, both owls and hawks. The
island lands are all privately owned. To avoid trespass-
ing, birdwatchers must confine their searches to rural
roadsides, but many impressive sightings have been
reported here, especially during hard winters when
owls are forced south. To reach Amherst Island take the
ferry from Highway 33 at Millhaven, west of Kingston.

Little Brown Bats at the Bonnechere Caves

Myths associating bats with otherworldly doings transform these helpless creatures into blood-sucking monsters. Contrary to much popular belief, they do not represent a serious rabies threat —in fact they carry hardly any parasites.

Whether in a downtown Toronto attic or a spindly spruce tree on the shore of James Bay, the little brown bat is found across much of Ontario and in many varied habitats. Their tendency to seek summer roosts near water makes them a common sight in cottage country, and their ability to tolerate high temperatures enables them to seek daily refuge in hot attics. Bats are a familiar, if somewhat startling, sight to many people.

You can visit a real Ontario bat cave on the shores of the Bonnechere River near Eganville in eastern Ontario. The Bonnechere Caves were carved out of the limestone when the river washed away sand and other soft deposits. Long known to native people and loggers, the caves were first documented by Alexander Murray who charted the river in 1853. A century later the enterprising Tom Woodward installed a system of pumps, wooden walkways and electric lights to enable visitors to tour the network of caves that winds for 30 metres under the hill. On a hot summer day the cool caves with their trickling waters are particularly inviting, but to see the bats you should visit in the fall. Chris Hinsperger, who now owns and manages the 6-hectare site, keeps a chalkboard at the ticket entrance to chronicle the bat arrivals. In 1998 the first little brown bat had returned by August 28. By mid-September the bats arrive by the dozen, and by the Thanksgiving weekend hundreds hang in crevices in the ceiling among the little stalactites and flow formations.

A guided tour of the caves takes about an hour, beginning with an explanation of the area's geology and some locally collected fossils, and followed by a walk through the winding caves.

When Chris closes up the caves after the Thanksgiving weekend, he turns off the pumps, allowing the cave to flood two-thirds full of water, sealing off the passageway. This prevents the cold air from entering the cave and keeps the temperature at an even 8 to 10 degrees Celsius for the bats' winter slumbers.

Roughly 850 species of bats exist worldwide. At least eight of these are found in Ontario—little brown bat, big brown bat, red bat, hoary bat, silver-haired (or tree) bat, small-footed bat, northern long-eared bat and eastern pipistrelle. The most common is the little brown bat. Not much bigger than a field mouse with wings, this voracious insectivore consumes half its body weight in insects during night flights.

Some species migrate south each winter to warmer climes, but the little brown bat is a year-round resident, spending the frigid months in caves or abandoned mines where temperatures remain stable—cool, but above freezing. In a state of torpor, the bats roost in vast colonies, sometimes in densities of hundreds of thousands, until they become active again in spring.

Although little brown bats do not migrate out of Ontario, they do have different summer and winter ranges. The bat you see zigzagging over the lake on a summer night might have travelled hundreds of kilometres from its winter hibernaculum where it mates. As insects become available in spring, groups of females seek out summer roosts, often barns or attics, to give birth to their young. Males tend to be solitary.

"Twinkle, twinkle, little bat! How I wonder what you're at! Up above the world you fly, Like a tea tray in the sky."

— LEWIS CARROLL, *Alice in Wonderland*

The newborn bat clings to its mother's chest as she flies about in pursuit of insects. By the time the youngster is three weeks old it can fly on its own. Bats that survive their first winter may easily live ten years, perhaps even as long as thirty. Their biggest threat, especially for the young, is starvation. Those that awake from hibernation too early cannot find enough insects to eat to replace the energy used in their nightly flights.

Few people have done as much to promote an understanding of bats as Dr. Brock Fenton, a York University professor who has been dubbed Ontario's own Batman. In recent years he has introduced thousands of people to the mysterious world of bats through his evening demonstrations with live bats at Kleinburg's Kortright Centre for Conservation. The evening is a great opportunity to examine bats up close. The doctor and his students bring live specimens of little brown bats. Glow-in-the-dark detectors are carefully attached to the bats before they are released outdoors so visitors can see their seemingly erratic flight patterns in the dark.

An evening program is also offered at least once during the summer at Mountsberg Wildlife Centre near Milton. Visitors can see hundreds of bats fly overhead as they leave their daytime roost in an old barn for a night of insect hunting.

First-Hand Experience

The Bonnechere Caves are located south of Eganville via Highway 41. From Eganville, follow the signs. For information call (613) 628-CAVE or toll-free 1-800-469-2283.

The Kortright Centre for Conservation holds its informative bat evening in mid-August. Advance book-ing is required and costs about $10 for adults and $6 for children. The Kortright Centre is near Kleinburg, on Pine Valley Drive, south of Major Mackenzie and west of Highway 400. For details call (905) 832-2289.

The Mountsberg Wildlife Centre is west of Campbellville near Milton, south of Highway 401. The bat evening should be booked in advance by calling (905) 854-2276. There is a fee.

Listening to Spring Peepers at the Kortright Centre

Amphibians are particularly vulnerable to environmental degradation because they have permeable skins through which they can breathe. This skin is thought to be sensitive to increased acidity in lakes caused by various forms of pollution, and to the rising ultraviolet radiation that is due to the thinning of the earth's ozone layer.

One April evening I stopped the car to admire a springtime waterfall rushing over rocks near the village of Apsley. As the car slowed, a loud squeaking noise filled the air. Thinking it might be a worn fan belt, I shut off the engine, and only then did I realize how much noise a tiny frog can make. The shrill and steady chirping of spring peepers can be heard in the woods each spring night throughout Ontario as far north as James Bay, when these tiny frogs strike up their mighty mating chorus.

Among the earliest of the frogs to awaken, peepers emerge in April from their hibernating places under the leaf litter. Often heard, but seldom seen, they can be difficult to observe because they are most active at night. Your best bet for frog watching is to take part in a naturalist-guided program at a conservation area. At the Kortright Centre near Kleinburg naturalist Dan Stuckey leads guided hikes to peeper ponds. Each evening begins with a slide show that teaches about the life cycle of the frogs. Stuckey tries to find a few beforehand to display in an aquarium. No bigger than 2 to 3 centimetres, these pale brown frogs can be identified by the dark X-shaped markings on their backs.

Peepers don't breed in marshes or other lakes, but in woodland pools created by melting snow. These vernal ponds usually evaporate later in the summer, so the peepers need to breed early and complete their life cycle before the ponds dry up. Because fish cannot survive in these pools, amphibian eggs have a much greater chance of survival here. The ideal pond is in a wooded area where the frog can live out its entire life. Although they are technically tree frogs, the spring peepers prefer to live close to the ground, using their large toe pads to cling to wildflower stems and low shrubs.

Squishing across the wet ground in rubber boots, Stuckey leads the spring frog-finders to a pond with emerging aquatic vegetation. "Cattails and sedges provide the frog with a safe place to sing," explains Stuckey. "It climbs up the vegetation to broadcast its song, safely surrounded by water."

Males migrate across the thawing ground to find their ancestral ponds. There they call to females who are drawn to the most vigorous chirps. Occasionally a silent male lying in wait at the edge of his rival's territory will intercept a female.

The sound can be deafening. Stuckey brings a decibel meter to the pond to measure the noise, which has sometimes been in excess of 80 decibels. "That's into acoustical trauma," says Stuckey. "Many people experience discomfort and want to leave after a short while."

The Ontario Herpetological Society organizes outings to observe amphibians. Membership costs $25. Contact the society at P.O. Box 244, Port Credit L5G 4L8, or visit their Web site at www.geocities.com/ rainforest/6560/ ohs1.htm.

First-Hand Experience

An excellent guide to frogs is *Familiar Amphibians and Reptiles of Ontario* by Bob Johnson, published by Natural Heritage Books.

Evening frog-finding programs are often offered in spring at conservation areas such as the Kortright Centre for Conservation, near Kleinburg on Pine Valley

Drive, south of Major Mackenzie and west of Highway 400. Call (905) 832-2289. The Mountsberg Wildlife Centre near Milton also offers evening peeper programs (see page 89). Call (905) 832-2289 or (905) 854-2276. There is a fee for the evening frog programs at both Kortright and Mountsberg, and you should book in advance.

ROCKY REMINDERS

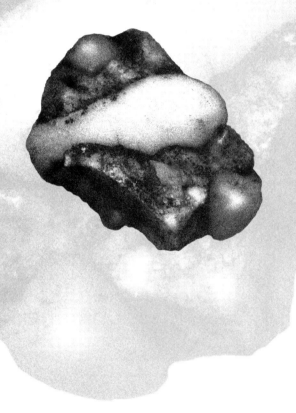

Finding Trilobites at Craigleith, Georgian Bay

As grey waves slap against Georgian Bay's rocky shore, lying at your feet are reminders that human beings are recent developments on this planet. Here at Craigleith Provincial Park, the fossil-rich shales remind you of the vast scale of geological time. Ordovician rocks at the base of Blue Mountain, near Collingwood, are filled with the fossils of small marine creatures that inhabited the place roughly 445 million years ago.

Often beautifully preserved in the shale are the outlines of trilobites, early arthropods distantly related to today's crabs, lobsters, spiders and centipedes. You find their fossils embedded in the rock under your feet as you explore the park's shoreline. Nearly half a billion years ago, long before fish and dinosaurs, the trilobites were the most common marine creatures. They teemed in the shallow seas that covered much of Ontario.

Trilobites take their name from their chitinous exoskeletons—the equivalent of lobsters' shells—that are divided longitudinally into three parts. Typically, the trilobites were small creatures, usually 5 to 8 centimetres long. As they grew they moulted periodically, leaving behind their exoskeletons to become potential fossils. The most easily identifiable trilobite fossils are those that show the dorsal (back) side like a slightly convex shield. With so many articulated segments in the thorax, the trilobite could roll up into a ball like a

Known for its dramatic scenery, Kakabeka Falls, near Thunder Bay, is also the site of some of the world's oldest fossils. Microscopic single-celled organisms are preserved in two-billion-year-old rock.

pill bug. By flexing its segmented body, it probably propelled itself through the water like a crayfish.

These ancient animals first appeared early in the Cambrian period (500 to 570 million years ago) and thrived and increased in diversity. Many varieties became extinct during the Ordovician period that followed, and by the end of the Devonian period (360 million years ago) only one order survived. Because so many different trilobites developed, most with relatively short appearances on the geological stage, their fossils prove useful in identifying various biological zones.

Hundreds of millions of years after their demise, the trilobites began to play a role in Ontario's human history when it was discovered that their fossilized remains and the black, organic muck that held them were rich in petroleum. Fuelled by fantasies of wealth, a nineteenth-century industrial experiment began. In 1859 entrepreneurs built a large plant on the site of the park to extract oil from the rocks. The process turned out to be too costly, and within four years the ill-fated experiment was abandoned, leaving the fossils for paleontologists.

But you don't have to be a paleontologist to experience the sense of awe that comes from touching such ancient creatures.

First-Hand Experience

Craigleith Provincial Park is located on Highway 26, roughly 10 kilometres west of Collingwood. The park offers picnic shelters, a playground and 172 campsites. Swimming is not recommended here, but the park is within a short drive of Wasaga Beach. For information call (705) 445-4467.

Rock Hounding Near Bancroft

Equipped with a geologist's hammer and sample bags, you can't help feeling like an old-fashioned prospector as you explore the mine sites and mineral deposits in the highlands at the north end of Hastings County. The town of Bancroft, with its annual Rockhound Gemboree, has been dubbed the Mineral Capital of Canada. With an estimated twenty thousand visitors and more than fifty dealers from across North America, the Gemboree is the largest gem and mineral show in Canada. While dealers sell stones, less experienced visitors can play at panning for gold and pick up tips on collecting. Held each summer on the August civic holiday weekend, the Gemboree is a great opportunity for budding rock collectors to get out into the field with a trained geologist who will show them how to collect samples from the old pits and quarries that once supplied corundum, graphite and mica.

The Bancroft Chamber of Commerce offers similar outings every Tuesday and Thursday during July and August. Geologists lead convoys of mineral collectors to various sites—usually two locations within the space of four hours. The trip typically begins with a short talk on minerals and includes tips on how to find them.

More than a decade before the great Klondike gold strike, this corner of eastern Ontario witnessed a massive mining boom. Iron-ore mines were built in the 1800s, and by 1866 gold was discovered at Eldorado.

The New Age fascination with crystals as an energizing force and source of inspiration dates back to ancient civilizations. Wealthy warriors once wore diamonds into battle, probably because the gem's hardness represented invincibility.

Between 1880 and 1935 Bancroft area mines were quarried for a host of minerals, including beryl, corundum, feldspar, fluorite, granite, nepheline, syenite, sodalite, lead and uranium. Marble was excavated to construct the Royal Ontario Museum. Mica was used in the production of formica. Known for its lightweight properties, graphite, a form of pure carbon, proved serviceable in a host of products from pencils to fishing rods—and even synthetic diamonds.

In 1866 the first discovery of gold in Ontario was made north of Madoc. The site was promptly named Eldorado.

The wealth of minerals in the area is attributable to numerous geological forces: volcanic activity, faulting, folding and intense pressure and heat more than a billion years ago. Roughly 80 percent of the minerals found in Canada are represented in the Bancroft area.

Although most commercial activity ended decades ago, there are still several local sites where collectors can search for their own specimens.

Mineral finds vary with each location. At the Faraday Mine visitors may find quartz, selenite, ilmenite, magnetite and uranophane; the Quadeville area has rose quartz, beryl and tourmaline. At the Bear Lake diggings west of Tory Hill visitors can excavate earth-filled veins that cut through the gneissic bedrock. Water seeping through fallen leaves becomes acidic, so when it filters through the veins it wears away the calcite. Harder, silicate materials remain: crystals of apatite (hexagonal green crystals), hornblende (shiny black crystals), titanite and feldspar. Collectors may keep their finds.

You can also experience some of the area's mining history at an abandoned open pit mine in Murphy's Point Provincial Park, located on a mineral-rich spur of the Canadian Shield. Mica, feldspar and apatite were among the minerals dug here before the mine closed more than seventy-five years ago. Visitors are not allowed to remove mineral samples, but you may follow the 2-kilometre trail to the Silver Queen Mine on one of the conducted hikes offered during summer months. Hard hats are provided for the slippery climb down into the mine. There the rock glistens with silvery sparkles of mica, which was once used as electrical insulation. The feldspar produced a pottery glaze, while the apatite was used to make fertilizer. Because apatite consists mainly of phosphate of lime, it is often found with lush greenery growing over it.

As mining boomed in the late nineteenth and early twentieth century, the Central Ontario Railway expanded north. Although the trains no longer run, the old COR rail-bed remains as a 156-kilometre recreational trailway stretching from Lake St. Peter south through Maynooth and Bancroft to Glen Ross. The four-season, multi-use trail passes through woods and over some lovely creeks.

First-Hand Experience

The Bear Lake site is operated by the Bancroft Chamber of Commerce. Collectors pay $5 each per day or $12 per family. The collecting season runs from May 1 to October 31.

A mineral museum is located in the chamber of commerce office in Bancroft. There you can purchase the hammer and sample bags you will need for rockhounding excursions. The price of the hammers ranges from about $18 to $50. A good alternative is to bring a regular carpenter's hammer, chisel and garden claw. The chisel is necessary to get a clean cut and the claw helps pry rocks loose.

Visitors register for rock-hounding excursions at the Bancroft Chamber of Commerce at 9:30 a.m. on the morning of the outing (sometimes a different location is used during Gemboree). The group departs, convoy-style, at 10 a.m. to visit two of the nearly three dozen local sites. Participants travel in their own cars and may leave whenever they have had enough, although the excursions officially wind up around 3 p.m. The trips cost $7 per person or $15 per family. For details call the Bancroft Chamber of Commerce at (613) 332-1513.

Murphy's Point Provincial Park is located 19 kilo-metres south of Perth via Road 21 (Elm Grove Road). Call (613) 267-5060.

Stories in Stone at Petroglyphs Provincial Park

With its mysterious carvings in white stone, Petroglyphs Provincial Park holds some of Ontario's most precious archaeological treasures. On a large outcrop of quartzite lined with fissures, hundreds of stylized figures of animals and spirits have been carved. These mystic and mysterious images will likely never be fully understood, but they continue to intrigue and remain a source of spiritual teaching for First Nations people.

Since the site first came to public attention in the 1950s, many anthropologists have speculated on the petroglyphs' origins. Today it is generally believed that the images were carved five hundred to one thousand years ago by Algonquin-speaking aboriginal people. The exact meaning of the carvings has vanished with the nomadic people who created them, but anthropologists and present-day First Nations people have many interpretations of the sacred site.

Unusual geological formations such as this well-weathered outcrop of crystalline marble are of special significance to many native people because manitous, or spirits, are believed to reside within them. The gurgling of underground waters and other sounds from the eroded cavities within are the voices of these manitous.

Creating images on rock is an ancient native tradition and there are more than three hundred sites of rock art, mostly pictographs (paintings on rock, as opposed to carvings), in Ontario. These include Agawa Bay, Bon Echo Provincial Park, Lake Superior Provincial Park, Mazinaw Lake and Quetico Provincial Park.

Such a site would likely have been visited by shamans (spiritual leaders) who carved the images over many years, as suggested by the faintness of some of the images compared with the relative clarity of others. Roughly three hundred images are clearly visible and another six hundred remain indistinct. It is the largest concentration of native rock carvings in North America.

Today the main site of the petroglyphs is protected by a modern shelter, which allows enough sunlight for a good view of the images. An elevated path allows visitors to walk on concrete walkways around the carvings to see them from many angles. Staff are on hand to explain the significance of the images. Some are stylized depictions of recognizable creatures while others are highly symbolic or otherworldly.

One of the most repeated images is the mythical turtle on whose back the earth was built. Sometimes it is surrounded by dots, thought to represent its eggs. Another easily discernible creature is a massive, long-legged bird, almost 2 metres long. Possibly a heron or a crane, it may be a clan symbol.

Mythic figures include a man-like creature with long rabbit ears. It suggests Nanabush, the teacher and trickster, as he takes on a rabbit's form. The Great Spirit, or Gitchi Manitou, is thought to be depicted in a tall, standing creature with an elongated neck and a head that resembles a sun with rays emanating from it. Although the Gitchi Manitou does not have a constant form, it is believed to reside in the sun.

Because park staff have tried to accommodate present-day aboriginal people and their spiritual beliefs, the site is frequently used by members of the Ojibway Anishinabe Nation, who call this place Kinomagewap-kong, "the rocks that teach." It is not unusual to see tobacco set out on a ceremonial stone in preparation for

burning, to cleanse and purify the site after the day's visitors have left.

A separate building intended to serve as a visitor
centre was built in 1988, but no exhibits were installed.
Now, after a period of consultation with the local Curve
Lake First Nation, plans are underway to install an ex-
hibit that will prepare visitors to approach the sacred
site with an understanding of First Nations' beliefs and
spirituality, not just as rock art. Completion is depen-
dent upon funding.

After seeing the petroglyphs, you can walk through
some of the landscape that helped inspire their cre-
ators. The park's extensive network of rugged trails
leads hikers through forests of old white and red pines,
alongside wetlands populated by beavers and across
scenic ridges. Birdwatchers will find many northern
species here, including grey jays and ravens. Bald eagles
have also made a comeback. During winter months the
neighbouring Peterborough Crown Game Reserve (see
page 183) shelters many white-tailed deer. Deer carcasses—left by wolves or winter starvation—attract
both bald and golden eagles as well as ravens, who often
lead the way to the site of the kill.

First-Hand Experience

Petroglyphs Provincial Park is 55 kilometres northeast
of Peterborough via Highway 28 and Northey's Bay
Road. The petroglyphs site is well signposted. The park
is in operation from mid-May to Thanksgiving. Call
(705) 877-2552. There is no camping at Petroglyphs,
but there are both campgrounds and modern yurts
(winterized shelters) at Silent Lake, 32 kilometres north
(see page 220).

Discovering Devonian Fossils at Rock Glen and Rock Point

Although no dinosaur fossils have been found, they could have inhabited Ontario and died off during the great Cretaceous extinction sixty-five million years ago. However, geological records of life on earth are incomplete. In Ontario few rocks from this period exist. Either they were never formed or subsequent erosion and glacial scouring has worn them away, along with any fossil evidence.

Each new rain washes down a fresh supply of fossils in the mud at Rock Glen Conservation Area. With bare hands and a simple guidebook, the amateur fossil finder is well equipped to search for remnants of Devonian life, and possibly make some rare discoveries.

Long before dinosaurs roamed the earth, much of southern Ontario was covered by a warm, tropical sea. Corals, snails and shellfish thrived in the waters that covered the present-day farms of Lambton County. Some 350 to 400 million years ago the simple life forms of the Devonian era predominated. Their fossilized imprints are visible today, embedded in the soft limestone and shale along the banks of the Ausable River.

At Rock Glen Conservation Area the river's course has worn a gorge through the 25 metres of sedimentary deposits formed when the remains of the Devonian creatures were deposited in the shallow, salty sea. As layers accumulated over the millennia, increased pressure turned the calcium carbonate of the animals' shells into limestone.

The exposed sediments in the walls of the gorge make for prime fossil hunting, and even complete novices will find some excellent specimens. Among the most common are the brachiopods (early bivalves whose

open shells resemble butterflies) and two types of coral
(horn and staghorn).

Many fossils are found in pieces. Crinoids usually
turn up as little rings that look like stone Cheerios.
These rings are cross-sections of a stalk that grew from
the bottom of the sea. At the top of each stalk were
food-gathering tentacles. Though they looked much
like plants, the crinoids are classed as animals. Without
much effort at all you can uncover dozens of specimens
simply by picking through the mud with your fingers,
feeling for the hard, fossilized shapes of shells and other
small marine animals. But once you have become familiar with some of the frequent finds, you will probably
want to concentrate your search on rarer specimens.

Less common are platyceras (marine snails) and
specimens of some of the world's earliest fish. Although
fish lived in this sea, their delicate skeletons crushed
more easily than the shells of snails and bivalves, so they
are seldom found in complete fossils. Although common at other sites, trilobites are a special find here.
Segmented like crayfish, these thumb-sized invertebrates
varied greatly between species. *Phacops rana*, the species
found at Rock Glen, is noted for its large, bulging eyes.
The numerous prisms gave the creature 180-degree
vision.

The easiest way to find fossils is to walk along the
riverbank in either of the two areas designated by the
Ausable Bayfield Conservation Authority. The fossils are
so plentiful that you can't help stepping on them, but
the best specimens are usually washed down in the mud.
Visitors are asked not to use picks or shovels. You can
take home some of your finds as long as you remove
only one sample of each species.

Bring a picnic and plan on spending the day. An excellent on-site museum boasts a collection of roughly a

thousand Devonian-era specimens, among the best in North America. Besides fossil finding, you can hike through some beautiful woods. Rock Glen's 25-hectare site boasts many species of southern Carolinian forest plants, including common hackberry and chinquapin oak. Several trails and stairways border the gorge, offering a view of the dramatic 11-metre waterfalls.

Embedded in the limestone slabs at Rock Point Provincial Park on Lake Erie's north shore are some large patches of tabulate colonial corals resembling stone honeycombs, as well as impressively large Devonian horn corals, also known as solitary rugose corals. Some grew to lengths of 60 centimetres. Unlike colonial corals, these creatures lived apart from each other. Their horn-shaped bodies were anchored to the sea floor at the narrow end. Tentacles filtered food at the wide end.

Fossils can be found along most of the park's shoreline, but the best specimens are at the eastern end of the park. Take the stairs that lead down to the beach from the 2.5-kilometre Woodland Trail. A sunset walk along the park's 600-metre beach is a magical experience. Multitudes of shorebirds dabble in the rocky pools, and the breeze carries a maritime scent. From the main fossil site you can see the historic Mohawk Island Lighthouse, built in 1848. Today the island is a sanctuary for gulls and cormorants. Deer, pheasants and opossums inhabit the lush woods.

First-Hand Experience

The Rock Glen Conservation Area is located nearly 50 kilometres west of London near the village of Arkona. From Highway 402, turn north on Middlesex County Road 6 to Keyser, then west on County Road 12 to

Rock Glen. Fossil hunting is permitted year-round, but some facilities, including the museum, are closed during winter. For information call the Ausable-Bayfield Conservation Authority at (519) 235-2610 or Rock Glen at (519) 828-3071.

Rock Point Provincial Park is on Niece Road, 11 kilometres south of Dunnville via Regional Road 3. The park has two groomed picnic areas, a snackbar, store and 178 campsites. It is open from mid-May to Thanksgiving. Visitors cannot remove fossils. For more information call (905) 774-6642.

Exploring the Drumlins of Peterborough County

Looking at a drumlin rising out of a cow pasture gives one pause to think about the ever-changing surface of this planet. The tranquil, green hills of Peterborough County grew out of the massive flux of global warming and cooling, the change from tropical sea to ice-shrouded land. Twelve thousand years ago a vast glacier covered southern Ontario. Glaciers are powerful rivers of ice that slowly scrape across the landscape, bulldozing terrain under their tremendous weight, grinding behemoth boulders into gravel. When they melt, they dump vast quantities of crushed stone and silt in heaps and ridges, forming drumlins.

Drumlins are found in many places in Ontario, including Collingwood. But one of the most notable drumlin fields can be seen in Peterborough County. Covered with maple woods and surrounded by lush farmland, drumlins appear softly unspectacular. But look closely and you can see the telltale pattern of glacial activity. Long, ovoid hills lie parallel to each other like humpbacked whales all swimming in the same direction in a sea of green fields. Many drumlins can be observed from numerous county roads and highways, but excellent examples can be seen at Serpent Mounds Park on the north shore of Rice Lake. Many of the islands in Rice Lake are drumlins, now surrounded by water. Serpent Mounds' shoreline offers a fantastic view of these waterbound drumlins, and also chronicles the prehistoric occupation of the area by the Point Peninsula people two thousand years ago. They came to these rolling hills each summer to hunt and fish among the abundant rice beds that gave the lake its name. A ground-level midden, or garbage dump, of clam shells stretches 60 metres along the shoreline. These crushed shells—and the occasional bits of bone and rare pottery shards—are the remains of many thousands of meals harvested from the rich forests and fertile lake.

The Point Peninsula people also used the site for ceremonial burials. Archaeologists discovered human remains interred with copper work, silver work and even conch shells, revealing an extensive trade network that must have stretched from the Gulf of Mexico to north of Ottawa.

Another popular park located in the drumlin field is Mark S. Burnham Provincial Park, east of Peterborough. It sits on the side of a drumlin covered with old-growth woods and boasts some of the oldest stands of maple, beech and hemlock in Ontario.

First-Hand Experience

Serpent Mounds Park is administered by the Hiawatha First Nations Band. It is located south of the village of Keene on Peterborough County Road 34. Camping is available during summer months. There is a parking fee of $6 per vehicle. During winter months the park closes, but visitors may park their cars at the general store just outside the park. For information call (705) 295-6879.

When melting glaciers leave large chunks of ice in their wake, they create unusual lakes that have no inlets or outlets. At Kettle Lakes Provincial Park near Timmins the forests are dotted with twenty small lakes formed by a retreating glacier that dropped huge islands of ice behind. Kettle Lakes is 40 kilometres (25 miles) northeast of Timmins on Highway 67. Telephone (705) 363-3511.

Mark S. Burnham Provincial Park is located on Highway 7, just east of Peterborough. It is a day-use park—great for hikes and picnics, but with no overnight camping. It is open from mid-May to the end of October. Telephone (705) 799-5170.

Hiking the Niagara Escarpment

With its numerous waterfalls and clifftop vistas, the Niagara Escarpment is one of Ontario's most impressive geological features, snaking through 2,300 kilometres of southern Ontario from Niagara Falls up through the Bruce Peninsula to Sault Ste. Marie. Ontario's most famous tourist attraction, Niagara Falls, lies at the southern end of the escarpment. While fifteen million tourists throng to the falls each year, the inaccessibility of the sheer cliffs in many other sections of the escarpment have preserved them in their wild state. Ancient cedars cling to steep walls, rare ferns grow in shaded nooks, and turkey vultures nest along the cliffs.

The Niagara Escarpment offers remarkable views from its many trails. The most famous is the Bruce Trail, which follows the escarpment from Niagara Falls to Tobermory, a distance of roughly 740 kilometres. It is maintained by local trail clubs who clear the path and mark it with white blazes. Along the trail are numerous conservation areas where waterfalls tumble over the limestone cliffs and unusual plants and animals inhabit the cliff face. At Rocklyn Creek Management Area, west of Meaford, hikers can see a rare old-growth forest of ancient cedars estimated to be more than a thousand years old. These gnarled, often stunted trees are not what we usually think of as old-growth forest. Their slow growth rate is likely attributable to steep, inaccessible

On the first Sunday of October, Ontario Hiking Day celebrates the joys of walking in the woods. Trail clubs are encouraged to organize hikes and welcome new ramblers to their ranks. For information contact Hike Ontario, a non-profit organization that promotes hiking throughout the province, at 1220 Sheppard Avenue East, Willowdale, M2K 2X1.

cliff faces and dry conditions. Slower growth in trees is often associated with greater structural integrity, so these twisted little cedars have often outlived much larger trees growing on the gentler lands below.

In addition to the cedars there are numerous rare ferns. Black's Park, a small park near Owen Sound, boasts a remarkable twenty-nine species of ferns, including the long flat leaves of hart's-tongue and the delicate fronds of maidenhair.

Explore many interesting detours by following the Bruce Trail side loops marked with blue blazes at places such as Cootes Paradise, a restored wetland in Hamilton, or the nineteenth-century industrial ruins of old mills along the Cataract River in the Caledon Hills at Forks of the Credit Provincial Park.

For sheer drama you can't beat the cliffs and caves along Georgian Bay where the Bruce Trail winds through Bruce Peninsula National Park. Delicate blooms of columbine emerge from cracks in the slabs of limestone overlooking the turquoise bay below. The 3-kilometre stretch of the trail from Halfway Rock Point to Overhanging Point is the most scenic along the length of the Bruce. Here ambitious hikers can follow the difficult descent down to a boulder beach and explore caves carved by Georgian Bay's pounding waters. Agility is needed to scramble up the ledges.

Six hundred million years ago the area that is now the escarpment was a warm, inland sea. Sediments settled on the sea floor and eventually compressed into limestone, shale and sandstone. Forces deep within the earth sucked this bowl-like formation deeper and deeper. When those forces reversed, layers of sedimentary rock were thrust upward, creating the escarpment. You can find fossil remnants of ancient sea creatures at many of the caves along the trail.

Georgian Bay's rough waters have also eroded the cliffs to create strange "flower pot" islands—layers of stone towering above the water, with tufts of vegetation on top. Although the Bruce Trail ends at Tobermory, the escarpment continues across the north shore of Manitoulin Island towards Sault Ste. Marie. From Tobermory, hikers can continue their rambles by taking one of the many tour boats that will drop passengers off at Flowerpot Island for a few hours of hiking along quiet trails— about 3 kilometres in all. The escarpment continues underwater, creating steep underwater cliffs on the island's east shore. Here you can see the towering rock formations that give Flowerpot its name. The sea stacks were carved by eroding forces five thousand years ago when lake levels were much higher. Harmless garter snakes are often seen in great number on the trail. More than twenty species of orchids, including the calypso, bloom on Flowerpot.

First-Hand Experience

For information on the Bruce Trail contact the Bruce Trail Association. Their office is located in the Royal Botanical Gardens in Hamilton (page 167). Write to P.O. Box 857, Hamilton L8N 3N9, or call (905) 529-6821. A copy of the *Guide to the Bruce Trail* is essential for hiking. It is sold at outfitting stores, such as the Mountain Equipment Co-op, for about $20.

For information on the Niagara Escarpment and its parklands, contact the Niagara Escarpment Commission at 232 Guelph Street, Georgetown L7G 4B1, or call (905) 877-5191. The commission's Explorer series of brochures are particularly helpful.

SMALL BUT SIGNIFICANT

Blackflies and Blueberries on the Canadian shield

Sure as geese fly north, trout lilies bloom, sure as spring itself is the blood-sucking onslaught of blackflies. Venture onto an Algonquin hiking trail on a May morning and it won't be long before droplets of blood appear in the part of your hair, on your wrists and on the back of your neck. Soon the spring serenity gives way to grim musings about how many blackfly bites you can stand and still stay sane.

Unlike the mosquito whose bite leaves a swelling but no bloody trail, the blackfly does some serious visible damage. That's because blackflies really do bite. While the mosquito merely pierces the skin with a fine tube, the blackfly actually chews up the surface of your skin with mouth parts that work like scissors. Teeth added to the scissor blades help the blackfly dig right in until sufficient bleeding allows it to simply lap up its liquid meal, feeding at the wound for up to five minutes. Only females do the biting and sucking; they need the nutrients in your blood to build their strength up for laying eggs. Many of Ontario's fifty species of blackflies are specialists; one dines exclusively on loon blood.

But as big a nuisance as they are, the presence of blackflies can be reassuring. They are an indication of good water quality. Blackflies breed only in clean, fast-flowing water because their larvae must take oxygen directly from the water—unlike mosquitoes, who

Female blackflies lay two to five hundred eggs in water or on rocks and weeds just below the water's surface.

breathe at the water's surface. Filter-feeding blackfly larvae are very sensitive to sediments and therefore seldom thrive in areas contaminated by agricultural run-off. Blackflies are also an important source of food for swallows, warblers and other birds. But even if none of this consoles you through your post-bite itching, remember that blackflies feed not only on blood but on plant nectar, thereby helping to pollinate blueberries.

Come mid-July, when the worst of the blackfly plague is forgotten, sweet blueberries ripen on outcrops of the Canadian Shield. Thriving in thin soils, often springing up after forest fires, the blueberry is an important source of food for nectar-eating insects and berry-loving bears. In a bad berry year, hungry black bears are more likely to wander further afield in search of food— and often end up in confrontations with humans!

Blueberries were an important source of food for native people, who dried them for winter use. Pioneers mixed the crushed fruit with buttermilk to produce a blue-grey paint.

When picking blueberries be careful not to confuse them with potentially poisonous blue-coloured berries like clintonia. The lowbush blueberry, as its name suggests, grows on low shrubs seldom more than 30 centimetres high, though it may sprawl in the right sun-filled space. The blueberry has a five-pointed crown, the remnants of the corolla, or petals, from the tiny white bloom.

First-Hand Experience

The art of avoiding blackflies lies in understanding their habits. They tend to be most active in the morning and late afternoon on warm, overcast days with little wind. These pesky insects will crawl inside ears, noses and under collars, so a hat with fine mesh netting to cover your head and neck is essential. Blackflies can penetrate loosely woven fabrics or openings such as cuffs. Try

putting elastic bands around your shirt and pant cuffs
and stick to zipper-front jackets. Wear light colours.
Blue, red, purple and black are particularly attractive to
blackflies.

Blueberries thrive in the thin acid soils of the Canadian Shield. Obatanga and Windy Lake Provincial Parks
are both known for their blueberries. However picking
wild fruit is not encouraged in provincial parks, as it is
important food for birds, bears and other wildlife.

Blueberry picking is made easy at several southern
Ontario fruit farms such as Wilmot Orchards (see page
24) where acid is added to alkaline soils through irriga-
tion systems. For a list of pick-your-own berry farms
contact the provincial tourism office at 1-800-
ONTARIO or (416) 314-0944 from Toronto.

Blueberries are also
associated with
cleansing the kidneys.
They contain an
enzyme thought to
be helpful in treating
bladder infections.

Lichens Colour the Landscape

Lichens like it hot and cold. Some have survived absolute zero: -273 degrees Celsius.

Not nearly as glamorous as old-growth forests, lichens are easily overlooked—the stuff you step on while searching for bigger and better beauties. But a closer look reveals a fascinating organism that plays a crucial role in Ontario's wild habitats.

Until a century ago lichens were thought to be a separate plant form. Today we know that lichens are actually a symbiosis of fungi and microscopic algae growing together to form a composite structure. Both are needed to make a lichen, so lichens tend to have double-barrelled names, one for the fungus and another for the alga.

Varying in colour from green to yellow, brilliant orange to red, lichens can colour a landscape with vivid hues at times of the year when all else seems grey. Their shapes range from flat, leathery leaves, to clumps, crusts and tufts. One of the most distinctive and easiest to recognize for budding naturalists is the British soldier, often found on rotting logs, especially in pine woods. This lichen takes its name from the scarlet tips on its greyish-green clubs, which are no more than 2 centimetres tall.

Tough enough to thrive on sun-baked rocks that can support little or no other life, lichens are also remarkably sensitive. Like the canaries in coal mines a century ago, they cannot survive in polluted air, particularly air contaminated with sulphur dioxide, which causes acid rain.

Having no roots, they take moisture and minerals from the air; hence their sensitivity to air quality and inability to thrive in urban environments. Consequently most of the seven to eight hundred species of lichens found in Ontario are most often associated with northern landscapes: pale green patches of map lichen on a boulder in Algonquin Park, or grey tufts of old man's beard dangling from the branches of a balsam fir at Lake Superior Provincial Park.

In the north lichens play a vital role in the food chain. Reindeer lichens (*Cladina rangiferina* and *Cladina stellaris*) are important foods for caribou. During winter months woodland caribou paw away snow with their hooves to reveal mats of these ash-grey lichens, which sustain them when little else is available.

As well as food, lichens provide nesting material for birds and small mammals. A pretty blue and yellow warbler known as the northern parula builds its nest within the tangles of old man's beard in boreal forests. Some robins may use tufts of coral lichen in their nests.

When faced with starvation humans have also turned to eating lichens. Half-digested lichens from a caribou's stomach, boiled with water or blood, were a traditional food for some native people. Ill-fated northern explorers, like Sir John Franklin, turned to eating rock tripe to stave off starvation. However these flat, leaf-shaped lichens that turn leathery when moist need to be processed properly in order to prevent side effects such as nausea and severe gastric distress. After trimming off the base where it was attached to the rock, the rock tripe should be washed repeatedly in clean water. After a slow roasting during which the lichen becomes crisp, it is ready to be boiled for an hour. But eating lichens—even properly prepared—is perilous. Most species grow very slowly, not more than 2 to 4 millimetres a year. They absorb water from the air without the benefit of filtration, so poisons such as radioactive by-products from nuclear testing may slowly accumulate. Thus lichens should only be eaten in desperate circumstances. They have little nutritional value and serve merely to stave off hunger pangs.

First-Hand Experience

Although numerous books describe trees and wildflowers, finding a guide to the humbler forms of vegetation can be much more difficult. I found *Forest Plants of Central Ontario*, written by Brenda Chambers, Karen Legasy and Cathy V. Bentley, to be well worth its carrying weight in my backpack while hiking. Focusing primarily on plants of the Great Lakes forest zone, the book covers mosses, liverworts, lichens, herbs, sedges, ferns and shrubs, as well as trees and flowers.

The Five-Lined Skink, Ontario's Only Lizard

Lizards are often thought of as tropical creatures, but there is one species found in parts of eastern and southern Ontario. The five-lined skink is an elusive creature—a quick flash of a metallic blue tail may be all you see of a young skink as it dashes across a woodpile on a hot afternoon. It takes its eponymous name from the five cream-coloured lines that run from its head along the length of its brown body. On older skinks the lines may be barely visible.

Young skinks are identified by the brilliant blue of their tails, which are thought to provide a natural defence; if grabbed by a fox or a mink, the tail will break off and wiggle about to distract the predator while the tail-less skink beats a hasty retreat. The skink will grow a new tail later, although the loss of a tail—and any fat it contains—late in summer might signal the death of an Ontario skink. At the northern limit of its range, the tail-less skink probably would not have enough fat reserves to survive the winter.

Growing to a maximum length of about 20 centimetres, the skink lives a solitary life among sun-warmed rocks or old piles of decaying wood and fallen logs. They emerge from hibernation in May to establish their home territories. They do not travel far, but use a small range for all their feeding and basking needs. Early in the summer mature males develop orange colouring

Skinks really are leapin' lizards. They can be seen performing a variety of acrobatics—jumping, rolling and wrestling—most often in pursuit of insect meals.

on their throats to attract females. After mating, females leave their mate's territory. About a month later she will build a nest in a rotting log or leaf litter, hollowing out a space to lay her eggs, up to eighteen at a time. She promptly curls up around them and remains with them until they hatch, occasionally rolling the eggs. Once they hatch, the young are left on their own to forage for insects, spiders, millipedes and earthworms.

As they quickly flick their tongues while scurrying across a rock, skinks are thought to be following pheromone trails. Pheromones may help lead them to den sites where they overwinter underground, sometimes in small groups.

Skinks are extremely timid and will quickly scurry away to escape curious eyes. I suppose it is not coincidental then that I have always spotted them unexpectedly. They illustrate the value in taking time to stop and observe the ground around you. On a summer day you may see a skink sunning itself on a lakeside rock. Any movement will cause it to dart into a dark crevice in a rock or rotting log, but if you sit still and wait, chances are good that it will re-emerge.

In April 1998 the five-lined skink was one of eighteen species added to the list of endangered species by the Committee on the Status of Endangered Wildlife in Canada. Sightings of skinks are becoming less frequent due to poachers who sell them in the pet trade. It is illegal to hunt or even possess a five-lined skink under Ontario's Game and Fish Act.

First-Hand Experience

Scattered populations of skinks are found across southern Ontario. These lizards are occasionally sighted in

Bon Echo and Pinery Provincial Parks, but the most likely place to see one is in Point Pelee National Park on Lake Erie, where they typically live under the boardwalks, particularly in the areas of the De Laurier and Tilden's Woods Trails.

Migrating Monarchs at Presqu'ile

Monarch butterflies seem to drift south almost by accident. By choosing a flower somewhat south of the one it has just taken nectar from, the monarch gradually moves along. Toward the end of August they can be seen in the thousands as they congregate on southern points along the lower Great Lakes, preparing for their 4,000-kilometre migration.

The most difficult part of the journey is crossing large open bodies of water such as the Great Lakes, where there are no plants to provide nectar or shelter from wind and weather. To shorten this dangerous portion of their trip, monarchs seek out the shortest stretches of open water by following land formations that jut into the Great Lakes. These include Long Point and Point Pelee on Lake Erie, and Presqu'ile on Lake Ontario.

Along the beaches of Presqu'ile Provincial Park, Dr. Fred Urquhart conducted studies that recently revealed the destination of Ontario's migrating monarchs. Adapting bird-banding techniques, Dr. Urquhart's team attached tiny postage-stamp-like tags to the wings of half a million monarchs, then traced them to the Sierra Madre in Mexico.

Tagging monarchs continues each summer at Presqu'ile's Monarch Migration Festival, held on the first weekend of September. Visitors can watch naturalists affix tissue-thin discs to butterfly wings. In a good year thousands of monarchs will pass through, descending on trees to rest. They have difficulty flying in temperatures below 10 degrees Celsius so they will often roost overnight. Look for them early in the morning when the air is still cool along the Presqu'ile shoreline, particularly around Owen Point on the west side of the spit, where they are sometimes so plentiful that the trees seem orange. They will wait in the trees until warmer temperatures make it possible for them to cross the lake.

Aptly named, the monarch is the largest of Ontario's butterflies. Multiple generations of them are born on the journey north and in their summer range, which includes most of Ontario as far north as James Bay. Some of the previous fall's migrants may return north in the spring. The tired, tattered females lay their eggs on milkweed plants. From the eggs emerge ravenous black, yellow and white caterpillars that gorge themselves on milkweed before spinning their white cocoons to pupate into butterflies. The milkweed diet is thought to provide some natural defences: the caterpillars can absorb its toxins without harm to themselves, while becoming distasteful to predators.

Not all of Ontario's butterflies migrate. Some adult butterflies such as the American painted lady, the Compton tortoiseshell, the red admiral and the mourning cloak sleep through the cold season, hidden in leaf litter or under a layer of bark.

First-Hand Experience

Look for migrating monarchs in late August and early September along land spits that reach southward into the Great Lakes: Long Point Provincial Park, Presqu'ile Provincial Park, Point Pelee National Park and Tommy Thompson Park.

Presqu'ile's Monarch Migration Festival is held on the Labour Day weekend each September. However, butterflies don't always respect calendars. Weather conditions may prompt them to fly through sooner or later, or even to take a different route, so it's wise to phone ahead. Call (613) 475-2204. A nature centre displaying local fauna remains open until Labour Day. The park has nearly four hundred campsites, many of which are near the beach.

Monarchs migrate at an average speed of 15 kilometres per hour.

Seeking Salamanders in the Dundas Valley

The Dundas Valley is tucked into a corner under the Niagara Escarpment where it bends around the west end of Lake Ontario. Four-hundred-million-year-old walls of rock shelter 585 species of plants and 99 species of breeding birds. Early settlers used the relatively flat land above the escarpment walls for agriculture and quarries, but the steep cliffs, the talus slopes of fallen rubble and the riverbanks below were more difficult to reach. They have therefore endured in a state that, while not entirely pristine, is delightfully wild.

In the midst of this verdant beauty lies a ruin surrounded by ghost stories, the most notable about a coachman who committed suicide when denied permission to marry his employer's daughter. This stone mansion, known as the Hermitage, was built in 1855 by George Leith, the second son of a Scottish baronet, and was occupied by his descendants until it burned in 1934. Stone walls and the remnants of overgrown orchards from the estate can still be seen.

A 72-kilometre network of trails surrounding the ruined Hermitage provides hikers and cyclists with glimpses of some of Ontario's rarest flora and fauna. From Jefferson salamanders to sassafras trees, many of these species are at the northernmost tip of their range. But they can survive comfortably on the sheltered south-facing slopes of the Dundas Valley.

Salamanders were attributed with mystical powers by the ancients because of their phoenix-like emergence from burned ground after forest fires. But the salamanders' need for moisture keeps them largely in the dark under leaf litter, as close to the damp earth as possible. By burrowing deep into old root tunnels and rocky crevices they survive not only forest fires, but also the winter freeze-up.

Here, you are never far from gurgling waters.
Myriad creeks pour down from the Niagara Escarpment, eventually draining into Cootes Paradise on the
shores of Burlington Bay. Hooded warblers and rare
Cooper's hawks nest in the trees. Skunk cabbages grow
in the wet hollows and delicate branches of witch hazel
grace the hills. Hailed for its beautiful, pagoda-like
tiers, the witch hazel is also a source of an astringent
used on insect bites and swellings, as well as in beauty
products. It is one of the few plants to bloom in October
and November, producing ribbon-like, yellow blossoms
on its black twigs. Some of Ontario's largest deciduous
trees can be seen in the Dundas Valley, including a red
oak roughly 2 metres in diameter near the Hermitage
Gatehouse parking lot.

One of the most attractive features of the valley are
the large blocks of escarpment rock that have broken
away and fallen into the valley below, where they now
serve as moss-covered flower pots for a host of vegetation. On one slab alone I counted wild ginger, early
meadow rue, downy yellow violet and false Solomon's
seal. Joining them was a fascinating array of ferns: the
rock polypody fern typical of the Niagara Escarpment,
the fragile fern and the walking fern, which earns its
name by anchoring the points of its long, thin fronds
onto the rock then growing out and down in successive
steps. Wildflowers abound each spring: hillsides of green
violets, Jack-in-the-pulpits and even the rare yellow
mandarin, a delicate lily.

Here and there you find the stumps of American
chestnuts. Once one of the predominant trees in the
area, they suffered a blight in the 1930s and were almost
entirely wiped out. Occasionally a spindly new growth
sprouts from a stump, but the trees never reach maturity before the fungal blight enters their bark and they

die. The Canadian Chestnut Council is researching methods of inoculating trees with a fungus, and their U.S. counterparts are working to develop a disease-resistant tree. Besides its esthetic value, the chestnut provides excellent wood for making musical instruments and furniture, as well as tasty nuts (not to be confused with the inedible horsechestnut).

Silent and secretive, redback salamanders are seldom encountered by accident, but they occur in such great frequency in the Dundas Valley—often outnumbering all other vertebrates—that finding these amphibians takes only a little effort. I have found them by simply turning over rocks or rotting logs.

At 5 to 10 centimetres long, the redback salamander is not much bigger than a finger. Its slender, slate-grey body has a distinctive red stripe along the back and tail. Because they don't have lungs, redbacks require a moist environment. They breathe through their skin, which must remain moist to exchange oxygen and carbon dioxide. Unlike other salamanders though, they don't need standing water for breeding, and are therefore much more adaptable to life in urban areas. Their range extends as far north as Lake Superior's rugged north shore.

A fortunate few amphibian seekers may even spot the much rarer Jefferson salamander in the Dundas Valley. Roughly twice the size of a redback, the Jefferson is black with pale blue flecks on its legs and body. A rainy night in early spring prompts its migration to a breeding pond where it lays its eggs.

When looking for salamanders, take care not to damage them or their environment. Return rocks and logs to their original position and refrain from touching these delicate amphibians. Any insect repellant or even the salt on your hands can damage their sensitive skin.

First-Hand Experience

The Dundas Valley Conservation Area is located on Governor's Road (Highway 99) in Dundas; telephone (905) 627-1233. The Hamilton Region Conservation Authority is located at 838 Mineral Springs Road, Ancaster; telephone (905) 648-4427 or (905) 525-2181. To reach the Hermitage from the Queen Elizabeth Way, take Highway 403, then follow Mohawk Road west through Ancaster. Turn left at Wilson Street, then right on Sulphur Springs Road. Follow the Headwaters Trail to the Hermitage. Other major trails in the 40-kilometre system include the Spring Creek Trail and the John White Trail. Walkers should be aware that this is a shared-use trail system, and be alert for mountain bikers that occasionally zip down the path at startling speed.

The focal point of the trail system is the Dundas Valley Trail Centre on Governor's Road, east of Sulphur Springs Road. The centre is open on weekends and holidays. It features displays, washrooms, a picnic pavilion and snackbar. There is a $5 entry fee per vehicle. A combination of loonies, toonies or quarters is needed for the automated gate.

The Ontario Herpetological Society conducts guided field trips at least once a summer. Past outings have focused on the Rouge River, Bronte Creek and Sixteen Mile Creek. For information on upcoming outings, write to the Ontario Herpetological Society, P.O. Box 244, Port Credit L5G 4L8. A society member will write or phone you when the next trip is scheduled. Membership costs $25.

ON THE WATERFRONT

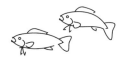

Smallmouth Bass in Baptiste Lake

On a warm summer afternoon we scooped tiny fish not much bigger than jellybeans from Baptiste Lake and poured them into a bowl for observation. Within minutes one fish chased after another nearly its own size and promptly swallowed it.

"Yup, that's a smallmouth," pronounced our resident fishing expert, as we all looked on in astonishment. A fearless predilection for preying upon fellow creatures distinguishes the smallmouth bass as one of the feistiest fish anyone can land.

The smallmouth is a favourite with sport fishers because it puts up a good fight, but its protective parenting instincts also make it an interesting fish to observe without using hook and line. In spring, long before the bass season opens, I have often watched a male smallmouth from a cottage dock, especially early in the morning when the water is still enough to allow one to peer down to the bottom. Look for a fish that seems to be nudging the stones on the bottom, or staying in one place while moving its tail back and forth. It's probably a male smallmouth preparing its nest. The male does the child rearing in this species. He begins as soon as spring sunshine warms the water, by fanning the bottom with his tail and prodding the gravel with his nose to fashion a saucer-shaped indentation 30 to 180 centimetres in

Caught in 1954 near Kinmount, Ontario's record bass weighed in at 4.46 kilograms and measured 61 centimetres. Bass that size are seldom seen today because many anglers keep them for trophies instead of throwing them back. Most caught in Ontario are now under 1.4 kilograms.

diameter. The obsessive fanning continues until silt and sand wash away, leaving a clean bed for his brood-to-be.

Once the nest has been built he must coax a female into it by rubbing and nipping her. Eventually she comes to rest in the bottom of the nest. The male stays with her to fertilize the eggs while she lays them in short intervals over a couple of hours. After spawning the female's job is done. She leaves the nest, sometimes to breed with another male. The two thousand to ten thousand pale yellow eggs are left in the care of the male, a devoted parent.

Anyone who has swum near a bass nest knows how vigorous the male's defence is. He will not be budged. This protective parent will nip at intruders much larger than himself, including feet dangling from the dock.

He continues to fan the lake bottom near his nest to keep it clean and prevent fungal growth. Even when the yolk sac is absorbed and the bass fry can eat food through their mouths, he continues to protect his school of young. The fry dine first on plankton, then on aquatic insect larvae and eventually other fish. Crayfish make up about 75 percent of the adult smallmouth's diet. In turn, the smallmouth fry feed turtles and other fish, including rock bass, yellow perch and catfish.

It will be between three to five years before the newly hatched male smallmouths are ready to nest. Once they are, they will likely return to the site of their original nest or a spot nearby.

First-Hand Experience

Bass can be found on many northern rivers and lakes, particularly those with good "structure," an angler's term for submerged branches, rocks and roots. Anyone plan-

The shallow waters of marshes and lakeshore are populated by teems of fascinating critters from dragonfly larvae to tadpoles and tiny red water mites. To better observe these creatures you can improvise an economical underwater lens by cutting the bottom out of a plastic ice-cream tub or a metal coffee can. Cover it with clear plastic film and secure with a rubber band. Hold the plastic-covered end in the water and it will work like a scuba mask, offering a clear view of the activity under the water's surface.

ning to fish should obtain a licence (generally available at bait and tackle shops) and a copy of the *Guide to Eating Ontario Sport Fish*, a free publication available at the Ministry of Natural Resources Information Centre at 900 Bay Street in Toronto.

Broere's Fly-Fishing arranges two-day trips from Toronto to Baptiste Lake. For information call Broere's Toronto office at (416) 604-3164.

If your main interest is in observing rather than catching fish, try watching underwater with a mask and snorkel. Bass are ideal for this because they typically nest near shorelines.

During spawning season you can see some pretty dramatic fish migrations along several Ontario waterways. A particularly favourite site is the Ganaraska River in Port Hope, where rainbow trout, brown trout and salmon swim upstream in mid-April. On a good day you can see hundreds of silvery fish leaping in the water as they make their way up the fish ladder at Corbett's Dam.

ONTARIO'S HOTTEST
BASS LURES
Long A Bomber
Black Bucktail
Mr. Twister
Popping Bug
Live Worm
Shad Rap or
    Rattlin' Spot
Mepps No. 3 or
    Bass Killer

— Ministry of
    Natural Resources

Frogs, Fowl and Dragonflies at Conroy's Marsh

In addition to their diet of insects, bullfrogs have been known to eat some rather large prey. They have swallowed mice, small birds and even other frogs.

Masses of cattails, pickerel weed and water lilies stretch almost to the horizon. Cumulus clouds reflect on the still marsh surface, and all seems incredibly peaceful until an osprey splashes down into the lake and soars off with a silvery fish. Surrounded for the most part by crown land, Conroy's Marsh remains a rich, natural habitat of 2,400 hectares accessible only by water. It also has its share of human history, and you can enjoy some of that aboard the *Maggie II*, a 1946 log-boom tug that once plied the Ottawa River. Now it carries tourists on hour-long cruises through the deeper waters of the wetlands. Remote corners, like some of the narrow stretches of the York River, where maples form a canopy over the water are best explored by canoe or a combination of pontoon boat and canoe.

Situated in eastern Ontario at the junction of the York and Madawaska Rivers, the marsh is probably wilder today than it was half a century ago. Irish and Polish settlers who first farmed the area used to cut hay on the marsh each fall to feed their livestock during winter. Miners once drilled for corundum (an almost diamond-hard grinding material) in the hills overlooking the marsh, while logging tugs drove rafts of lumber downstream to the Ottawa River.

Now the mine is no longer worked, although a few rockpile remnants of the supply dock remain in the marsh. A dam was built in 1955, which raised the water level so that hay could no longer be cut. Log drives are things of the past now that truckers haul on year-round roads. The marsh is pretty much left to the beavers and bullfrogs, as well as a handful of fishermen.

Ducks Unlimited has attempted to improve the marsh as a duck habitat by digging channels through emergent vegetation to establish protective islands where black ducks and mallards can nest safely out of the reach of predatory foxes. Both bald and golden eagles nest in the area.

Large, loud and quintessentially froggy, bullfrogs live in and around weedy bays in permanent bodies of water, particularly those with lily pads. Belonging to the true frog family *Ranidae*, bullfrogs are completely aquatic.

When springtime temperatures at the bottom of their lakes warm up to 13 to 16 degrees Celsius, usually in late April or early May, the bullfrogs emerge and become active. Males stake out territories at least 2 metres in diameter and start singing to announce their availability to females. The French name for bullfrogs, *ouaouaron*, best describes their mating call, although "jug-o-rum" is another popular approximation. If a male trespasses on another's territory he will be warned away first with a loud hiccup. If that doesn't clear off the stranger, the two wrestle like a pair of sumos, holding each other with their front legs in a powerful struggle until the weaker retreats.

A female chooses her mate on the basis of his territory, which should have plenty of underwater vegetation where she can lay a large, sticky raft of up to twenty thousand eggs. Most will become food for leeches, fish and dragonfly nymphs. Those that survive grow into

Dragonflies first appeared on earth more than two hundred million years ago. Except for size, the dragonflies we observe today are little changed from their ancestors, who were contemporaries of the great dinosaurs. Those early dragonflies had wingspans nearly the length of a man's arm (75 centimetres).

finger-length tadpoles, which may take two years to fully develop into adults. A wily bullfrog that escapes hungry herons, pike, snapping turtles and other predators can live up to six years, growing to a length of six inches. Females usually live the longest and grow the largest, as they lead somewhat more sheltered lives.

Dragonfly nymphs, bearing virtually no resemblance to their adult forms, emerge from their watery homes in the late spring. After parking themselves on a plant stem, boathouse or similarly secure spot, the nymphs' backs split open and the adult dragonflies emerge. These long, large insects with double sets of membranous wings are a common sight at almost any pond or lake. Most dragonflies overwinter in ponds. The female lays her eggs directly in the water. These grow into hungry nymphs, consuming worms, mosquito larvae, tadpoles and even tiny fish.

Harmless to humans, they do serious damage to mosquitoes and blackflies, both as flying adults and water-bound nymphs. Using their front legs like a little basket, they scoop the tiny insects out of the air.

First-Hand Experience

The easiest access to Conroy Marsh is via the village of Combermere, on Highway 62, south of Barry's Bay. At Combermere you can rent pontoon boats and canoes at Hydes Bay Marina, whose telephone number is (613) 756-1802. Cruises on the *Maggie II* riverboat depart from the Bent Anchor Bar, near the bridge in Combermere. Call (613) 756-2052. There are approximately 100 kilometres of navigable waters between Combermere and Barry's Bay; be sure to ask for a map when you rent a boat.

Island Hopping at St. Lawrence Islands National Park

Southern species meet northern landscapes in the St. Lawrence Islands National Park, a scenic stretch of the St. Lawrence River east of Kingston. More than a thousand islands lie scattered over the river, some not much bigger than haystacks. With their pink granite and rugged pines they display rare beauty. Part of the Frontenac Axis, a southerly extension of the Canadian Shield that reaches towards New York State's Adirondack Mountains, the islands are actually worn down mountain stubs that only show their peaks above the St. Lawrence.

By the late nineteenth century these idyllic islands attracted American industrialists seeking refuge from the grime and grind of urban living. So popular was this area that when English poet Rupert Brooke cruised through in 1913 he observed, "The Thousand Isles vary from six inches to hundreds of yards in diameter. Each, if big enough, has been bought by a rich man—generally an American—who has built a castle on it …"

Concerned that the area would be spoiled by overdevelopment, local residents sought to protect their recreational treasure. In 1904 the St. Lawrence Islands National Park was created and picnic pavilions and wharves were built to provide easy access for boaters.

Growing up to 2 metres long, the black rat snake is Ontario's largest snake. It's harmless, despite its somewhat startling habit of vibrating its tail and flattening out its neck when frightened. But chances of seeing this shiny black reptile are rare.

On the mainland at Mallorytown Landing, one of the park's original hexagonal picnic pavilions now serves as a visitor centre. Here you can see displays of the area's famed flora and fauna, much of which is unique to this tiny corner of Canada, including the black rat snake, the pitch pine and deerberries.

Island explorations can easily be arranged by hiring a local water taxi or a charter such as Island Hopper Charters. On a sunny June afternoon I set out with Ryan Wells, a former St. Lawrence Islands Park interpretive naturalist, who charters his 8-metre cruiser for guided tours of the islands. From the mainland park base at Mallorytown, a short cruise down the Canadian middle channel brought us to the largest of the islands, Grenadier. Once home to a thriving farming community, the family farms gradually dwindled after the island school closed. One farm has since become a golf course, while others have simply grown wild. A township road running the length of Grenadier Island makes for an easy 8-kilometre walk through many diverse habitats: mature forests in the east, a flat area of farmland in the centre and a rare stand of pitch pines at the rugged west end of the island.

We docked near the site of a rusted windmill, the last remains of the old Anglers' Inn, which was destroyed by fire in 1870. Today you can camp on the site —two tent pads are provided by the park—and walk the meandering paths that staff have mowed through the old farm fields. Startled leopard frogs jump up with each footstep, diving into tangles of vetch, buttercups, Timothy grass and grapevines. Early in the morning deer are often seen in these fields. Look for the shagbark hickory grove near the Anglers' Inn site. Shagbark hickory is one of many southern species found in the

park, along with chinquapin oak and rue anemone, a
white member of the buttercup family.

Pitch pines, whose sap was once used to seal
wooden boats, grow at the northern edge of their range
in the park. The decay-resistant wood was used by pioneers for flooring barns and building mine shafts and
water wheels. During night voyages, boaters used to
light their way by holding burning knots of pitch pine
in metal cages over the water. Smugglers used to ferry
cases of whisky across the border in the mists of night,
during the Prohibition years in the United States. Local
place names tell the story: Smuggler's Cove, Horse
Thief Bay.

Georgina Island, situated in the middle of the park,
is known for its microclimates: a dry southern side
where pitch pine and blueberries thrive, and a cool,
damp northern side where hemlock grows. A rugged
trail traverses Georgina's contrasting habitats. As you
walk, look for the rectangular-shaped holes pecked into
the hemlocks by pileated woodpeckers. These large,
crow-sized woodpeckers chisel out feeding holes so
neatly squared they look like they were made with steel
tools. Attractive picnic shelters make the island a
favourite with visitors.

Great blue herons are a frequent sight among the
islands. Plan to be in the vicinity of Ironsides Island
around 6 p.m. and you will see dozens of these long,
graceful birds arriving to roost for the night. You can
recognize the island by its numerous dead trees—the
result of prolific heron droppings.

Birdwatchers enjoy the park year-round. In spring
they can turn their binoculars on an assortment of warblers: cerulean, pine and Blackburnian. Bald eagles frequent the area in winter. Parks Canada and the U.S. Fish

and Wildlife Department jointly organize a bald eagle watch each March, with spotting scopes set up at the Brockville Sky Deck to observe the nesting eagles. Also nesting in the park, after near extinction, are numerous osprey. Five nesting platforms have been erected to simulate the high treetops they require.

Cruising past Hill Island, lucky birders may even glimpse one of the wild turkeys that have been reintroduced to the park. Hill Island Marsh is a great place to see red-spotted and yellow-spotted salamanders. It is also one of the few hibernacula sites in Canada for black rat snakes. Five-lined skinks and Blanding's turtles are among the rare reptiles found here.

With a total of roughly 3 kilometres of docks available to boaters on the twenty-one park islands, it's easy to combine a day of cruising and hiking. Most of the islands boast relatively easy, scenic hiking trails. Several islands have a few primitive campsites. The waterside campsites at Camelot Island offer idyllic sunsets and rugged Canadian Shield terrain.

Standing at least 1 metre tall, the wild turkey is much brighter than its domestic cousin, which was a subspecies Spanish conquistadors brought back to Europe in the sixteenth century. Wild turkeys forage for acorns and seeds, but are also quick enough to catch lizards and frogs.

First-Hand Experience

Without ever abandoning the comfort of their cars, motorists may easily enjoy the St. Lawrence Islands by driving the dramatic Thousand Islands Parkway. But to really explore the islands, you either need your own boat, and a good set of charts, or you should hire one of the local water taxis. Island Hoppers specializes in dropping passengers off at various park islands for picnics and explorations, and charges roughly $50 per hour for charters. Call (613) 923-5713 or (613) 340-1049.

The park's main base is easily accessible via Highway 401 at Mallorytown Landing and offers two trails, each a kilometre in length. One is fully wheelchair accessible and offers tactile signage for the blind. There is also a beach suitable for children, a picnic site and campground. For information call St. Lawrence Islands National Park at (613) 923-5261.

Exploring the Grand River

In 1994 the Grand became the first largely urban river to be designated a Canadian Heritage River. It joined other Ontario waterways—the Missinabi River, French River, Mattawa River and Boundary Waters—better known for their wilderness. But the 290-kilometre Grand River is rich in human history, and attempts are underway to restore its natural heritage. Rural rather than wild, the Grand gurgles past the Scottish stone masonry of Fergus and the pretty shops of Elora, picking up force as it churns through the Elora Gorge, where it once turned many a millstone. At West Montrose it flows under the wooden covered bridge, past rolling farms, then through the cities of Kitchener, Cambridge and Brantford. It meanders south through Six Nations Indian Reserve—lands the Iroquois were deeded for their allegiance to the British Crown during the American Revolution. Gradually it widens into muddy marshes then pours into Lake Erie south of Dunnville.

Flowing from marsh to marsh, the Grand's headwaters emerge north of Luther Marsh, near Dundalk, one of the largest inland marshes in southern Ontario. Its weedy waters make it an important resting area for migrating waterfowl and a major destination for birders. During summer months the least bittern and great egret are among the waterfowl that nest here. Luther is one of the few places in southern Ontario where you might glimpse a Wilson's phalarope, a long-billed shore-bird that migrates from the lakes high in the Bolivian and Argentinian plains to breed in Canada. Look for them swimming in tight circles, stabbing the water with their needle-like beaks in a search for insects. Besides the marsh and swamp, the area also boasts a bog, unusual in southern Ontario. Until fairly recently Luther was relatively inaccessible, but gravel and grass roads are being developed around the perimeter of Luther Lake to create better birdwatching opportunities. Visitors should be aware that duck hunting is allowed on some days.

The Grand has more species of fish (eighty-five) than any other river in Ontario, thanks to its varied topography. Trout favour the cool, fast and shallow waters around Elora, while catfish, or "mudcats" as the locals call them, prefer the slow, turbid waters near Dunnville. Here you can feel the Carolinian influence on the river. Southern species such as shagbark hickory and chinquapin oak abound.

The Grand River marshes, sprawling over 1,618 hectares, are a vast coastal wetland that attracts numerous birds and serves as an important staging area for migratory waterfowl. Noisy red-winged blackbirds squawk in the cattails and stately great blue herons silently study the water for frogs and fish. The best way to see the marsh is to paddle a canoe through the dense cattails of the channels.

A walk through the woods at Byng Island Conservation Area brings visitors to the Dunnville Fishway, an innovative conservation project designed to enable fish to migrate to spawning beds upstream, beyond the local dam. The world's largest freshwater fishery is on Lake Erie and, as a major tributary, the Grand River is

GRAND STATS

- 750,000 people live in the Grand River watershed

- 250,000 people drink water from the river

- 600,000 dump treated sewage into the water

vital for many breeding fish. During the spring run, rainbow trout have been known to travel from Lake Erie to New Hamburg via the Nith River. Later, as the water warms, bass and catfish will swim upriver via the fishway. In fall 60-centimetre-long chinook salmon make an exciting spectacle, jumping out of the river, seemingly standing on their tails and wiggling their noses in the air. Large enough to accommodate a 3-metre sturgeon, the fishway is more frequently used by smaller species such as gizzard shad and mooneye. Though somewhat less glamorous than the behemoth sturgeon and the leaping salmon, they nevertheless play an important role in the food chain, providing meals for herons, pike and walleye.

You can use a rapella lure to troll for catfish just as you would for walleye, but kids will appreciate the fact that these whiskered fish will happily nibble at dough balls squashed onto a hook tied on a length of string.

First-Hand Experience

Hunting is permitted in Luther Marsh from September to February on Monday, Wednesday, Friday and Saturday. Luther Marsh is located north of Orangeville via Highway 25. Turn west onto East Luther Township Sideroad 6 and follow the signs. Call (519) 928-2832.

The Byng Island Conservation Area is located in Dunnville and offers picnic and camping facilities as well as many good fishing spots. Call (905) 774-5755. Canoes may be rented at the Grand Island Bar BQ, 100 Dover Road, Dunnville. Call (905) 774-6051.

Ecotours featuring highlights of the Grand River are offered through the Conservation Lands of Ontario. Call 1-888-376-2212 or (519) 621-2761.

The 250-kilometre Grand Valley Trail follows the river from Alton to Lake Erie. Contact the Grand Valley Trails Association, 75 King Street South, Box 40068, RPO Waterloo Square, Waterloo N2J 4V1.

Return of the Swans to Wye Marsh

Paddling through the vast beds of cattails at Wye Marsh, you can't help but be impressed by its fecund beauty. Wild trumpeter swans serenely move through the rushes, a painted turtle basks on a floating log, and a tiny green frog sits almost invisible in the duckweed. But the naturalists here are quick to point out that wetlands are more than just a pretty place.

Cattail marshes are one of nature's most efficient cleansers. They remove excessive levels of nitrogen and phosphorus, which are introduced to the water system through fertilizer, sewage and industrial discharge. Unless filtered, water containing high degrees of these nutrients becomes thick with algae. Oxygen is depleted, creating foul, stagnant water. During rapid summer growth, a dense stand of cattails can remove up to 90 percent of the nitrogen and phosphorus in raw sewage. Even the humble duckweed, which covers still or slow waters with little dots of green, plays an important role in purifying the marsh by absorbing complex chemicals. High in protein, duckweed is also an important food source for waterfowl and aquatic mammals.

The 1000-hectare Wye Marsh is both large enough to support many species and accessible enough to be enjoyed by visitors. Located on the shores of Georgian Bay near Midland, the marsh is a favourite place for professional wildlife photographers and ardent naturalists.

Native people roasted young cattail shoots to eat them like corn on the cob. They also washed and dried the roots, then pounded them into flour.

The best way to explore Wye Marsh's wetlands is on one of the guided canoe excursions offered three times a day during summer months. The 45-minute paddle takes you past sedges and towering cattails, where you may see a muskrat swimming through the rushes or an American bittern swooping through the maze of channels. With a naturalist steering and a crew of seven or so visitors paddling, the canoes quietly pass floating flowerbeds of pickerel weed and arrowhead.

Iridescent blue frogs are one of the more surprising sights at Wye Marsh. They are a local genetic variant of the green frog, lacking yellow pigment on some parts of its skin.

Dykes and trails make for easy walking, as does the long boardwalk that winds through the marsh. Dip nets are provided along the walk during summer months so visitors can scoop up dripping masses of duckweed, insect larvae and tadpoles. There is a primeval feel to some of these lush woodland trails. The Identification Trail signposts such curiosities as the scouring rush, a coarse horsetail fern that pioneers used for scrubbing pots. Children will delight in finds of apricot jelly fungus and the little American toads hopping across the woodchip-covered path.

Wye Marsh is best known for its success in breeding trumpeter swans, which were reintroduced after a 250-year absence. Once common in Ontario, the swans' numbers were quickly depleted by hunting when the first Europeans arrived. The trumpeter swan reintroduction program has been gradually increasing the bird's numbers since its inception in 1988. Only two trumpeter swans were born that first year, but thirty-eight were born in 1998. Even though more swans are hatching, many fail to thrive. A problem that plagues many wetlands across the continent is affecting them: lead poisoning.

Hunters and fishers had been scattering lead shot and sinkers into the marsh at an alarming rate. Muscular weakness, anemia and neurological problems, all symp-

tomatic of lead poisoning, were observed in the swans.
Radiographs revealed lead pellets in the crops of ailing
birds. Lead shot has been successfully banned in the
marsh, but the problem won't go away quickly. Swans
who have ingested lead can be treated with an antidote,
but success is by no means certain. Of the six swans
treated over the winter of 1997–98 for lead poisoning,
only three survived.

In spring the trumpeter swans build huge nests out
of dead cattails packed with mud. While they may not
seem very large from the surface, the nests are actually
sitting on the bottom of the marsh, and the piles of cattails may be as high as 2 metres. The female lays half
a dozen off-white eggs, each the size of a man's fist.
Unlike the ugly duckling of the children's story, trumpeter cygnets are far from ugly. Covered with pale grey
down, the fluffy young birds have pink bills and legs.
Swankeeper Michelle Knegt talks about the swans with
obvious affection. Each has a name: Pigpen, Big Guy
and Sidekick. Sidekick has been treated twice for lead
poisoning.

"You can really see their individual personalities,"
said Michelle. "By the end of the summer they are learning to fly. Usually the adults teach the young, but one set
of parents had clipped wings so their babies had to learn
by watching other birds. Once they got up you could
see their expressions, as though they were thinking, 'Oh
no. How do I get down?' The female was afraid to fly for
a couple of days after that. Another was trying to come
in for a landing on a windy day. He came down with
such a strong tail wind that he couldn't slow down. All
the other swans were ducking out of his way."

Since the swans are underwater feeders, they usually migrate when the marsh freezes up in winter. They
don't go far though. Most head for the open waters of

Burlington Harbour, where they are monitored by Hamilton-area biologists.

In addition to the trumpeter swans, many other species of waterfowl feed or breed in Wye Marsh. Widgeons, ringnecks, wood ducks and green-winged teal are plentiful. Black terns and Caspian terns are among the rarer finds. In winter months staff find otter tracks covering considerable distances overland. The otters come to hunt along the creeks and open water of the marsh.

Over 13 kilometres of trackset ski trails and guided snowshoe hikes attract visitors during the winter. The rewards for snowy explorations are the discovery of animal tracks in the snow: coyote and cottontail, red fox and ruffed grouse, porcupine and white-tailed deer. Bird feeders attract tame chickadees who will eat from your hand.

First-Hand Experience

Wye Marsh Wildlife Centre is located on Highway 12, 5 kilometres east of Midland. Telephone (705) 526-7809. No experience is necessary to join one of the guided canoe trips, as the paddling is very easy. All equipment, including life jackets, is provided. To maximize your chances of seeing birds and other wildlife, try one of the special early morning canoe trips that depart at 7:30 a.m. Admission is $5 for adults.

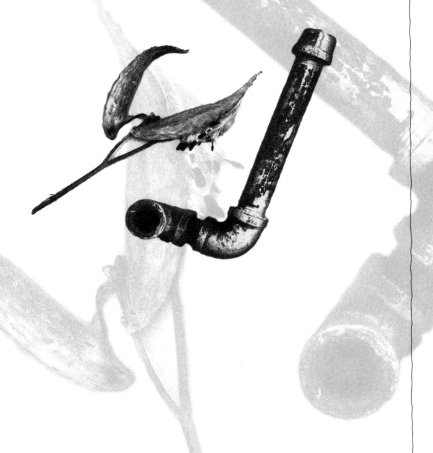

URBAN WILDERNESS

Rambling Through Toronto's Rouge Valley

Rouge Park is the wilderness next door. In this remarkable river valley on the eastern edge of Toronto you will find mature woodlands, abundant wildflowers, rainbow trout, wood ducks, and even a herd of white-tailed deer. That the Rouge River system remains in such good condition is nothing short of a miracle, considering the pressures of urban development. A municipal dump, a gravel quarry and suburban sprawl have all encroached on the area. But in recent years the special value of the Rouge as a wilderness area has begun to be appreciated. Steps have been taken to preserve it in the most pristine state possible by officially declaring half of the 4,800-hectare area a park.

This is as close as you can get to being in the wilderness while still standing within the boundaries of Toronto. Several great hiking trails—and the city's only campground—are found at Glen Rouge Park on Highway 2. At first glance the area looks pretty tame. but leave your car in the parking lot and walk past the mown lawns and paved paths toward the sound of the rushing river. On a May afternoon returning warblers can be heard amongst the black willow trees, a tangle of vines cascades down an old pine, and the spring air smells sweet with the fragrance of balsam poplar. Here you can ramble along grassy riverside paths or hike hillside trails through ever-changing woods that illustrate the blend of northern and southern that characterizes the Rouge.

On a May morning a hike up the hill known as the Hog's Back shows this strange juxtaposition. North-facing slopes shaded with hemlocks look distinctly northern, while the sunny, south-facing slopes favour maples and a host of wildflowers: trout lily, trillium, mayapple and violets. More than seven hundred kinds of wild plants are found in the park, including several southern species, such as the sycamore tree, that are at their northern limits here. Take a sunset hike on a summer afternoon and you will likely see a fox loping along the river, perhaps eyeing a family of merganser ducks dabbling near a patch of riverside coltsfoot.

In Rouge Beach Park, at the mouth of the Rouge River where it opens into Lake Ontario, pale pink sea rockets bloom on the sandy beaches. Numerous gulls, ducks and swans frequent the river-mouth marsh. This is where birdwatchers come to spot green and great blue herons, common and Caspian terns, bufflehead, merganser and goldeneye ducks, to name a few. The Lower Rouge Marsh is also home to map turtles, mink and northern water snakes.

The Hillside Nature Centre off Meadowvale Road is used by school groups during the week in their nature studies. You can park your car on the road and explore the nature trail that begins across the street. A woodland path meanders through patches of meadowsweet, ostrich ferns and shady forests to a riverfront bluff where bank swallows build nesting tunnels in the steep bank.

The Rouge River has its source in the glacier-shaped hills of the Oak Ridges Moraine, north of Markham. From these ridges, cool groundwater trickles down the river valleys to Lake Ontario. Relatively clear despite their urban proximity, the Rouge waters are a spawning

Also known as cough-wort, coltsfoot is a highly esteemed herbal remedy, particularly when used as a cough treatment. French apothecaries displayed its leaf on signs to identify themselves as vendors of herbal treatments. The leaves, which appear later in the summer, long after the yellow blooms have disappeared, can be dried for tea, or boiled with water and sugar to make candy.

ground for rainbow trout, one of the fifty-five species of fish found in this river system. Through habitat restoration, park managers hope to bring back such indigenous species as Atlantic salmon and river otters. They have already succeeded in bringing back eastern bluebirds by installing hundreds of nesting boxes.

First-Hand Experience

Although some of the best known sections of Rouge Park are in Scarborough, the system winds through at least six municipalities. There are numerous access points. The Finch Meander, on Finch just east of Sewells Road, is the site of rare Carolinian woods. Pearse House, on Meadowvale Drive near the Metro Zoo, is a place to follow trails through meadows and down the wooded riverbank. From Twyn Rivers Drive hikers can get onto trails that offer spectacular views of the valley. Glen Rouge Park, which is the only area offering overnight camping within Toronto, is a great place to fish, explore the river and hike some beautiful trails, such as the Hog's Back. Rouge Beach and the marshes at the mouth of the Rouge River can be reached via the eastern end of Lawrence Avenue.

Numerous informative events are held at the park throughout the year, including an environment week in June, when community groups do restoration work, and a Rouge Park Day in July that focusses on hiking.

To learn more about Rouge Park contact the park office at 361A Old Finch Avenue, Scarborough M1B 5K7, or telephone (416) 28-ROUGE.

"An infusion or tea of black alder bark is a wonderful tonic, and a healer of the skin, inside and out ... a bracer for the feeble constitution."

— E.T. SETON,
The Book of Woodcraft

Back to Nature in Toronto's Don Valley

Although you are only a few metres from bumper-to-bumper traffic, when you stroll through the Don Valley past tangles of new growth abuzz with insects, you can almost imagine it as it was in the 1870s, when young Ernest Thompson Seton roamed this still-virgin wilderness. Seeking escape from an oppressive father and a miserable school life, Seton spent time in the valley studying birds and imagining himself leading the traditional Indian way of life, which he may have read about in James Fenimore Cooper's novels. His early love of wildlife grew into a lifelong passion. Seton became one of the pre-eminent naturalists of his day, and was known for his realistic wildlife paintings and animal tales devoid of the prevailing Victorian sentimentality. He established the original Woodcraft Movement to teach boys outdoor skills. The Woodcraft Movement eventually became the Boy Scouts, although Seton never agreed with Robert Baden-Powell's soldier-style training and khaki uniforms. "The Indian, not the army general, should be our ideal," wrote Seton.

Today traffic roars down the highway, and subway trains trundle high overhead on the busy viaduct connecting Bloor Street to the Danforth, but the Don Valley is slowly being given back to nature. Since the mid-1990s, natural regeneration and restoration projects have been gradually greening the Don Valley where it was scarred by industrialization.

One of the most impressive projects can be seen on the Bayview Extension, just north of where the viaduct traverses the valley. Here the Don Valley Brickworks has drawn world attention for its amazing fossils embedded in the interglacial deposits of clay and sand. A century ago a quarry at the north end of the site provided vast amounts of clay to the brickworks, which manufactured building materials for such landmarks as Casa Loma, Osgoode Hall and the Pantages Theatre.

Ice Age fossils of bison, bear, musk oxen, mammoth and mastodon have been found in and around Toronto—all contemporaries of the giant beavers about 11,000 years ago.

Now the site is a public park, with much work still underway. The north quarry hillside looks like an ordinary clay slope, with vegetation slowly spreading over its surface. But from a geological standpoint it provides a rare record of detailed climate change. A wide range of fossils, from tropical shellfish to post ice-age mammals have been found in the Don Valley beds. Perhaps the most exciting discovery was the Giant Beaver (*Castor ohioensis*). These massive rodents reached the size of present-day black bears, weighing as much as 200 kilograms and growing to roughly 2 metres in length. They had cutting teeth up to 15 centimetres long, and their tails were rounded, not broad and flat.

Today the 17-hectare site, which opened in October 1997, is easily recognized by its towering brick chimney, a remnant of the old industrial days. Beyond the buildings, crushed stone pathways wind along ponds and marshes. As part of the site's rehabilitation, a stream that was once buried underground like a sewer is being opened up and brought back to life. Mud Creek flows downhill from the neighbouring residential area of Moore Park through the wetlands and into an open channel between two of the old brickworks buildings. A handful of mallard ducks swim in the creek while Canada geese congregate on the shore.

Another restoration site, south of the Bloor Street Viaduct on the east bank of the river, is the newly restored Chester Marsh. From 1912 to 1925 the marsh served as the city's main garbage dump. Today the marsh is a testimony to Ma Nature's regenerative abilities—with a little help from organizations such as The Task Force to Bring Back the Don, a citizens' group working to improve the natural environment through projects such as planting tens of thousands of trees and wildflowers in the Lower Don Watershed, the south end of the Don River. On a September afternoon you can walk through chest-high stands of evening primrose and white sweet clover, or sit on a fallen log to watch a kingfisher diving for suckers and minnows. The marsh has been planted with cattails, arrowhead and water lilies to purify the water. By clearing out invasive exotics such as purple loosestrife and Japanese knotweed, task force members hope to enhance the native vegetation.

Cottonwood poplars may grow as much as 1.5 metres a year.

During dry spells you can walk the beach along the Don River past cottonwood poplars and massive willows, trees that like to get their feet wet. When spring rains bring floods, the overflow is more than just a nuisance for motorists driving along the low-lying Bayview Extension, it also brings seeds and new life to the regenerating river banks.

First-Hand Experience

The Lower Don Trail passes through Chester Marsh on the east shore of the Don River and continues south to Cherry Beach. The Don Valley Brickworks is located on Bayview Avenue, south of Pottery Road. Pedestrian

access is awkward, but not impossible. From the Broad-
view subway station, take any of the buses heading
north to Pottery Road. Walk down the hill into the valley and cross the bridge. The Brickworks is located on
the west side of the river, south of Pottery Road. It is
about a twenty-minute walk from the Todmorden Mills
Museum, which is on the east side of the river at the
foot of Pottery Road. The museum has free brochures
describing the brickworks site. Call (416) 396-2819,
Monday to Friday.

Paved paths in the valley are popular with cyclists.
You can follow one of these south from Pottery Road to
Chester Marsh, which is located on the east side of the
river. For information on the marsh and brickworks
call the Metro Toronto Regional Conservation Authority
at (416) 661-6600 or the Task Force to Bring Back the
Don at (416) 392-0401.

Coyotes on the Toronto Waterfront

Located on the industrial waterfront of Canada's largest city, Tommy Thompson Park, also known as the Leslie Street spit, is a prime example of nature taking a toehold, then colonizing an apparent wasteland. Once a stretch of rubble, in a few decades the spit has evolved into a wilderness. Hundreds of thousands of gulls nest on its rocky beaches, migrating warblers perch in the poplars and coyotes den among the piles of concrete rubble. A 5-kilometre paved trail, ideal for bicycles and rollerblades, meanders past woods and grasslands.

The spit was originally developed as an expanded Outer Harbour area for Toronto's shipping industry. Since its inception in the 1950s the spit has been used as a dumping site for material dredged from the Outer Harbour and surplus fill from city building sites. Four million loads of fill and nearly fifty years later, hardy grasses accustomed to drought conditions have established themselves in the gravel. Seeds of cottonwood poplars, named for their soft seed-bearing tufts, blew in on warm spring winds. Cottonwoods grow remarkably quickly and in doing so they stabilize the soil, setting the stage for further plant colonization.

The mounds of rubble make attractive hibernacula for garter snakes, and the beaches make popular nesting sites for colonial waterbirds such as ring-billed gulls, herring gulls, common terns, black-crowned night herons and double-crested cormorants. Roughly three hundred species of birds have been sighted in the park.

It is those birds that bring us to the coyotes, because with prey come predators. The coyotes are believed to have migrated down green corridors like the Don Valley, finding their way to the feast of gull eggs and chicks on the rocky beaches of the spit. Though it is unlikely that visitors would encounter the largely nocturnal coyotes by day, it is possible to see signs of their activity, such as gull carcasses and feathers scattered in front of dens hollowed in the landfill rubble. Although the park is closed at night, local naturalists have reported sightings of coyotes in the surrounding docklands at night. Since the early 1990s coyotes have been finding dens in the park—they typically change the site each year—and successfully raising litters of four to six cubs.

The coyote's ability to adapt to change has often made it successful in areas disturbed by man. When the introduction of agriculture changed the western prairie, wolves, grizzly bears and mountain lions declined in numbers, while coyotes increased their range and number. They are now found throughout most of Ontario.

Smaller than wolves, coyotes do not hunt big game. Instead these clever opportunists chase down a wide range of small animals including rabbits, mice, voles and, in the case of Tommy Thompson Park, nesting birds. They have even been known to eat fish, acorns and fruit. According to research by Ducks Unlimited, coyotes may even play a role in maintaining the breeding success of ground-nesting birds by preying on foxes. Foxes raid nests and kill more birds than they can eat at one time.

Should you be lucky enough to glimpse a coyote, it will probably be by surprise. There isn't much to distinguish it from a long, lanky German shepherd running with its tail down. I have never seen one when I was

Once found only in the American southwest, coyotes have expanded their range north as far as the Mackenzie River Delta and south as far as Central America. They first appeared in southwestern Ontario in 1890. In 1920 they appeared in eastern Ontario, and by 1945 they were seen in Quebec.

actually looking. In his delightful book, *Toronto the Wild: Field Notes of an Urban Naturalist*, Wayne Grady describes finding coyote tracks in a fresh snowfall not far from a row of Toronto townhouses. Silent and secretive in the city, the coyote has a talent for staying out of sight. But whether or not you ever see them seems almost irrelevant. Knowing that you may be sharing its paths, that you are both walking through the same landscape, is enough.

First-Hand Experience

Tommy Thompson Park is located at the southernmost end of Leslie Street. It is open year-round on weekends and most holidays from 9 a.m. to 6 p.m. Continued landfill operations in some areas mean that the park is closed during the week. Cars must be left at the main gate and it is a long walk—roughly 5 kilometres—from the parking lot to the lighthouse at the tip of the spit. A free shuttle van ferries visitors between the main gate at Leslie and Commissioners Streets and the bridge roughly halfway down the spit. The shuttle van runs from the first weekend in May to Thanksgiving. The schedule is posted on the information board at the main gate. On Sundays look for the Spit Cart, a mobile display of neat nature stuff found in the park, including owl pellets, bird eggs, turtle shells and animal skulls. Dog walking is not permitted, due to the potential for disturbing nesting birds. For more information call (416) 661-6600.

Return to Paradise in Hamilton

It's not far from the smokestacks and slag piles of Hamilton Harbour's steel mills, but tucked into a corner of Burlington Bay, Cootes Paradise seems a world apart. Here huge willows lean over a marshy shoreline, red-winged blackbirds perch on cattails and mallards paddle in the duckweed. Administered by the Royal Botanical Gardens, the 1,000-hectare area of field, forest and marsh is the site of one of the largest wetland rehabilitation projects in North America.

The wetland is named after a British captain who guarded the Niagara frontier in the early 1800s. Thomas Coote found the hunting exceptionally good and took every opportunity to bag a brace of ducks. Coote's contemporaries would also have found an excellent spawning ground for northern pike and largemouth bass in the cattails and wild rice.

But it wasn't long after Coote that the marsh suffered the first in a string of abuses. In 1837 the Desjardin Canal was dug, increasing erosion and muddying the water. In 1896 carp were accidentally introduced and quickly displaced the native salmon and other fish. While in many European countries carp is considered a tasty meal, it proves troublesome in Ontario marshes. Its messy feeding habits—sucking up mud then spitting it out—create murky water unsuitable for other fish and prevent aquatic plants from taking root.

The average carp weighs about 11.5 kilograms, but specimens weighing up to 45.5 kilograms have been found. They may live as long as 150 years.

Raising water levels on Lake Ontario to accommodate shipping has taken its toll on shoreline plants. Only an estimated 15 percent of the marsh's emergent vegetation remains. As populations grew in the neighbouring communities of Dundas, Burlington and Hamilton, so did the sewage load. Sewage caused large quantities of algae to bloom, making the water turbid. Between the carp stirring up mud at the bottom of the marsh and the increasing algae, the water became so cloudy that sunlight could not penetrate to the aquatic plants.

As part of the clean-up, a fishway designed to keep out carp was built where the marsh opens out into Hamilton Harbour. The fishway holds fish trying to swim in from the harbour. Staff check it periodically—usually twice a day in summer—and remove the undesirable carp while letting native species pass through to the marsh. Marsh plants have been re-introduced to improve water quality. The hope is that pike and perch, mink and muskrat will make this wetland their home once again.

Visitors can explore the area on two trails along the south and north shores. Observation towers and boardwalks offer expansive views of the wetlands and wildlife which includes a cormorant colony.

The range of habitats, from marsh to meadow, with mature maple and hickory woods, ensures a wide variety of visiting birds. Among them are colourful wood ducks, moorhens who cluck like chickens and orchard orioles who build finely woven nests that dangle from tree branches like pouches. At dusk you might see a black-crowned night heron feeding on insects and frogs. Green herons crouch in branches overhanging the shore as they wait for food. These fascinating birds have been known to drop tiny twigs on the surface of the water to lure their fishy prey. Many migrating shorebirds feed on the mudflats.

On a sunny day, watch for turtles—Blanding's, map and painted—basking on a log or rock.

First-Hand Experience

From Highway 403, exit north at Highway 6 and follow the Royal Botanical Gardens signs to the Arboretum on Old Guelph Road, where you can park. The North Shore Trail is a 2.9-kilometre loop, starting at the Nature Centre on Arboretum Road. The Nature Centre is open daily from 10 a.m. to 4 p.m. On the Grey Doe section of the trail you will find Carolinian trees such as butter-nut and blue beech, labelled for easy identification. Trails connect to the Bruce Trail, and the Bruce Trail Association's headquarters are located here, at Rasp-berry House. It is open during the week for anyone who would like information or the trail guidebook. For infor-mation on the Royal Botanical Gardens call (905) 527-1158. To reach the Nature Centre call (905) 527-7983.

Second Marsh and McLaughlin Bay in Oshawa

Marshes, swamps and bogs are all wetlands, but each has its own special features. In the marsh the predominant vegetation is aquatic grasses, sedges and rushes; there are no trees. Swamps, however, are wooded wetlands. Bogs are waterlogged wetlands where sphagnum mosses create acidic conditions in the stagnant water.

It is estimated that 80 percent of southern Ontario's wetlands have been lost to urban and industrial sprawl. That makes the 123 hectares of Oshawa's Second Marsh a rare, if somewhat tarnished, gem, but one that is being lovingly restored.

This wetland is not what you would expect to find neighbouring the corporate headquarters of General Motors of Canada. Situated on the north shore of Lake Ontario, the marsh is just visible to the non-stop surge of motorists on Highway 401, yet it provides a migratory stopover for more than 250 species of birds, including waterfowl and songbirds. In October elusive long-eared owls and northern saw-whet owls may be heard in the woods. The streams pouring into the marsh are spawning grounds for rainbow trout and coho salmon. The largest remaining coastal wetland in the Greater Toronto Area, Second Marsh is characterized by beds of cattails and sedges surrounded by wet meadows, swamps flooded by beavers and thickets of hawthorn and basswood. All these are protected from the surging waves of Lake Ontario by a barrier beach.

Human activity is responsible both for creating and damaging the marsh. Before European settlement, the marsh was a deepwater bay. A trading post was established on the west shore in the late 1700s, but the real environmental changes began after the American Revolution, when Captain Benjamin Wilson headed settlement in the area. As farmers began to work the land, erosion washed sediments into the bay, turning it into a wetland sheltered by a sandbar. Nearly two centuries of agriculture and urbanization led to environmental degradation: excessive sediment, murky water and declining variation in plant and animal species.

To rehabilitate the marsh habitat, islands have been built, an outflow gap at the southwestern shore has been opened and nesting boxes have been erected for birds. Sanctuary islands in the marsh have become home to nesting waterfowl and help direct the flow of water.

Rehabilitation projects have met with varied success. Because carp displace native fish, a barrier of wire fencing was constructed, but high spring water levels rendered it useless. However, underwater cells, or enclosures, built with submerged Christmas trees, have proved effective in discouraging the carp. They don't like to be poked with the pointy branches of the Christmas trees, so they stay out of the area. This gives aquatic plants such as milfoil and coontail a chance to take hold, creating habitat for indigenous fish such as pike.

In addition to encouraging wildlife, many improvements have been made to encourage human visitors. These include observation towers, picnic tables, interpretive signs and 2 kilometres of walking trails alongside the marsh and swampy woods. About 1 kilometre of the trail is wheelchair accessible.

You can easily spend a spring afternoon watching dabbling ducks among the reeds or colourful warblers darting through the hedgerows. Winter brings coyotes to the frozen marsh, and when the ice melts, swans feed in the open waters of Lake Ontario.

In the early 1600s Samuel de Champlain wrote, "During the day they bind the child to a piece of wood and wrap him in furs or skins ... under the child they spread the silk of a special kind of reed ... which is soft for it to lie on and helps to keep it clean."

On a September afternoon, when waves of migrating waterfowl and shorebirds pass through, you can easily spot a dozen great blue herons. Standing nearly 125 centimetres tall, this bird lives up to its name. On long legs it slowly walks through the shallows, pausing with deceptive stillness until a hapless frog or fish swims too close and is scooped up in the heron's pointed bill. With its Zen-like poise and elegant black crest, the bird is endlessly fascinating to watch. The great blue heron's smaller cousin, the black-crowned night heron, might also be spotted standing motionless in the mudflats. Joining the herons are sandpipers, plovers and yellowlegs, all gorging themselves on insects and other invertebrates in preparation for the long journey south. Hundreds of blue-winged teal—one of the largest sightings in the Greater Toronto Area—gather in the marsh on their autumn migration. These little ducks attract predators such as the northern harrier, a large hawk that courses over the cattails searching for its prey.

The Beaver Pond Trail on the west side of the marsh leads through meadows and woods to an observation tower overlooking an old beaver pond where green frogs can be spotted among the duckweed. In spring look for an outstanding display of wildflowers in these woods: showy lady's slipper, Jack-in-the-pulpit and Canada anemone.

Bordering the marsh to the east is the 40-hectare McLaughlin Bay Wildlife Reserve with its 5 kilometres of cinder walking path, which leads from the General Motors' parking lot through meadows and woods to Lake Ontario. Ancient willows shelter the path as it winds down to a pebble beach, where traffic sounds give way to the slapping of waves, and swallows dance on the breeze. Those who have a mind to keep walking can

continue along the Waterfront Trail right into Darlington Provincial Park.

First-Hand Experience

You can reach both Second Marsh and the McLaughlin
Bay Wildlife Reserve via Colonel Sam Drive in Oshawa.
From Highway 401, take the Harmony Road exit, and
follow Farewell south to Colonel Sam Drive where you
turn east. The Friends of Second Marsh is a not-for-profit
organization that coordinates habitat restoration and
community outreach programs. To learn more about the
marsh and the programs, contact Friends of Second
Marsh, 206 King Street East, P.O. Box 26066 RPO,
Oshawa L1H 8R4, or telephone (905) 723-5047.

There are no washrooms or snackbars at Second
Marsh but these facilities are available at Oshawa's Lake-
view Park, to the west of Second Marsh, at the foot of
Simcoe Street.

A network of paths that traverses much of the north
shore of Lake Ontario is described in *The Waterfront Trail:
Explore Yesterday, Today and Tomorrow Along the Shores of Lake
Ontario*, published by the Waterfront Regeneration
Trust. Call (416) 314-9490.

Feeding Chipmunks in Toronto's Edward's Gardens

The rate at which chipmunks collect autumn's bounty: nine hundred or more acorns per chipmunk per day.

Easily observed in a wide range of habitats from Algonquin Park to Toronto's Edward's Gardens, chipmunks are not usually considered prize sightings by seasoned nature watchers. But on a sunny September afternoon in one of Toronto's most popular parks, a chipmunk was charming first-time visitors to Canada with its gregarious nature, readily taking peanuts from an outstretched hand, then quickly returning for seconds, thirds and more until the supply ran out. Unaccustomed to such friendly wildlife, the visitors were smitten.

To park visitors and cottagers who delight in feeding chipmunks, it can come as a bit of surprise that the little critters are actually rough-and-ready loners, tough enough to tangle with small reptiles. Belonging to the oldest genera of living squirrels, which has remained unchanged since the Miocene epoch nearly twenty-five million years ago, chipmunks are versatile creatures who build tunnels, climb trees and scamper through the undergrowth in their relentless quest for food.

Indeed, much of a chipmunk's daily routine is consumed with the search for food. Anyone who has watched a chippie cram yet another peanut into already bulging cheek pouches has seen the compulsion that drives these little rodents from dawn to dusk. They eat a wide variety of seeds (such as maple keys) and nuts (including acorns, hazelnuts, beechnuts and hickory nuts). Some even eat small animals such as slugs, grasshoppers and fly larvae. While they love blueberries and raspberries, they don't eat the fruit pulp, but cut it away to get at the seeds, leaving the peel and pulp behind in a little pile. They store the seeds they don't eat—as much as a peck—in their underground nests.

A chipmunk's burrow is a crafty piece of engineering, designed to show no obvious signs of construction. Because chipmunks must be ever-wary of predators such as hawks, foxes, weasels and even house cats, they keep the entrance a carefully guarded secret, usually obscuring it under a low-lying branch or root. No matter how tame you may think a chipmunk has become by taking nuts from your hand, chances are it will never let you witness it entering its burrow. Most dangerous of all the chipmunk's predators are the slender weasels who can pursue it down the burrow's tiny tunnels.

Burrows are dug during summer months, but evidence of this activity is seldom seen because the excavated dirt is removed through a special work hole, carried off in cheek pouches and scattered well away from the burrow. The work hole is subsequently plugged. The entrance is a hole barely big enough to accommodate a golf ball. It drops straight down to a network of storage and nesting chambers that extend about a metre below the surface. A chipmunk usually inhabits the same burrow throughout its life, adding to it over the seasons, so that it may extend 4 metres or even farther.

While it doesn't actually hibernate, the chipmunk enters a state of torpor during the winter, sleeping curled up for about six days at a time and waking only to feed on its ample supplies or to eliminate waste in a corner specially reserved for that purpose. Females

Although they are solitary creatures, chipmunks use a variety of sounds to communicate. Short, high-pitched, rhythmic chips are thought to assert the chipmunk's presence. A similar, but lower-pitched noise is thought to express anger and fear. Startled animals may trill. During fights squeals are common.

may have two litters: one in spring and one in summer. Blind, bald, deaf and completely helpless, the young grow quickly, and by the time they are five or six weeks old, they are ready to emerge from the burrow for the first time. Not long after that they will be dispersed. The mother forbids them access to the burrow and chipmunks in the outlying area start vocalizations to encourage the young to move off.

Chipmunks guard their territory with vigour, shouting chipping noises. A defender will chase an intruding chipmunk to the edge of a lake, harassing it until it falls in. Or it will pursue the potential usurper until it succeeds in driving it away. Unlike the cartoon characters, Chip and Dale, real chipmunks don't share.

Northern and western chipmunks most likely belong to a species known as the least chipmunk. Their preferred habitat is upland, hardwood forests where the soil is soft enough for burrowing, preferably at the forest edge where shrubs such as hazelnuts provide additional food.

First-Hand Experience

Chipmunks can be found across most of Ontario as far north as the southern tip of James Bay. In Toronto they can be seen—and fed—at Edward's Gardens at the corner of Leslie Street and Lawrence Avenue.

MAJOR MAMMALS

Looking for Moose in Algonquin Park

An adult male moose is an impressive sight—imposing in size, but homely by design. This behemoth browser weighs up to 817 kilograms and sports a rack of antlers up to 2 metres across. The drooping snout and the fleshy dewlap dangling from its throat may seem more endearing than majestic, but you'll never forget the sight of your first moose.

Moose are surprisingly easy to observe. Visit Algonquin Park in the spring, and you're almost certain to see a moose, especially on a May or June morning. As you drive the Highway 60 corridor that cuts east to west through the park, watch the wetlands near the sides of the road, and you may easily see a dozen moose or more in the space of an hour. While it seems suicidal for moose to linger by the roadside, they cannot resist the same powerful cravings that hit so many junk-food addicts. During winter, road clearing crews use sand mixed with salt to keep the highways safe. When spring runoff drains the salt into low-lying areas beside the roads, it proves irresistible for moose. Northern herbivores who have spent a winter eating low-sodium twigs are desperate for a salt lick. Those who can't find a roadside sodium supply have been known to travel great distances in search of salt. Moose seek aquatic plants, like milfoil, which have greater sodium concentrations than woody plants.

Moose are not the only animals that crave salt. Mammals need salt in their nervous systems to transmit electrical impulses and to maintain pressure in cells. Powerful salt cravings drive porcupines to chew up canoe seats or any other wooden object with a lingering residue of sweat.

The moose's name is an Algonquin word that means "twig eater." While twigs are not its preferred food, moose browse on this woody stuff in winter, when little else is available. During summer months its taste-buds turn to fresh leaves and large volumes of aquatic plants such as water lilies. Moose will even dive and swim underwater—to depths of 5 metres or more—to get their favourite plants. Hence they are often found wading through the web of waterways, muskegs and swamps that characterize the boreal north.

Moose were uncommon in Algonquin at the turn of the century, although the reason for their relative scarcity was not well understood at the time. Now biologists think the low moose population was a result of very high deer numbers. In the early 1900s the white-tailed deer population was thought to run as high as one hundred thousand individuals. White-tailed deer carry a parasitic brainworm that does not affect them, but blinds, paralyzes and soon kills moose. Deer thrive on the secondary growth that springs up after a forest fire. When deer populations dropped as a result of forest-fire prevention and the logging of the conifers that provided winter cover, the moose population exploded.

Of course the classic way to watch Algonquin moose is from a canoe. Paddle the waterways and you are almost certain to glimpse one feeding on the aquatic vegetation. Unlike deer, moose are not skittish. They will stop, look and contemplate their next move, rather than leaping for cover in the bush. I've watched and waited for thirty minutes while a mother moose chomped great mouthfuls of water-dripping weeds, oblivious to the buzzing flies that hovered around her, ignoring our canoe, our conversations and eventually our loud shouts as we tried to persuade her to move away from the portage path.

Each spring females give birth to a single calf, which they defend with great maternal concern. Even though the calf is weaned by autumn, it stays with the mother over the winter until the following spring when the next calf is born. Though the male reaches maturity in two to three years, it still has to wait another two to three years for an opportunity to breed.

First-Hand Experience

A rack of moose antlers weighs up to 32 kilograms.

While Highway 60 presents an easy opportunity for spring moose-watching in Algonquin Park, it also presents a real danger for motorists, particularly at night. Moose do not turn to face the headlights of on-coming traffic, so the light seldom catches their eyes. Drivers should be extremely alert at this time of year and drive at 10 to 20 kilometres below the posted speed limit.

Seeing a moose on a canoe trip is always a special joy. With more than 1,500 kilometres of canoe routes, Algonquin is an ideal park for paddlers. But even without canoeing experience or equipment, you can still explore the park on a guided canoe excursion. Numerous outfitters offer canoeing and hiking trips for both novice and experienced campers.

Guide Steve Sana of Pow-Wow Wilderness Trips offers canoe trips with lots of stops for swimming, fishing and hiking. He provides all the required gear and happily shares his wilderness know-how with tips on how to build a sweat lodge, and cure headaches with birchbark tea. He cooks hearty meals over an open fire, including dishes made from wild foods, such as milkweed fritters. Each trip is customized to suit your interests, whether they include watching wildlife or learning how to smoke beef jerky on the trail, and includes round-trip transportation from Toronto, meals, tour guide and canoes. Camping equipment rentals are offered. Special weekends can be arranged for singles and for mothers and children. Expect to spend about $200 per weekend per person. Call Pow-Wow Wilderness Trips at (416) 754-9998, or visit their Web site at www.pathcom.com/~powow.

If you want a shorter experience, try the one-day guided canoe trips offered by The Portage Store at Canoe Lake in Algonquin Park. For roughly $40 a day, the gear, guide and lunch are included. Complete outfitting packages are also available. Call (705) 633-5622 or visit the Web site at www.inforamp.net/~portage.

Watching White-Tailed Deer in Ontario's Deer Yards

While a glimpse of a white-tailed deer darting across a rural road is a common sight for many early risers, the most deer any wildlife watcher will see at any one time will be in the late winter months. That's when many of Ontario's white-tailed deer gather in large, natural areas know as yards where they seek shelter from the cold and a means of surviving heavy snowfalls.

Winter's deep snow puts deer at a serious disadvantage. Snow more than 50 centimetres deep or snow that is crusted, requires a great deal of extra energy for movement and food-seeking activities. Deer that sink in the snow are easy prey for large-footed predators that can remain above the crust. Where snowfall is lighter in the south, deer may remain in small groups, but further north they congregate in wintering yards.

Yarding is thought to offer deer the advantage of well-packed trails formed by the collective movements of hundreds or thousands of deer. They choose areas where canopies of intermingling evergreens shelter the ground from snow and provide insulated resting places.

At the Peterborough Crown Game Reserve dozens of deer may be sighted together on a March afternoon, searching for winter browse, the tender shoots and twigs

Each summer a buck grows a new set of antlers. Velvety skin covers the growing antlers, which remain sensitive until September when the buck begins aggressive territorial displays in preparation for rutting. After rutting, hormone levels drop and the antlers fall off, but few are ever found by people. The calcium-rich antlers are eaten by mice and other rodents.

of trees and shrubs. Watch roadside clearings for movement in the fading sunlight of a late winter afternoon.

White-tailed deer populations and their ranges have fluctuated wildly in the province as a result of human activity, particularly logging. When a massive influx of European settlers began opening up the dense forests in a serious way during the first half of the nineteenth century, the stage was set for major population changes. At first the clearings increased deer habitat by encouraging the secondary growth on which deer thrive. But as unrestricted hunting increased, white-tail populations fell in the south. At the same time railroad construction and more northerly logging was creating improved deer habitat further north. Deer moved into the western part of the province, around the Rainy River area, from Minnesota.

The regulation of hunting has allowed southern herds to recover to such an extent that some people now consider them a nuisance. They are accused of overbrowsing sensitive parklands, particularly in the rare areas of Carolinian habitat along Lake Erie's north shore. Populations continue to fluctuate locally with changes to climate, habitat and hunting regulations.

Today one of the largest herds of white-tailed deer is found south of Lake Nipissing. Known as the Loring herd, it contains an estimated eight to fourteen thousand individuals. While deer are observed in the area year-round, March is the best time to see them. Many local people feed the deer and they are often seen in the towns of Loring, Commanda and Restouille. Drive along Highways 522, 524 or 534 between 4 and 6 p.m., and you will likely see dozens of deer.

Deer have survived in Ontario because of their adaptability. Their short, wiry, reddish-brown coats of summer become longer, thicker and grey each fall.

One theory on the declining Algonquin deer population suggests that when large quantities of hemlocks were felled for the construction of Toronto's subway in the 1950s, the resulting loss of winter cover affected deer numbers.

Dappled fawns can hide on the forest floor, undetected by predators. Adults have keen senses and can flee from danger at speeds of up to 48 kilometres per hour.

Deer feeding-habits change according to their seasonal needs. After winter they seek high-protein grasses in woodland openings. Spring is when deer graze. They still eat grasses, but unlike other ruminants like elk who graze year-round, the deer change their diets. In May they nibble on emerging aspen leaves. In summer, when they require carbohydrates, they eat the tips of cherry, oak, maple, willow and other trees and shrubs, especially young yellow birch seedlings. Deer who inhabit agricultural areas will turn to crops. In the fall they seek foods that will fatten them up for winter: orchard fruits, acorns and mushrooms. Winter is a time of scarcity when they must get by on twigs that offer some nourishment in their bark and the underlying cambium (the thin, formative layer below the bark).

First-Hand Experience

Three well-known Ontario deer yards are the Peterborough Crown Game Reserve Yards, the Loring Yard and the Bonnechere Deer Yard. The Peterborough yards can be seen from Highway 28 between the towns of Apsley and Burleigh Falls. Drive south from Apsley along Highway 28 and watch the roadside clearings. As soon as you spot one deer, you will likely see dozens more foraging in the brush. Park along the roadside and the deer will probably stop to watch you with as much curiosity as you watch them.

The Loring Deer Yard covers roughly 500 square kilometres in an area south of Lake Nipissing. To reach the yard, turn west off Highway 11 at Trout Creek. The

yard has been managed since the 1960s, with supple-
mental food provided. The yard begins west of the village of Commanda on Highway 522.

East of Algonquin Park, the Bonnechere Deer Yard
is located in Hagarty and Richards Townships.

Spring Porcupine Sightings

My first sighting of a porcupine was not what I had expected. Instead of a quill-throwing confrontation, we eyed each other with solemn curiosity—the porcupine from its perch high in a treetop, and I from the roadside where I'd stopped to admire a waterfall. Porcupines can be found throughout the forests of Ontario, and they are not as dangerous as they may seem. Contrary to common belief, the porcupine cannot throw its quills. When approached it will turn its back to the enemy, protecting its head, then display its bristling quills. Should the opponent come too close, the porcupine quickly lashes out with its powerful tail, impaling the attacker. Each quill is tipped with backward-projecting scales, much like the tip of a fish hook, making it virtually impossible to tug out. Dogs or livestock that get a muzzle full of quills may starve to death unless they are surgically removed. Snipping the end off the offending quill makes the extraction process easier by releasing air within the hollow quill. Because they are barbed, quills continue to work their way through the body. They can be fatal if they pierce a vital organ, but they often emerge from a different part of the body days later. The porcupine grows back the lost quills within six months, often sooner.

The porcupine is one of Canada's largest rodents, weighing 6 to 13 kilograms and measuring up to 1 metre long. Only the beaver is bigger. The porcupine is

According to Chippewa legend, the world's first porcupines had no quills. Trying to protect himself from predators, Porcupine covered his back with hawthorn branches. Nanabosho saw how well this defence worked and decided to help. Using clay, he stuck thorns onto the porcupine to offer him lasting protection.

usually nocturnal, but warm spring sunshine may stir it from its den to go in search of fresh food. After a boring winter diet of bark and pine needles, the hungry porcupine craves the tasty buds of sugar maples and new aspen cattails.

Large and lumbering, the porcupine moves slowly across land, shuffling in a pigeon-toed waddle to its next meal. When that meal is a bed of luscious water lilies, the porcupine proves to be a surprisingly strong swimmer, aided by roughly thirty thousand hollow quills that keep it afloat. It is also an adept climber, using the bristly underside of its tail to help push it upward. Porcupines spend much of their day high in the trees, munching or resting. They find shelters on the ground in rocky crevices, caves, culverts, brush piles and tree hollows—particularly hemlock. You can identify a porcupine den by the profusion of peanut-shaped scat in front of the entrance.

Despite its awesome ability to stick its opponents, the porcupine is not without its predators. The fisher, a large weasel, specializes in preying on porcupines, biting their faces and heads. When fishers are overtrapped, the porcupine population can soar out of control, much to the aggravation of farmers, who see their corn and clover trampled by porcupines in search of an easy summertime meal.

During bleak winter months they must make do with twigs. If they are lucky enough to find a rack of antlers, they will gnaw away with great relish to supplement their vegetarian diet with minerals. Their quest for salt leads them to roadsides each spring where they often end up as roadkill.

A porcupine that meets such an untimely end may still prove useful to traditional native craftspeople. The porcupine's hollow quills can be trimmed and sewn

When food has been scarce, woodsmen have often turned to porcupines because they are easy to catch. The porcupine's fatty flesh tastes of the food it eats—pine or aspen bark. In their book *Wilderness Cooking*, Berndt Berglund and Clare E. Bolsby advise parboiling the animal before fixing up a mess of Porcupine Ribs, glazed with a mixture of mustard, brown sugar, cream and rye whisky.

onto bark baskets in decorative or pictorial designs. At the community museum at the Golden Lake Reserve in eastern Ontario, visitors can learn about the laborious process of decorative quill work, starting with how to use an old blanket to gently lift off quills from roadkill. The quills are cleaned and the ends snipped off, with each dangerous hook carefully put aside. They are arranged so that their natural grey and white colours form artful designs, then they are sewn in place.

First-Hand Experience

Porcupines reside throughout the forested parts of the province, including many provincial parks such as Algonquin. In late winter and early spring you can often see them high in tree tops munching bark.

Fine examples of traditional quill work can be found on Manitoulin Island at shops and galleries that specialize in quality First Nations art such as Kasheese Studios in West Bay: (705) 377-4890.

North of Peterborough, the Whetung Gallery at Curve Lake Indian Reserve often has porcupine quill boxes. Located off County Road 23, Whetung displays fine arts and crafts from reserves across Canada. During summer months a restaurant serves traditional foods such as corn soup. Call (705) 657-3661. Golden Lake Reserve is located at the town of Golden Lake on Highway 60.

Besides the North American animal, another twenty species of porcupines have been found living around the world, some with quills 30 centimetres long. Crested porcupines in India have been known to get the better of a Bengal tiger.

Black Bears and the Aspen Valley Wildlife Sanctuary

Humans are unlikely to outrun, outswim or outclimb black bears. They have been known to travel at speeds of up to 56 kilometres an hour over short distances.

I could almost wish myself a dormouse, or a she-bear, to sleep away the rest of this cold, cold winter, and wake only with the first green leaves, the first warm breath of the summer wind.

——ANNA BROWNELL JAMESON, *Winter Studies and Summer Rambles in Canada*

On a slushy February morning, who doesn't envy the black bear hibernating in its cosy den? The bear's ability to virtually shut down its bodily functions for half the year is one of nature's most intriguing mysteries.

As the daylight hours dwindle and the air chills between mid-October and early November, black bears prepare to enter their dens. Unlike the large caves of ursine cartoon characters, real bears prepare a small den, just big enough for the individual, or with enough extra room to accommodate a litter of cubs, if it is to be a maternal den. Smaller spaces are more efficient for the conservation of body heat. A bear will dig a hole about 1.5 metres deep—usually under tree roots—then line it with branches, leaves and lichens. After the bear settles into the den, it masks the entranceway with more vegetation.

It is popularly believed that black bears remain in their dens for five or six months. During that time they do not eat, drink or eliminate any waste. Heart rates slow to half the normal level and body temperature decreases. Now some biologists think that black bears do not always remain holed up for the entire winter. A flooded den or similar disturbance may prompt a bear to go in search of new shelter and possibly food. Reports of black bears roaming through the Rouge Valley in eastern Toronto on Christmas Day, 1997, seem to substantiate the theory.

During their time in the den, bears shed their foot pads, growing tender new ones. The mother bear gives birth to her young without ever waking. A newborn cub weighs little more than a large grapefruit, but rapidly plumps up by nursing on its mother's milk, which is rich in fat and protein.

Black bears probably came to the New World about a half million years ago, crossing the Bering Land Bridge from Siberia.

When the mother and her cubs emerge in the spring they will spend the first few weeks near a home site where at least one large tree provides a quick escape for cubs. The first foods of April, new grasses, insects and poplar catkins, provide little nourishment. A few weeks later they will eat new leaves from trembling aspens, sometimes bending the saplings by straddling them or simply breaking them. During this time the bears continue to lose weight.

Not until the berry crops of summer do bears begin to fatten up. Later in the year they dine on hazelnuts and hawthorn, and in fall they look for ridges of oak and beech trees for feasts of acorns and beechnuts. Feeding predominantly on vegetation, black bears eat mammals only occasionally, and often as carrion.

Bears are at their most social as a young family. The female is deeply protective of her offspring, who stay with her until they are at least 16 months old, sharing a winter den during their first year. Female offspring may remain near the mother's range, and one may eventually inherit it.

Spring bear hunts were permitted in Ontario until 1999, so it was not unusual to find orphaned cubs. Muskoka's Aspen Valley Wildlife Sanctuary takes in orphaned and injured animals, then rehabilitates them so they can return to the wilderness.

"In one week alone, we received three orphaned bear cubs," said Aspen Valley Director Audrey Tournay. "They will be kept in an enclosure way back in the bush where they have no human contact except for their caregiver. We only keep them for as long as they would naturally remain with their mother—usually until they are 18 months old—then we tag and release them at a site far away from people."

Not all the sanctuary's bears can be rehabilitated. Three bears that were declawed and defanged by their previous owners to train hunting dogs now remain permanently in a 1.5-hectare wooded enclosure complete with pond. "Human beings amuse them. When visitors come, the bears will sit and watch them," Tournay says.

The sanctuary is no doubt the safest way to watch black bears. Most bears avoid human contact, but nuisance bears, those who come into potentially dangerous contact with humans, are more frequently sighted when the bear's natural food supply is low. In years when wild berry yields are poor, hungry bears are more likely to be lured by the smell of an unwashed barbecue grill or poorly stored garbage. Males, especially subadults, are the most frequent nuisance visitors to campgrounds and dumps. Weighing between 120 to 128 kilograms, an adult male is powerful enough to do some serious damage.

Bears have poor vision, but they can smell carrion more than 1.6 kilometres away.

Younger males tend to steer clear of older, larger bears. When a youngster meets an older male at a prime feeding site, such as a dump, he'll head for a tall tree. Driving into the dump in Sleeping Giant Provincial Park, I watched a dozen large adults snuffling through campers' refuse. Three young bears were perched 10 metres up a birch tree. The bored-looking youngsters each sat in the crotch of a branch, leaning back on the trunk, while they waited for the feast below to finish.

First-Hand Experience

Black Bears live in wild, forested areas across most of the Canadian Shield, the Bruce Peninsula and Northern Ontario. The animals generally prefer a young, mixed forest, one with a great variety of trees and shrubs, both for concealment and food. They are particularly common in Sleeping Giant Provincial Park (see page 199).

While sensible back-country campers and hikers don't go looking for bears, they should understand bear behaviour to prevent dangerous situations. The Federation of Ontario Naturalists publishes a pamphlet titled *Bear Facts*, which offers advice on preventing bear problems and how to handle bear encounters. Call the Federation of Ontario Naturalists at (416) 444-8419.

A fascinating book for anyone who hikes, bikes or paddles in bear country is *Backcountry Bear Basics* by Dave Smith. He advises readers to be responsible for their own safety by understanding the animals' natural behaviour patterns.

The Aspen Valley Wildlife Sanctuary is located east of Rosseau via Muskoka Road 3 (Cardwell Road) and Crawford Street. In addition to bears, the sanctuary rehabilitates wolves, porcupines, squirrels, skunks and many other animals. The sanctuary is open for public visits on Wednesday and Sunday afternoons from 1 to 4 p.m., from the Victoria Day long weekend to Thanksgiving. No admission is charged, but donations are welcome. Call (705) 732-6368.

A Beaver Changes the Algonquin Landscape

Both revered and reviled for its industrious ways, the beaver comes second only to humans in its ability to alter the landscape. By cutting down vast numbers of trees, damming streams and flooding dry land, the beaver seems relentless in its efforts to re-invent the landscape to suit its own needs.

Though maintenance crews decry the massive work that goes into removing beaver dams from culverts, and cottagers complain about the tree-cutting activities that flood their properties, the work of the beaver creates a habitat that is needed by many other species. Although beavers kill trees by flooding an area, those dead trees will likely become occupied by birds such as wood-peckers. Then wood ducks will nest in the vacated woodpecker holes. The waters will be populated by insect larvae, minnows and frogs who in turn attract herons. Eventually moose will come to feed on the aquatic vegetation. So many creatures are tied to the beavers' activities, that one can't imagine the Ontario landscape without them.

Beavers fell trees to get leaves, buds and bark for food and to build their dams and lodges. Master engi-neers, beavers can readily construct a 33-metre dam, blocking the flow of water to flood the surrounding land. The resulting pond provides them with protection from predators such as wolves. The pond must be deep

Beaver pelts have two kinds of hair—short, soft fur and coarse, long guard hairs. Hatters working with beaver pelts removed the long guard hairs with mercury, leaving behind a soft, water-resistant felt that would keep the rain off a gen-tleman's head. The mercury caused brain damage to the hatters who worked with it, leading to the expres-sion, "mad as a hatter."

enough so that the bottom won't freeze during winter months. Beavers must be able to access the underwater entrance to their lodge.

Beavers are abundant at Algonquin Park and are most active on October evenings when they work on their winter food piles. They must cut huge amounts of branches in the fall to survive the winter. Aspen and willow are their preferred foods, but they will take other species if needed. Branches are stored in an underwater food pile that serves as a well-stocked larder to get through the lean winter months. Contrary to popular opinion, beavers are not natural lumberjacks; they cannot determine the direction in which a tree will fall. Odds simply have it that trees growing on the shoreline incline towards the water.

Life inside the well-insulated lodge is dark, but dry, with above-water platforms for eating and sleeping. As many as a dozen beavers will inhabit the lodge, usually two mated adults, their kits and yearlings. They don't actually hibernate, but they do slow down during winter months, only making forays to the food pile. Although they rely on bark for much of their nutrition, beavers add a little variety in spring by munching aquatic plants such as duckweed and water lilies.

A hefty rodent, weighing between 18 to 27 kilograms or more, the beaver is supremely adapted to the aquatic life. Its large, flat tail serves as a rudder, its webbed hind feet act as flippers, its ears close tight when it dives, and its luxurious fur is waterproofed by oil glands.

It was the beaver's fur that brought Europeans deep into the continent and nearly led to the extinction of the animals. As broad-brimmed felt hats became popular in Europe during the latter part of the sixteenth century, beavers were hunted to extinction in western Europe.

The first animal to ever appear on a postage stamp was a beaver on Canada's three-penny red in 1851.

No other pelt could match the beaver's as a hat felt; tiny barbs on the soft underfur keep it matted and durable.

The relentless quest for beaver pelts pushed fur traders beyond the Great Lakes into the north and west. By 1893 beavers were trapped to near extinction in the Algonquin area. But the formation of the park that year offered the animals protection and signalled a rebound in beaver populations. Today there are an estimated twenty thousand beaver ponds in Algonquin Park, with an average of five beavers per pond—roughly equivalent to the population of Pickering. Trapping for beaver and other fur-bearing animals (including mink, marten, muskrat and otter) in Ontario can be undertaken only with a Ministry of Natural Resources licence.

First-Hand Experience

The Beaver Pond Trail in Algonquin Park is a 2-kilometre loop past two beaver ponds, plus a lesson in beaver pond ecology courtesy of a trail brochure with comments relating to markers on the trail. It is located just west of the visitor centre at KM 43 on Highway 60. The trail brochure is available at the park gates or the visitor centre for roughly 35 cents. For information call (705) 633-5572 or 1-800-668-7275.

Another excellent trail for spotting beavers is the Mizzy Lake Trail, near the east end of the park at KM 15 on Highway 60. Mizzy Lake is an 11-kilometre loop that requires a full day, but its nine ponds promise excellent opportunities for spotting wildlife.

Beavers are common through most of Ontario, north to the treeline. There is even a beaver lodge in Toronto, in Tommy Thompson Park.

In medieval Europe beavers became the subjects of some fantastic myths. Because the aquatic rodent's testicles are internal, it was supposed that the animal had somehow disposed of them. A medieval bestiary, translated by T.H. White, explains that when the beaver is "pursued by the hunter, he removes his own testicles with a bite, and casts them before the sportsman, and thus escapes by flight."

Watching Wildlife at Sleeping Giant Park

Situated on the Sibley Peninsula, east of Thunder Bay, Sleeping Giant Park takes its name from a series of dramatic mesas that when viewed from across the bay resemble the form of a sleeping man. Legends have grown up about the sleeping giant. Some say it's Nanabosho, the son of the west wind who led the Ojibway people to the north shore of Lake Superior, away from their Sioux enemies.

The park is known for its dramatic cliffs, some of the most accessible of which can be seen from the Thunder Bay Lookout. Here you can stand on a 137-metre-high platform above Lake Superior and look down on the aspen growing on the tallus slopes of fallen rubble at the foot of the cliff. Rugged hiking trails circle the giant formation at the south end of the park, where peregrine falcons have been sighted nesting along the cliffs. At some points these cliffs tower up 240 metres, making them some of the highest cliffs in Ontario.

Sleeping Giant's forest is primarily boreal, featuring many of the evergreens found in the north. Large stands of balsam fir are draped with thick masses of old man's beard lichen, making them look like shaggy ghost trees. Many of the pines were cut down by lumber operations, which continued until the 1960s, but large trees still remain in a few places. One such area is Piney Wood Hills, where you can still see massive red and white pines that are 150 to 300 years old—trees so large you want to put your arms around them just to see how far you can reach. Measuring 4.8 kilometres return, Piney Wood Trail takes you past signs of the large scale lumber operation, including a trail made by horse teams dragging lumber out of the bush many decades ago.

Altogether the park boasts more than 80 kilometres of hiking trails, ranging from the rugged 16-kilometre return Chimney Trail, a steep climb that crosses the knees of the giant, to the 2.4-kilometre return Sibley Creek Nature Trail with its views of marsh life and beavers. Thunder Bay Bogs Nature Trail offers a look at a small northern lake, whose edges are slowly filling with sphagnum moss. Few plants tolerate the thin acidic soils, but among them are lush quantities of blueberries, elegant pink lady's slippers that bloom in early July, and Labrador tea, which is named for the beverage that can be brewed from its leaves.

Only 2.4 kilometres return, the Ravine Lake Trail is known for its wildflowers. Open areas along the path are thick with thimbleberry and sarsaparilla (used to make an early form of root beer), as well as the large-leaf aster, whose ample foliage has earned it the nickname "toilet paper of the north woods." More delicate finds include the one-sided pyrola growing at the base of a white cedar, bunchberry, starflower and tiny pairs of pink twinflowers. Blunt-leaved and other orchids have been spotted in these woods. Arctic arnica is one of the northern plants that grow in the park hundreds of kilometres south of their normal arctic habitat. Look for little piles of sawdust at the base of balsam trees. These indicate an infestation of sawyer beetles, whose larvae can be heard munching inside the tree.

The peninsula formation of Sleeping Giant Park reaches 40 kilometres south into Lake Superior and acts

Squeeze one of the blisters on the bark of a balsam fir and sap oozes out onto your finger. Taste it and you will recognize the unmistakable flavour of a cough mixture known for its unpleasant taste. The sap is a key ingredient in the remedy.

as a funnel for wildlife moving south from the mainland. This funnel effect combined with the park's diverse habitats makes the peninsula a haven for wildlife. Timber wolves have been sighted along the west shore of Marie Louise Lake and can be heard howling in the spring and fall. Bald eagles nest at the north end of the lake, while cormorants make their home at the south. Numerous fox dens are located along Highway 587 near Pickerel Lake, and the foxes are so numerous that park staff must constantly remind visitors not to feed them.

White-tailed deer can be found throughout the park, wandering through campgrounds and even grazing in front of the visitor centre. Black bears are abundant, particularly around the dump. I saw a large female so obese she virtually dragged her belly under her.

A century ago, before logging, woodland caribou were the most populous large mammals on the peninsula. But caribou are very sensitive to human activity and have since disappeared from the area. Moose thrive on the shrubbery that grows up after logging, and they soon predominated. Today the moose are giving way to the white-tailed deer, who carry a parasitic brain worm that does not affect them, but kills moose. Also coming back to the park after the cessation of logging are the marten and the fisher, two large weasels known for their hunting skills.

Because of its peninsula formation, the park is visited by many migrating birds. These are studied at the Thunder Cape Bird Observatory on the southernmost tip of the peninsula, just outside the park. Also just outside the park, toward the south end of the peninsula, is the village of Silver Islet, a rugged little cottage community whose origins date back more than a century ago to a time when the Silver Islet Mine, located under Lake Superior, was the most productive silver mine in

Juniper cones look like greyish blueberries. Sometimes used to season strong foods such as sauerkraut, the berries make fragrant incense when burned.

the world. The Silver Islet General Store has been in operation since 1871 and is popular for afternoon tea.

First-Hand Experience

Sleeping Giant Provincial Park is located 42 kilometres east of Thunder Bay, south of Highway 11/17 via Highway 587, which runs directly down the centre of the park. The park has two hundred campsites at Marie Louise Lake, while more ambitious campers can backpack into the rugged interior. For information call (807) 977-2526 or (807) 475-1506.

Observing Wolves in Haliburton Forest

Wepwawet, the ancient Egyptian wolf god, piloted the sun boat and judged people's lives on giant scales.

While wolves may be heard on a late summer's night, they are seldom seen. The Haliburton Forest Wolf Centre offers an exceptional opportunity to observe in daylight a pack of captive timber wolves that have not been socialized. The modern facility, which opened in 1996, offers an indoor display and observation area where visitors can watch the wolves through large picture windows overlooking the 6-hectare forested compound. One-way glass allows the wolves to play undisturbed and a microphone transmits the occasional yelp or howl—or birdsong—from the pen. Occasionally the sounds of other wolves from a video playing in the visitor area will start the pack howling.

Timber wolves are considerably larger than those normally found in the area around Algonquin Park. A collection of skulls in the centre's display area illustrates how the animals vary in size according to how far north they are found in the province; the smallest in the south and the largest in the boreal forests of the north. This phenomenon has been explained as a possible result of wolves interbreeding with coyotes. In Ontario some biologists suggest the tweed wolf may be such a creature, but recent genetic analysis suggests that the Algonquin area wolves are a distinct species, the Eastern Canadian red wolf. Wolves weighing as much as 50 kilograms have been found along the shores of

Hudson Bay, while wolves in the south weigh almost half that.

The pack on display at the Haliburton Forest Wolf Centre came from Michigan's Upper Peninsula, where they were the subject of a seventeen-year university research project. When the wolves had to go, the Haliburton Forest stepped in and brought the pack to Canada. While the wolves were not socialized to humans, they had never learned the hunting skills required by a wild pack.

Wild wolves prey upon the most numerous and vulnerable large mammals in their environment, typically the large ungulates (hoofed animals). In Ontario, this means deer in the southern part of the wolf's range and moose or caribou in the north. All wolves will eat beaver and other small mammals. Though a skilled predator, the wolf is by no means certain of success in a hunt. It may be outrun and outswum by both deer and moose. A wolf runs at a top speed of roughly 40 kilometres per hour, but can sustain that speed for no longer than twenty minutes. Moose often fight back, kicking their attackers with powerful blows. The element of surprise and pack tactics play an important role in a successful hunt, and the pack must work together to bring down a large prey animal.

Wolves at the centre are fed once a week, except during the spring-summer nursing season when feeding frequency is increased. Beaver carcasses supplied by fur trappers and road-killed deer brought in by the OPP are the staples of the pack's diet and fairly close to what wild wolves in the area would eat. The captive wolves also catch mice and squirrels for themselves in their compound.

Social animals, wolves usually live in packs led by the alpha couple, a male and female that lead travel,

"The strength of the pack is the wolf. The strength of the wolf is the pack."

— RUDYARD KIPLING,
The Jungle Book

initiate the hunt and decide when to end it. They also tend to be the first to explore new stimuli. The pack is small —usually about five to ten animals—so the alpha male can keep control. Only the alpha pair breeds, passing on their genes through one litter a year.

A subordinate wolf expresses its social position through postures familiar to most dog owners: flattening its ears back or rolling onto its side to expose its belly in a display of vulnerability to the dominant animal. Wolves are also said to show at least thirteen facial expressions.

The largest grey wolf recorded in North America weighed 79 kilograms and was found in Alaska. A more typical wolf weight is 27 to 60 kilograms.

While summer visitors at the centre watch a group of rambunctious pups jumping around an older wolf, staff explain their interaction. The large wolf is an older sibling "babysitting" a pair of ten-week-old cubs. Occasionally the pups muzzle-bite their older playmate in a behaviour that prompts the older wolf to regurgitate partially digested food, helping to slowly wean the pups.

The display area at the centre offers some fascinating tidbits of wolf mythology and art from around the world. North American artifacts include a Hopi wolf kachina doll, a Haida wolf rattle and Ojibway wolf paintings. Children enjoy the computer games that ask them to think like wolves seeking out water and food, and they love the touch table where they can touch a real wolf pelt and skull.

After watching the wolves, visitors can walk a trail through woods and marshes, gathering raspberries and looking for moose footprints. Haliburton Forest also offers an offbeat forest canopy tour. It combines a van tour of the forest, a short hike, a boat ride and a walk through the treetops 20 metres above the ground along a plank and rope walkway more than half a kilometre long. Safety harnesses are provided for the treetop portion of the four-hour guided tour.

First-Hand Experience

Haliburton Forest and Wildlife Reserve is a privately owned 20,235-hectare forest in the Haliburton Highlands south of Algonquin Park. It is home to the Haliburton Forest Wolf Centre, which is located 20 kilometres north of West Guilford via County Road 7 (also known as the Kennisis Lake Road). Because the wolves are in such a large 6-hectare enclosure, sightings are likely but not guaranteed. The day before or the day of a feeding are the most probable times to see active wolves. Free wolf howls are offered on Thursday evenings in July and August.

During summer the centre is open daily, from 10 a.m. to 5 p.m. The remainder of the year it opens on weekends. Admission is $7 per adult, $5 per child and $17 per family. The forest canopy tour costs $65 per person, with a minimum of four people. The price includes admission to the wolf centre. For information call (705) 754-WOLF.

GREAT FORESTS

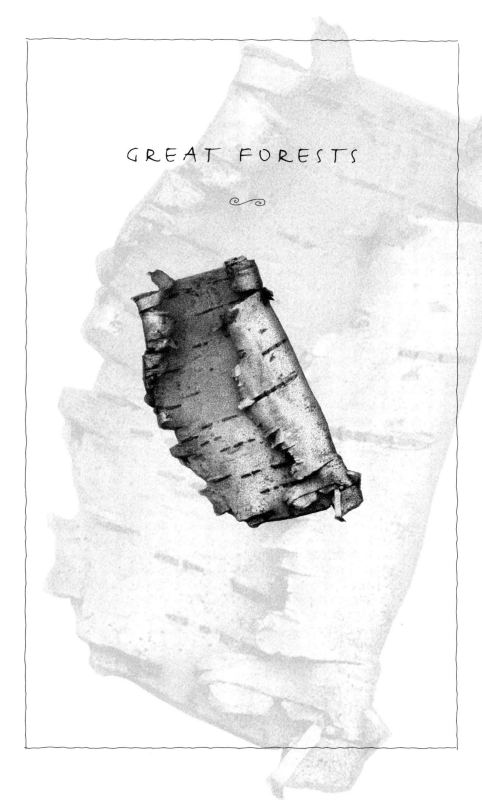

The Old-Growth Forests of Temagami and Shaw Woods

Magnificent white pines take the high ground, dominating ridges like stately sentinels towering over the forest below. The province's official tree, white pines grow to heights of 40 metres or more over the course of lives that span two or three centuries.

Tall and straight, the mature trees produce excellent lumber. They made ideal masts for sailing ships in the days when Britannia ruled the waves. Their soft, straight-grained lumber is easy to work with and is extensively used in residential construction. The value of the lumber means that few of these giants remain.

Concerns over the cutting of old pine forests have centred on the Temagami area in recent years. Finlayson Point Provincial Park, south of the town of Temagami, is an easily accessible gateway to the wilderness. The park is known for its beautiful camping on a peninsula that extends into Lake Temagami. Here you can pitch your tent among stands of 200-year-old red and white pines along the lakeshore. Finlayson Point makes a great base for exploring one of the finest tracts of old-growth forest, the 800-hectare White Bear Forest on the shores of Cassels Lake, east of the town of Temagami.

The forest is named for a nineteenth-century chief of the Teme-Augama. When the Gillies Brothers' logging

Until recently Ontario's tallest tree grew in the Kirkwood Forest, north of Thessalon. Estimated to be 350 years old, the white pine stood nearly 50 metres high. Even though it finally toppled, it remains a tourist attraction.

company began cutting the surrounding area in 1928, they set aside the White Bear Forest for their employees' recreational use. Today the area attracts hikers and canoeists who come to experience the beauty of an old-growth forest.

Hikers can get to the White Bear Forest either by road, following signs from Highway 11, or by boat. Doug Adams, a local trapper, photographer, politician and the proprietor of Northland Paradise Lodge, rents canoes to do-it-your-selfers and arranges motor boat drop-offs for hikers. He also offers guided tours along the trails of White Bear. He advises leaving plenty of time for a relatively short walk, not because the trails are difficult, but because "there's just so much to see." He'll show visitors the remains of a moose skeleton killed by a pack of wolves, and some exquisite northern orchids including rattlesnake plantain and purple-fringed.

Foresters often define old growth as red or white pines more than 120 years old. In the White Bear Forest many trees are considerably older. The crowns of these centuries-old giants rise above the canopy and younger trees fill in the gaps below. While the white pines dominate the sandy hills, a host of other trees find their own specialized niches: black spruce thrive in the shady wet areas and cedars form groves in lowlands.

Even when the great old pines die, they are still an important part of the forest ecosystem. Dead trees that have lost their bark but remain standing are known as "snags." They provide perches for large hawks. When the tree tops break off, owls and osprey nest in the bowl-like cavities that are left. Pileated woodpeckers eat the insects that inhabit the decaying snag. Woodpecker holes eventually become nests for squirrels and other animals. When the decayed tree finally topples over, assorted fungi spring from its soft, spongy wood,

Early in the century the Temagami woods were home to a British immigrant who succeeded in inventing a new identity for himself. A careful observer of wildlife, he learned to speak Ojibway, donned buckskin clothes and renamed himself Grey Owl. He claimed to be the son of a Scot and an Apache. In this role he became an early advocate for wilderness conservation. After his death, his persona was proved a fiction, but his love of the wilderness was genuine.

and salamanders and centipedes burrow in the moist rot underneath the log.

Forest fires, once thought to be unmitigated disasters, are now understood to play a role in the forest ecology of Ontario. Fire is often required for red pine seeds to germinate, because the fire burns away the duff (dead leaf layer) on the ground so that the seeds can root directly in the sandy soil they require. Many fires do not burn a forest completely. Instead they consume the understory of balsam fir, cedar and spruce. Because of their thick, insulating bark, many of the big old red and white pines survive fires, though they get somewhat scarred. The scars, known as "church windows," are shaped like gothic cathedral windows, blackened where the bark has been burned away. Walking in the shadows of these fire-scarred survivors, you can't help but be filled with a sense of awe at their endurance.

Both currant and gooseberry bushes provide a base for white pine blister rust, a fungus that lives part of its life in the berry-bearing shrubs, then attacks the inner bark of the pine tree. Removing all currant and gooseberry shrubs within half a kilometre of the white pines prevents the fungus from spreading to them.

White Bear is just a corner of the vast Temagami area, which is criss-crossed with a vast network of canoe routes, many of which have been used by native people for thousands of years. Canoeists can explore ancient pine forests at wilderness areas not accessible by road, including Obabika River Provincial Park or the north end of Temagami Island in Lake Temagami.

Although many of Ontario's remaining old-growth forests are primarily pine, a fine example of deciduous old growth can be seen in the Ottawa Valley, south of Pembrooke at Shaw Woods. Surrounded by farms, Shaw is a rare forest of mixed hardwoods that have never been cut. Massive maple, beech and oak trees provide a rich supply of food for animals and birds. As they die, their hollows shelter owls and squirrels. When they fall they are left to decay and replenish the rich soil. On a late summer afternoon a walk along Shaw's gentle trails is filled with the rich sights and smells of fecundity. Ferns and mosses fill the forest floor with greenery. Hundreds of tiny, brown stump puffballs grow on decaying logs. Amphibians abound, from the salamanders that live under the leaf litter, to the American toads that leap along the path.

First-Hand Experience

The highest elevations in Ontario can be found in the Temagami area, including Maple Mountain and Ishpatina Ridge, each about 760 metres above sea level.

Finlayson Point Provincial Park is located on Highway 11, south of the town of Temagami. It offers one hundred and fourteen campsites and guided nature hikes. Call (705) 569-3205.

At Northland Paradise Lodge, on Stevens Road in Temagami, you can arrange motorboat transportation. For $15 proprietor Doug Adams will ferry passengers to a drop-off point at Cassels Lake and arrange to pick them up further down the trail three to four hours later. The walk is only 2 kilometres, but there is plenty to see. Older people often prefer the .7-kilometre guided hike, which costs $25 per person, with a minimum of four people. You can rent a canoe for $25 a day. The lodge has motel-style suites and an all-you-can-eat dining room. Call (705) 569-3791, or write to Northland Paradise Lodge, Dept. N.O., Box 472, Stevens Road, Temagami P0H 2H0.

If you are driving to the White Bear Forest trails, park your car (at no charge) at the Caribou Mountain chalet off O'Connor Drive and follow the signposts from Highway 11.

For more information call the Welcome Centre in Temagami at 1-800-661-7609. Leave your address on the voice mail, and they will send a package of tourist information on the Temagami area.

Lady Evelyn Outfitting specializes in both summer (canoe and hiking) and winter (dog-sledding) trips into the magnificent Temagami-area wilderness, particularly in three provincial parks—Lady Evelyn-Smoothwater, Obabika and Solace. For information telephone (705) 569-2595, or e-mail evelyn@onlink.net.

Temagami-area canoe trip specialists, Wanapitei, offer guided six-day canoe trips through Obabika and Wakimika at a cost of $655. A five-day, guided canoe trip and hike in Temagami is based at Wanapitei's heritage log chateau, deep in the wilderness on the northern tip of Lake Temagami, and costs $795. Self-guided trips, family trips and outfitting services are also available. Call 1-888-637-5557 or (705) 745-8314.

Smoothwater Outfitters, located 14 kilometres north of the town of Temagami, operate a base camp with accommodations to suit all budgets—from a dormitory-style bunkhouse to charming private rooms. Easily accessible by Highway 11, their base is situated in a stand of old-growth maple and yellow birch. They offer guided and self-guided canoe trips in old-growth areas. Call (705) 569-3539.

The Canadian Nature Federation offers a free, four-page guide, titled *Ontario Old-Growth Ecotour*, which describes ten old-growth forest sites. For a copy call 1-800-267-4088.

To reach Shaw Woods drive south from Pembrooke on Highway 41. As you approach the north end of Lake Dore, look for Renfrew Road 9, where you turn east, continuing 1.5 kilometres to the trail entrance. There is no parking lot but you can leave your car at the roadside. No admission fee is charged to walk through the site. For more information call the Ottawa Valley Tourist Association at 1-800-757-6580.

Backus Woods,
A Carolinian Forest

Often found along stream banks in Carolinian woods, pawpaw trees produce a fleshy fruit that is irresistible to raccoons and opossums. The sweet, yellow pulp earns the pawpaw its nickname of false banana.

As you first walk through these lush woods, you won't find them much different from any other central Ontario hardwood forest with sugar maple, red oak and beech. But when you stop seeing the forest and start noticing the individual trees, you will begin to pick out the Carolinian species that are seldom seen in Ontario. Large tulip trees, black gum, sweet chestnut, sycamore and swamp white oak are all southern species at the northern limits of their range. This is Ontario's banana belt—the Carolinian zone.

The southernmost of Ontario's forest regions, the Carolinian zone stretches from the southern portion of Lake Huron, along the north shore of Lake Erie, as far west as Toronto's Rouge Valley. The area contains the province's prime agricultural land, as well as the highest population density. Only .22 percent of Canada is considered to belong to the true Carolinian temperate broadleaf deciduous forest. While agriculture and urban development has led to the destruction of many of these woodlands, remnants grow along the steep banks of creeks such as Bronte Creek near Burlington and Highland Creek in Scarborough

An unspoiled tract of Carolinian forest is a rare find, and that's what makes a large woodlot like Backus Woods so special. The 500-hectare forest contains some of the largest Carolinian trees found in Canada and is considered the finest remaining Carolinian woodland in the nation. Situated in Canada's deep south near the north shore of Lake Erie, Backus Woods survived the pressures of agriculture and urban development because its former owner, John C. Backhouse, was a conservationist with a passionate interest in protecting and preserving large trees. He succeeded admirably. In the swamp you will find black gum trees four hundred years old.

Among the most stately of the southern species are the tulip trees. They are the tallest deciduous trees in eastern North America, reaching heights of 40 metres. Unable to thrive in shade, they shoot upward quickly, trying to outgrow their rivals to tower above the forest canopy. In June they bear large, greenish-orange flowers, shaped somewhat like feathery tulips. Related to the magnolia, the tulip tree was prized by early settlers for its fine, straight-grained wood, ideal for furniture-making. Aboriginal people used the trees to make dugout canoes. Pileated woodpeckers favour the tulip trees for their high nesting sites.

Maple seeds are the favourite food of the white-footed mouse, the most populous mammal in Backus Woods' sugar bush.

Sassafras thrives in the sandy soil. Easily identified by its lobed leaves that look like mittens, the sassafras was widely used by early settlers. Its durable lumber was used to make buckets, a tea was brewed from the roots, and the bark produced an orange dye.

Just as central and southern species of trees mix in Backus Woods, so do birds and mammals from both regions. Vireos, orioles and the Louisiana waterthrush join northern species like the yellow-bellied sapsucker. Southern flying squirrels join their more northerly black and red cousins. Even opossums, Ontario's only marsupial, can be found in these woods, although you are most likely to see the critters scurrying across a road at night.

Adjoining Backus Woods is the Charles Sauriol Carolinian Forest, a 60-hectare tract of former agricultural land. In 1991 a forest regeneration project was started with plantings of red oak, sycamore, green ash and other trees. Named for a prominent local conservationist, Charles Sauriol Carolinian Forest is an important step in restoring some of Ontario's most valuable forest habitat, and it provides a protective buffer for Backus Woods.

When a lightning strike felled one of Backus Woods' tallest tulip trees, a ring count revealed that it predated Columbus's 1492 journey to the New World.

First-Hand Experience

The Backus Heritage Conservation Area is located 2 kilometres north of Port Rowan on Regional Road 42. Historic buildings once owned by the Backus (formerly Backhouse) family now serve as a Heritage Village. Exhibits relating to the local Carolinian habitat and the area's numerous waterfowl can be found at the Conservation Education Centre. A campground is open from May to October.

To the north of the village is Backus Woods, with parking at the Highway 24 entrance. A 3-kilometre walk along the Sugar Bush Trail loop takes you past two-hundred-year-old beeches and towering tulip trees. For information contact the Backus Conservation Education Centre, c/o Long Point Region Conservation Authority. Call (519) 428-4623, or fax (519) 428-1520.

At the Edge of the Boreal Forest in Mississagi Provincial Park

Roughly 25 kilometres north of Elliot Lake the road dwindles, the hydro poles end and the hardwoods slowly start to give way to the vast green expanse of the boreal forest. In a wide swath stretching across the province along the rugged edge of the Canadian Shield is a vast transitional zone where the deciduous basswood, yellow birch and sugar maple inhabit warmer south-facing slopes, and conifers grow along the cooler shorelines of lakes.

Mississagi Provincial Park straddles that transition zone where the Great Lakes forest region merges with the northern boreal forest as it rolls over the Penokean Hills. Richly diverse, the 4,900-hectare Natural Environment Park offers some exceptional hikes. The 7-kilometre Helenbar Lookout Trail is easily managed on a morning's outing. It winds through woods of maple and hemlock en route to a scenic clifftop lookout. On a moist September morning the well-trodden trail shows many signs of animal life. Long cones from white pines have been well nibbled by a squirrel. Further up the slope low-growing striped maples have been browsed by a moose who left ample evidence of its woody diet in

Leaves of three, let it be. That's the old adage for identifying poison ivy, a vine-like shrub belonging to the cashew family. Each compound leaf is made up of three leaflets that are rounded at the base and pointed at the tip. Touching poison ivy can result in a painful, itchy rash and blisters. Native people used poison ivy as a defence against enemies, by burning it in a firepit to release its toxins in air-borne droplets.

its fibrous droppings near the trailside. On south-facing, sun-warmed slopes the moose feed well into the winter until the snow becomes too deep for walking.

For eyes that pick out the small details, the forest floor is full of wonders: scattered puffballs growing on a mossy log, brilliant red mushrooms with yellow gills, a bed of club moss that looks like an ankle-height spruce forest for fairies. It's a layered world where the fallen plants feed new generations and new species, like the yellow birch that grows out of the rotting stump of an old white pine. White pine was logged here a century ago. With the pine gone other species began to spring up: aspen, white birch, balsam fir, cedar and sugar maple.

One of the most startling finds along the trail is a massive glacial erratic, a boulder seemingly dropped on the path by a retreating river of ice. Now covered with moss, this pink and grey conglomerate rock stands roughly 5 metres high, but looks as though it was tossed as casually as a pebble into its new setting.

A spectacular lookout point roughly 130 metres above Helenbar Lake offers remarkable lake and forest vistas. Towering white pines grow out of white quartzite rock. Hikers stop to watch osprey swooping down to nab trout that inhabit the cool lake below. Picnic tables are provided for a lunch stop before heading downhill. On an autumn afternoon you can actually see where the orange maples of the Great Lakes Forest give way to the more boreal greens of spruce and Jack pine.

Helenbar is only one of many diverse trails in the park. The 1.2-kilometre Semiwite Creek Trail takes you past old log chutes. For more logging history you can explore the Semiwite Lake Trail, a 12-kilometre loop that passes through the old logging camp. Long-abandoned copper mines are a feature of the 11-kilometre Cobre Lake Trail. The short Flack Lake Trail passes by fasci-

POISON IVY
ANTIDOTE
Washing with strong soap is recommended, but seldom possible on the trail. Many hikers use jewelweed to relieve the itching. Jewelweed is easily identified by its mottled orange blooms that dangle like cone-shaped sacs from slender stalks. It is also known as touch-me-not, for its seed pods that burst open with the lightest touch. To treat ivy poisoning, crush the fresh leaves and rub them gently on affected skin.

nating geological formations like the ripple rock of a 2-billion-year-old beach.

First-Hand Experience

Mississagi Provincial Park is 24 kilometres north of Elliot Lake via Highway 639. During summer you can call the park at (705) 848-2806. During winter months call the Ministry of Natural Resources at (705) 356-2234 ext. 229. The park offers approximately one hundred campsites. None are equipped with electrical outlets, but you can rent a solar panel from the park office. Pamphlets describing the trails are also available at the park office.

Autumn Colours at Silent Lake

Along the line of smokey hills
The crimson forest stands,
And all the day the blue-jay calls
Throughout the autumn lands.

— WILLIAM WILFRED CAMPBELL,
"Indian Summer" 1889

September days bring a special magic to the hilly landscape south of Algonquin Park. This is the southern edge
of the Canadian Shield, a rocky apron stretching across
the midriff of the province, where acidic soils are spread
thinly over Precambrian granite. The thin soils support
a remarkable variety of forest plants: conifers grow along
lake edges and cool lowlands, while maples and oaks
thrive on the sun-warmed hills of billion-year-old rock.
As September's daylight hours dwindle, the hills burst
into their full autumn glory: aspens and birch turn luminous yellow, staghorn sumac covers rocky slopes with
scarlet, and sugar maples say farewell to summer with a
blaze of orange and red.

Colour change comes about as the season triggers
chemical changes within each leaf. As days grow shorter
and temperatures fall, a special layer of cells forms at the
base of each leaf stalk in readiness for separation from
the tree. The leaf's water intake is restricted, so chloro-

phyll breaks down, revealing the colourful collection of chemicals that were previously masked by the green chlorophyll. Now the carotenoids can reflect their yellow and orange. Anthocyanins are the source of the purple colouring in beets, grapes, plums and cherries, and also bring shades of red, scarlet and purple to some hardwood leaves. Anthocyanins respond to intensity of light, bringing about redder colours with bright sunlight. Although cool temperatures may also increase anthocyanin, frost does not colour leaves. Freezing temperatures merely cause leaves to fall before reaching their full colour change.

On a sunny autumn afternoon at Silent Lake Provincial Park near Bancroft, you can walk along rocky shores and rugged hills to see orange sugar maples and yellow birch and aspen leaves. Staghorn sumac covers rocky hills with crimson. First Nations people taught early European settlers how to use the sumac's fuzzy red berries to produce a refreshing drink, often referred to as "Indian lemonade." Elizabeth Simcoe wrote in her 1795 diary: "I gathered bunches of flowers of the Sumach last year and poured boiling water upon them which tasted like lemonade, it has a very astringent harsh taste."

To enjoy the park's rugged Canadian Shield scenery you can rent a canoe and explore the rocky islands that dot the lake. At this time of year the last loons are about to head south and a beaver moves across a misty, early morning lake with another branch for its winter stockpile.

You can also walk the park's three hiking trails. Nature lovers especially enjoy the 3-kilometre Bonnie's Pond Trail, which meanders past woods and beaver ponds. Look for a mature stand of beech trees near the start of the trail. Many of the smooth, grey trunks show the unmistakable signs of black bears—claw marks left

SUMAC LEMONADE
Pour one litre of boiling water over one quarter cup of berries and steep for about five minutes, then sweeten with sugar. The key to a good batch of sumac lemonade is tasting the brew frequently to see when the best flavour has been reached. Leaving the berries in the water too long results in a bitter brew. The drink may cause some people to experience stomach cramps.

by bears climbing up the trees to feed on beechnuts. They'll find a large comfy branch to lie back on while they feast, tearing branches into pieces and leaving the resulting debris in a bundle resembling a large nest.

For a short hike with a great view, try the 1.5-kilometre Lakehead Loop, which takes you to a rocky point. The trail is easily managed by young children and passes through lovely stands of sugar maples. The rugged 15-kilometre Lakeshore Trail circles Silent Lake, where the autumnal colours are reflected in the lake's still, black waters. Three mountain-bike trails stay open until Thanksgiving Monday.

First-Hand Experience

Silent Lake Provincial Park is located on Highway 28, roughly 25 kilometres north of Apsley. The three hiking trails remain accessible through the Thanksgiving weekend. All-season camping is made easy at the park with the recent addition of a yurt, the ultimate in alternative accommodation. Based on the traditional felt-covered dwellings of Mongolian nomads, the modern yurt is a round, fabric-covered shelter erected on a wooden platform. Ten-foot high ceilings, skylights, Scandinavian-style furnishings and propane appliances give the interior a feeling of luxury that goes way beyond ordinary camping, without the cost of cottaging. Six can sleep comfortably in the fully furnished Howling Wolf Yurt. Cookware and utensils are provided—all you need bring is your food and a sleeping bag. The yurt can be booked for $60 to $75 a night, including park fees and parking. The yurt is insulated for winter use.

Other Silent Lake accommodations include 167 campsites and the Old Pine Lodge, which sleeps as

many as fourteen people in dormitory-style accommodations with such comforts as a large kitchen and
dining area, lounge and showers. The lodge is popular
with groups ranging from wedding parties to mountain-
bike clubs. It costs $420 per night per group, for up to
14 people. For information about Silent Lake Provincial
Park call (613) 339-2807 or (613) 332-3940.

Ontario's Ministry of Economic Development,
Trade and Tourism offers a Fall Colour Progression
Report that tells callers where and when colours have
reached their peak across the province. Call (416) 314-
0998.

Discovering Niagara's Hidden Glen

Pioneer woodsman
Daniel Boone made an
18-metre dugout canoe
from a single tulip tree.

While camera-toting tourists throng to Niagara Falls, the scenic woods of Niagara Glen Nature Reserve just downstream are a quiet haven where hikers can enjoy birdsong and wildflowers in a dramatic riverside setting. Steep, rugged paths dissuade many tourists from descending into this quiet corner of the Niagara Gorge, but those who clamber down the rocky paths are rewarded with a rare Carolinian forest, fossils, ferns and stunning riverside scenery.

More than six thousand years ago Niagara Falls tumbled over the escarpment at the site of the present-day glen. Thundering torrents of water gradually eroded the softer shale, pushing the falls upriver and leaving behind the massive boulders that litter the glen. Today the rocks are covered with ferns, mosses and wildflowers. Trees more typical of southern forests thrive alongside the Niagara River. Chinquapin, or yellow oak, grow along the Wintergreen Flat at the top of the glen and are easily identified by their serrated leaves, which are not lobed like those of the red and white oaks also found in the area. Beech trees provide plenty of nuts to feed the glen's chipmunks, squirrels and birds.

For environmentalists like Carla Carlson at Niagara Nature Tours, the glen is a special place. Much of the Niagara's original vegetation has survived because of its relative inaccessibility. Carla told me, "Virginia Moun-

tain mint once grew wild throughout this area. In the
1930s the Niagara School of Horticulture introduced
many foreign species as it began manicuring the area, so
these prairie remnants are now found on the side of cliffs
where mowers and clippers can't get at them."

Carla leads challenging two-and-a-half-hour hikes
into the Niagara Glen to bring nature lovers in touch with
both the majestic and the minuscule, from centuries-old
tulip trees to the fascinating world of tiny insect larvae.
The walk begins with a steep descent down a metal stair-
case from Wintergreen Flat to the Cliffside Path. Along
the cliff-face tiny clumps of cliff break and walking ferns
erupt from the stone. Virginia creeper and staghorn
sumac thrive on the stony hillsides. Near the bottom of
the shaded glen the air cools and the sound of the rushing river can be heard. The path continues to descend
along a series of stone steps, past pitted boulders, down
to the shores of the Niagara River. Giant boulders that
once whirled in the river's eddies have been dumped
here by the forces of erosion. Beach-like ripples mark
the rocks, remnants of the Ice Age known as the "chat-
ter effect."

Many plants thrive on the rocks, including wild ginger, named for its fragrant rhizomes. Less attractive is
the smell of wild ginger's burgundy, cup-shaped flower,
whose odour of rotting meat attracts flies to pollinate it.

From the swirling waters of Crips Eddy in the
Niagara River, Carla leads hikers north along the river
shoreline. Turquoise waters cast up white spume as the
water surges through the gorge at 43 kilometres per
hour. Towards the south, the path leads to a stand of
tulip trees that are centuries old. Two adults can just
barely hold hands around the base of a single tree, and
when they look up, it is almost impossible to see the top
of the tree towering above.

First-Hand Experience

The Niagara Glen is located on the Niagara Parkway, north of Queenston, opposite the Royal Botanical Gardens. Parking and admission is free. Should you choose to explore the glen on your own, be sure to take a trail map with you. Trail maps are available from the Niagara Glen gift shop, near the parking lot, for $1. The shop also sells the *Niagara Glen Nature Reserve Official Trail Guide*, with many colour photos, for $10. Poison ivy abounds in the glen, so stay on the trails.

If you want to make sure that you don't miss any of the area's special attributes, take a guided tour with Niagara Nature Tours who specialize in the habitat of the Niagara Glen. Tours cost $11.50 and should be booked in advance by calling 1-888-889-8296.

Exploring the Oak Ridges Moraine in Durham Forest

Pine forests cover its sandy ridges, and cool, clean water trickles through its springs. North of Toronto the Oak Ridges Moraine stretches from the Niagara Escarpment at Caledon, across the northern fringes of Toronto's sprawl all the way to the Trent River, near Trenton. Sculpted by glaciers these hills are perfect for hiking, skiing and even mushroom hunting.

The place seems so idyllic that it's difficult to imagine the devastation that was once here. But when early settlers cleared the vast white pine and oak forests in the nineteenth century, they had no idea they were about to unleash an ecological nightmare. Without tree roots to anchor the soil, heavy rains and winds swept it away. Within a few decades farmlands turned into deserts. After the erosion came the flooding, especially along rivers like the Ganaraska, whose headwaters are in the moraine.

Formerly productive farms were turning into wastelands at such a rapid rate that by 1911 Ontario County started buying them up in search of a solution. In 1926 white and red pine seedlings were planted in massive numbers, and the Durham Region Forest was created. Today those trees have matured, and a new forest is growing up through the understory. Durham Forest provides

Not all wood is equally effective as firewood. Sugar maple is one of the best, with 29 million BTU, while white pine delivers a mere 17.1.

an outdoor ecology lesson for local schoolchildren, a film set for movie crews and a network of trails for thousands of hikers, mountain bikers and cross-country skiers.

By walking the 2.8-kilometre Red Trail you can see how the forest is changing. Pine plantings of the 1920s and 1930s were effective in stabilizing the soil and creating shady, moist conditions in which native species could take hold, but the monoculture of pines lacked biodiversity. The tidy rows of trees had all the esthetic appeal of a cornfield. Forest managers studied means of improving the forest's natural renewal process by selective cuttings that would enable the pine plantings to act as a nurse crop for the more diverse forest growing underneath. Now red oak, black cherry, sugar maple, basswood and beech thrive where the canopy of pines has been thinned to make space and sunlight. The cut pines are sold as utility poles or building logs, and the revenues are used to maintain trails and keep up forestry work.

The increased diversity of tree species has led to a greater diversity in wildlife. The mast (nut-producing) trees, such as the oaks, attract numerous white-tailed deer. Look for their footprints in the sandy soil. Brush piles are built into lean-to structures to provide shelter for cottontail and snowshoe rabbits. Downy woodpeckers can be heard hammering holes in the trees, and on an autumn walk you may flush a flock of ruffed grouse. Earthstar fungi spring up through the dead leaves on the forest floor.

If you hike up some of the hills at the north end of the trail you will see some leftover sandy areas where 2 metres or more of soil has been eroded. Little will grow here. Even attempts to introduce Jack pines, Scots pine and poplars have had only modest success.

Melting glaciers can leave many curious marks on a limestone landscape. Rockwood Conservation Area on the Eramosa River is a prime example. The land is riddled with hundreds of sinkholes ranging from the size of a large kitchen bowl to walk-in caverns. Rockwood Conservation Area is located on Highway 7, near the village of Rockwood. For information contact the Rockwood Conservation Authority, telephone (519) 856-9543.

If you work up a thirst on your hike, you can sample some of Ontario's best spring water at a free tap at the Lakeridge Ski Resort on Lakeridge Road (Durham Road 23), north of Ajax. Bring your own bottles and look for the taps in the concrete cap directly below the ski resort sign. The water comes from an aquifer deep within the moraine. Sandy hills filter precipitation, then store it in underground aquifers that provide clean drinking water for many southern Ontario communities and some excellent springs.

First-Hand Experience

The Durham Demonstration Forest Main Tract is north of Ajax. From Highway 2 drive north on Lakeridge Road (Road 23) to Road 21, where you turn east (left), then south on Road 7 to the Head of Trail. The Red Trail can also be reached from the entrance off Durham Road 21. It is one of seven demonstration trail loops in the Durham Forest, and the hiking is relatively easy on wide, well-groomed paths.

For information and a free map of outdoor activities in the Durham Region, call the Durham Economic Development Department at 1-800-413-0017 or (905) 723-0023.

One of the easiest ways to enjoy the Oak Ridges Moraine is via a scenic train trip on the York–Durham Heritage Railway. The tourist train has cars dating back to the 1930s and 1940s and travels 20 kilometres between Stouffville and Uxbridge. The route is particularly pretty in autumn. Telephone (905) 852-3696.

REMOTE ADVENTURES

Taking the Train to James Bay

Those of us who live close to the Great Lakes sometimes forget that Ontario has a saltwater shoreline on its northern extreme. You can go whale watching, and seal watching too, on the tidal waters of the Moose River where it flows into James Bay. Each summer thousands of tourists take the Polar Bear Express, a 4.5-hour train trip that runs from Cochrane to Moosonee through the dense muskeg that covers the northernmost part of Ontario; more than 650 square hectares criss-crossed with tea-coloured rivers, stunted spruce, tamarack and myriad peat bogs. The land here is on the rebound, still rising after the crushing weight of the glaciers that melted away more than six thousand years ago. Flat land drains poorly, causing bogs and fens to build up over the cold clay base. Growing conditions here are so harsh that century-old tamaracks may measure no more than 6 centimetres in diameter.

Winter frosts and summer thaws in the boggy terrain can heave train tracks out of alignment, so each spring extensive work is done to align them. Numerous boxes of shims, used to prop up sinking rails, are stationed along the length of the line. But Polar Bear Express passengers travel in relative comfort, complete with dining car. For anyone familiar with the Toronto–Montreal run in the late sixties, the cars on the Polar Bear Express will seem very familiar. This is vintage stuff.

Until the railway was built in 1932, the trip from Cochrane to Moosonee had to be done by canoe in summer, or on snowshoes during winter, and took between eight to ten days.

There is even an old cabaret car with live entertainment—a children's singalong on the morning trip up and an adult version with alcohol served on the evening run back to Cochrane.

The community of Moosonee, on the Moose River near the mouth of James Bay, is both a transportation hub for the James Bay region, and a base for tourists who wish to explore the area on hikes and boat trips along the river, which flows brown with the tannins it collects as it passes through the acidic muskeg.

Rising and falling tides are felt 32 kilometres up the Moose and average 1.5 metres at Moosonee. The tides sometimes bring pods of beluga whales with them. The whales swim in from James Bay, looking like white flashes in the brown river. You can spot them best on a calm day when they can't be confused with whitecaps. Bearded seals may be seen basking on the gravel beach along the river's shoreline. At low tide the river reveals large, island sandbars where shorebirds gather.

With powerful currents and strong tides, the Moose River can be perilous to navigate, but locals familiar with its rhythms use motorized freighter canoes. They take tourists from Moosonee to some of the river's better known islands, including Charles Island, popular for its shoreline hiking trails through Tidewater Provincial Park.

Islands in the Moose River have long sustained the Cree people. Their adaptations to the harsh landscape can be seen at Moose Factory, once a strategic British outpost in the booming fur trade, now a Cree reserve. On the reserve, visit the Cree Cultural Centre where you will find traditional bark-covered teepees. A guide explains how the Cree thrived in this seemingly inhospitable terrain before European contact. He demonstrates geese calls, teaches games of skill using animal bones and shows winter clothing made from three layers of animal fur and hides. Strips of tanned rabbit fur were woven with a pointed caribou bone into a soft undergarment. Over that went a moosehide garment tanned with a paste of moose brains and ash, followed by an outer coat of unprocessed fur.

The huge flocks of Canada geese and snow geese that gathered on the tidal flats provided a staple for hunters, who used decoys made of tamarack twigs and vocal calls to attract them. Tamarack twig decoys are still a popular local craft, although most are made now as tourist souvenirs.

Geese still play a large role in the local diet and are roasted over a fire in a teepee designed for cooking. Several locals do a brisk summer business selling bannock from their backyard cooking teepees. For children one of the best meals of the trip is a smoky piece of bannock baked on a stick leaning over an open fire.

The freighter canoe trip to Fossil Island, 6.5 kilometres upriver from Moosonee, is easily accomplished in an afternoon. With wind whipping your hair and spray from the choppy river blowing into your face, try scanning the river for the famed seals. While you may not always see the large sea mammals, you may glimpse an osprey perched on an overhead cable.

The island's tangle of chest-high willows and wild roses is too dense for inland walking, but the shoreline's beautiful beaches offer a multitude of horn corals and other fossils from the semi-tropical sea that covered this area 375 million years ago. It seems strange to be this far north and still find the same Devonian-era fossils that are found in southwestern Ontario, but here they are: corals, crinoids and assorted shellfish fossils, all in abundant supply.

To journey into James Bay you need to take a cruise on the tour boat MV *Polar Princess*, down the Moose

RECIPE FOR
BANNOCK BREAD
(from the Polar Bear
Express)
Mix together 3 cups
of all-purpose flour,
$^1/_2$ teaspoon of salt,
1 teaspoon of baking
powder, 2 tablespoons
of shortening, $^3/_4$ cup
of water and a handful
of raisins. Knead into
a pliable dough then
mould hot-dog sized
pieces around the end
of a sturdy stick. Bake
over hot coals, turning
often.

River past Ship Sands Island, the site of a major bird sanctuary. Each spring the tremendous force of ice breakup on the Moose River gouges away great chunks of shoreline and scours much of Ship Sands Island of tall vegetation, leaving great marine marshlands and mud-flats, where flocks of migrating geese gather. Whimbrels probe the beaches with their downward curved beaks, and flocks of red knots and hudsonian godwits can be seen during their spectacular migrations, a virtual non-stop trek spanning two hemispheres, from Hudson Bay to Patagonia at the southern tip of South America.

To learn about day-to-day life in Moosonee take the evening school-bus tour around town, which concludes with a visit to the local dump to spot black bears forag-ing for freebies.

First-Hand Experience

To catch the Polar Bear Express, you can either drive to Cochrane or take the overnight Ontario Northland train from Toronto to Cochrane, which takes nearly eleven hours. It departs from Toronto's Union Station at 6:20 p.m. and gets you into Cochrane at 5 a.m. the fol-lowing morning. There are no sleeping cars. You'll have to hang around the local coffee shop until you can catch the Polar Bear Express which departs at 8:30 a.m. The Polar Bear Express operates during the summer months. Call Ontario Northland at 1-800-268-9281 or (416) 314-3750. The round-trip train fare is $46 for adults and $23 for children ages 5 to 11. The school-bus tour, Fossil Island tour and *Polar Princess* cruise excur-sions can be booked in Moosonee at Two Bay Enter-prises. Call (705) 336-2944 or (705) 336-2521.

CreeWay Wilderness Experiences offers tour services to explore the variety of life found along the James Bay coast. Telephone (705) 658-4390. Moosonee serves as a base for local air explorations, including trips to Polar Bear Provincial Park, which is accessible only by air and by special arrangement.

Rossport and Slate Islands in Lake Superior

The north shore of Lake Superior is one of the most dramatic landscapes in Ontario, with a beautiful string of islands scattered across the northern end of the lake, east of Nipigon Bay. The Rossport Islands, south of the community of Rossport, are a small part of this area, which is now under consideration for status as a National Marine Conservation Area. Many of the islands are accessible through local ecotourism operators. You can arrange to cruise or kayak past their dramatic cliffs and sheltered bays, explore their cool boreal woodlands and view the mysterious remnants of ancient cultures.

One of the most accessible islands is Battle Island, whose sheltered bays on the north side face the mainland, and whose steep cliffs on the south side face the vast, open waters of Lake Superior. Sea kayaking is a great way to explore the islands, with their fascinating coves, cliffs and rich history. Outfitters such as Superior Ecoventures often bring parties of kayakers to Battle Island to experience the lake's drama.

Although Superior is a freshwater lake, it is so vast that it behaves like a sea, breeding sudden storms and thick fogs. In November, the lake's storms are famed for their savagery. High atop Battle Island's towering pink cliffs sits a lighthouse. When we paddled past on an August afternoon the water was almost mirror calm. It was shocking to learn that the beacon at the top had been battered by waves that must have reached heights of roughly 40 metres or more during the storm that sunk the *Edmund Fitzgerald*. Immortalized in song by Gordon Lightfoot, the wreck of the *Edmund Fitzgerald* was one of most shocking shipping disasters on the Great Lakes. At 222 metres long, the massive freighter was just barely within the maximum length permitted passage through the St. Lawrence Seaway. Carrying more than 26,000 tonnes of iron and a crew of twenty-nine, she was caught in a furious storm that produced gusts up to 160 kilometres an hour and waves as high as any seen on the North Atlantic. On November 10, 1975 she sank suddenly, breaking in half as she disappeared into the lake. The crew didn't even have time to make a distress call. Coves on the southeast shore bear silent reminders of Superior's famed fury: rusting remnants of a steamer broken apart decades ago.

SUPERIOR FACTS

Average water temperature: 4.4 degrees Celsius

Volume: 11.3 quadrillion litres of water

Maximum Depth: 406 metres

The chilling effect of Superior's frigid waters is evident from the island's vegetation—scruffy-looking balsam fir trees draped in old man's beard lichens, and delicate blooms of twinflower, which is found only in cold northern woods. On the islands, visitors can see arctic plants that established themselves after the last ice age, about eleven thousand years ago.

Ancient aboriginal cultures left pictographs and Pukaskwa pits throughout the area. Located on old shorelines, the stone pits are 1 to 2 metres deep, surrounded by walls. Though their function remains unclear, anthropologists have speculated that they were shelters or possibly observation posts.

Further east, toward Pukaskwa National Park, lie the Slate Islands. Separated from the mainland by 11 kilometres of open water, the islands are inhabited by very different species. There are no wolves, deer or moose on the islands. Instead, numerous beaver and a

small herd of woodland caribou, probably stranded earlier this century after crossing an ice bridge, survive
without predators. The herd's biggest challenge is finding food. They have nibbled away the dense underbrush,
making the islands' forests much more open than they
would be otherwise. Sudden booms in the population
are typically followed by periods of starvation.

First-Hand Experience

The village of Rossport is roughly 200 kilometres east
of Thunder Bay on Highway 17. Located on Lake
Superior's scenic north shore, Rossport is a great base
for island explorations, with some good bed and break-
fast accommodations, marina facilities and canoe and
kayak rentals. Both the Rossport and Slate Islands can
be explored on sea kayaking tours through Superior
Ecoventures. Call (807) 683-7499. No experience is
needed: instruction is provided along the way. Kayakers
carry all their gear in waterproof compartments in their
craft. Nights are spent camping on the islands. For information about facilities in the Rossport area call North
of Superior Tourism at (807) 626-9420.

First Nations Culture at Camp Jeegibik and Golden Lake

On the north shore of Lake Huron, south of Elliot Lake, traditional healers share their spiritual beliefs and knowledge of healing plants at a native teaching lodge. Blaine Commanda and Isabelle Meawasige live on the Serpent River Band's reserve, which has seen its share of social problems. Looking to their traditional roots, Blaine, an expert woodsman, and Isabelle, a social worker, decided to use their skills to create a healing experience both for themselves and their community.

They welcome anyone who feels the need for the experience and who is willing to respect their cultural beliefs. They believe that sharing brings healing for Mother Earth. Situated on Lake Huron, Camp Jeegibik overlooks the dramatic North Channel, with John Island in the distance. The beauty of the white birch woods and hillsides covered in pine sets the mood for a spiritual experience.

On the site are a ceremonial spruce-pole teepee and a sweat lodge dug into the ground and covered with a framework of yellow willow. Blankets and tarps cover the sweat lodge to keep it dark and to hold the heat of the rocks that have been prepared in a sacred fire: a fire not used for cooking, but one that has been blessed with a tobacco offering. Water and healing herbs are placed

All are welcome to the Serpent River Band's traditional powwow. Non-competitive, with an emphasis on spirituality, the powwow is held on the second weekend in August.

Other annual native powwows include the Wikwemikong powwow, held on Manitoulin Island over the August Civic Holiday weekend, and the Cape Croker powwow on Bruce Peninsula.

on the rocks. These include cedar, for its cleansing properties, and mukwah root, which smells like ginger.

Ceremonial feasts and rituals involving pipes, drums and feathers are held at the camp. The feather ritual is one that ensures everyone has an opportunity to speak. An eagle feather is passed from one person to the next, giving whoever holds it the right to speak for as long as they require on the subject of their choice. During ceremonies members of the band sing their ancient songs to summon the spirits of the bear and wolf, their power animals.

Before taking visitors on a medicine walk to find healing herbs, Blaine guides everyone in performing a smudging ceremony to cleanse bodies and minds, and to focus thoughts and energy. A little dried sweet grass is placed in a large shell, then lit. As it smoulders, one by one participants use their hands to gather the fragrant smoke toward themselves, stroking it over their minds, their eyes, their mouths and their hearts.

The purpose of this walk is not to cover distance or to harvest herbs, but to learn and share. While Blaine walks through the bush to find specific plants, Isabelle explains their uses. Horsetail ferns can be used to make a vitamin-rich tea. She calls juniper berries "brain food," because they are believed to stimulate memory. The red furry berries of staghorn sumac are thought to be effective when used in diabetes treatment. Isabelle explains how yarrow, which the native people call squirrel tail, has been used to stop bleeding. According to Blaine, cedar is a multi-purpose plant that may be used in ceremonies, as medicine and to aid tired hikers who put it in their shoes to give them stamina.

No plant is picked without thought of the creator. An offering of tobacco is left behind with a prayer of thanks for each root or leaf that is taken. More than just a lesson on woodland lore, this walk creates a real sense of connection with Mother Earth.

Throughout Ontario many native communities are undertaking tourism ventures that promote cross-cultural exchanges. One of the most successful of these is the Anishinabe Native Experience at the Golden Lake Reserve in eastern Ontario. Whether you come for a lunch of fried bannock or camp overnight in one of the teepees, the Anishinabe Native Experience provides some great insights into Algonquin culture. Linda Sarazin brings visitors into her community to broaden their understanding of First Nations people. That begins as soon as you order your food at the Anishinabe Midjim (People's Food) restaurant, where everyone meets and where Linda offers a discount to anyone who orders in Algonquin. Over a cup of fragrant *kijikminabo* (cedar tea) she asks visitors what activities they might enjoy. Whether it's making a wild rice casserole or learning how to stitch a pair of moccasins, she arranges the activities. Overnight guests begin by choosing their teepee, either at a forest camp just a short walk from the road, or near Linda's waterfront log home. The teepees are already erected, so the real work begins as guests prepare beds of fir and cedar boughs. Linda provides sleeping bags and pillows, and her husband makes sure everyone is kept warm with a fire. Pinned on each of the teepee's fifteen spruce poles is a paper slip naming one of the traditional teachings, which include obedience, respect, humility, happiness, love, faith, kinship, cleanliness, thankfulness, sharing, strength, hope and good child rearing.

Guests who plan to stay for several days may have an opportunity to join a community social, hear traditional storytelling, try making bannock over an open fire or learn how to tan hides. A local canoe maker wel-

In his fascinating first-hand account of eating wild foods, *Stalking the Healthful Herbs*, author Euell Gibbons describes his attempts to ingest various parts of the white pine, from bark to new shoots. He recommends a tea made from the needles, rich in vitamins A and C. To make this mild-tasting tea, pour a litre of boiling water over half a cup of chopped, fresh white pine needles. Steep a few minutes then flavour with sugar and lemon.

comes visitors to watch how he stitches a birchbark canoe with spruce roots. But even on a short visit there is time to talk about the medicine wheel while making your own dream catcher, a sinew of net woven like a spider's web to trap unpleasant dreams.

First-Hand Experience

Isabelle and Blaine Commanda offer their services through Marie Murphy Foran at Discovery North, an Elliot Lake tourism agency. Call (705) 848-2908.

The Anishinabe Native Experience is located at Algonquin Territory, 104 Mishomis, Golden Lake. Call (613) 625-2519 or (800) 897-0235.

The Boreal Forest of Wabikimi

It has been called the largest wilderness canoeing reserve in the world. Three times the size of Quetico, Wabikimi is a place of spruce bogs and lonely lakes so remote that woodland caribou still roam its tangled forests. One of Ontario's newest provincial parks, Wabikimi covers 900,000 hectares of boreal wilderness.

Wabikimi's mystique is enhanced by its inaccessibility. Although canoeists may be flown in by float plane, it is far more economical to be dropped off along one of the wild stretches of the main CN railway line. When you read, "access to park via CN railway," you might get the impression that there is a railway station there. In fact, Wabikimi Provincial Park is so remote it has no highway access, no visitor centre and no train station. You must hop out of the baggage car at a remote spot on the main CN line, roughly 300 kilometres north of Thunder Bay.

The experience is a study in contrasts. At 8:30 a.m. you can be nibbling fruit cocktail on a linen-covered table in the dining car. At 9:30 a.m. you head down the train to the baggage car and prepare your gear, while the engineer looks for the railway mile marker where he brakes the train. You jump down onto the gravel embankment, the conductor briskly assists unloading packs and canoe, and in seconds the train has trundled down the

A member of the honeysuckle family, the twinflower takes its name from its bell-shaped pink flowers that hang in pairs. Its Latin name, *Linnaea borealis* is a tribute to the eighteenth-century Swedish botanist Carolus Linnaeus who founded the modern, binomial system of classification of plants and animals.

line. You listen until the last sounds of civilization die
away, then contemplate the wilderness. A canoe trip
into Wabikimi should not be undertaken lightly. There
are few signs of civilization once you paddle beyond the
odd cabin or lodge near the railway line. Even experienced canoeists would be wise to hire a knowledgeable
local guide or outfitter, such as Wild Waters Wilderness
Tours, to plan a route. When you have a guide to show
you the way, Wabikimi has some wonderful rewards:
meals of freshly caught walleye, pristine lakes for swimming, pink blooms of twinflower, and deep mats of soft,
green moss for the perfect tent site.

From the rail line you portage into a network of
elongated lakes and whitewater in the Ogoki River basin,
which connects to the Albany River system. Paddling
these lakes takes you past islands of stunted, twisted
spruce that look like scenes from mythic northern
sagas. Shallow, sandy bays are populated by freshwater
sponges and tiny frogs no bigger than your fingernail.
Occasionally you see a windthrown spruce that has
lost its footing and toppled over to reveal roots spread
through little more than a carpet's thickness of sand. In
this nutrient-poor soil trees two hundred years old are
no thicker than a man's arm.

This is the great green north, the vast boreal forest
that stretches across the continent from Labrador to the
Rocky Mountains. It covers most of the northern half of
Ontario, but is the preserve of only a rugged few. The
sense of vastness is enhanced by the monotony of the
vegetation. There are no sugar maples, oaks and other
hardwoods—these belong in kinder, southern soils.
Even the towering white and red pines are too delicate
for the harsh climate. This is a landscape of spindly black
spruce, black lakes, green bogs and dense carpets of

moss, with the occasional Jack pine gaining a foothold in one of the gentler glacial spillways. You can identify the Jack pine by its cone, which is curled tightly around the twig, like a large brown insect larvae. These tenacious pines do not give up their seeds easily. Temperatures of more than 50 degrees Celsius are required to open the cones. That's a rare sun-baked day with heat reflected from the rocks, or more likely, a forest fire, part of the natural cycle of these woods.

Low areas within the woods are filled with soft mats of emerald-coloured moss punctuated by incredibly beautiful flowers: tiny, white, star-shaped blooms of one-flowered wintergreen and luscious orchids. Rocky shores are covered with blueberries and lichens.

Lichens are food for the woodland caribou, one of Ontario's most threatened animals. Extremely sensitive to the pressures of logging, the caribou thrive only in a vast, pristine wilderness. Roughly three hundred caribou live in Wabikimi. Here they find a variety of large spaces to meet their seasonal needs. Travel corridors along rivers are used for spring migrations. Islands in large swamps and lakes provide sheltered areas for calving, away from predators. Areas of ample shrubbery and sedges are ideal for rich summer browsing. Sphagnum swamps are favoured for autumn rutting. The caribou travel as far as 100 kilometres to their wintering grounds, where they seek snow deep enough to hamper predators such as wolves, but soft enough to allow it to be scraped away to reveal patches of cladina (reindeer) lichens that are their winter browse. Paddle through Wabikimi and you are bound to see places where the caribou have nibbled clumps of lichen from the rocks.

Snow adaptation is the key to survival in the boreal forest. Like the caribou, all mammals must adapt to the snow. Those with large feet, like the snowshoe hare and lynx, stay on top, while those with small feet, like the white-footed mice, tunnel below the snow. Moose and caribou step through the snow on long legs like stilts.

Few birds remain over the winter months. The grey jay survives by feeding on seeds it stored away during summer months. Great grey owls prey on mice and voles tunnelling under the snow. Seed eaters, such as the pine sisken or the crossbill, specialize in opening up spruce cones. But early in the summer the migrants return, and paddlers can hear warblers proclaiming their nesting territory.

First-Hand Experience

Wabikimi Provincial Park is accessible through local outfitters. Bruce Hyer of Wild Waters Wilderness Tours has studied the park's caribou population and has been a keen advocate for the park. He outfits and guides nature tours and expeditions, and operates a water-access base camp on the outskirts of the park. If you want to go it on your own, he will provide detailed topographical maps, with planned routes and suggested campsites. To contact Wild Waters call (807) 767-2022.

For information on Wabikimi Provincial Park call the park superintendent at (807) 475-1634.

By prior arrangement, two of Via Rail's Ontario passenger trains will drop off wilderness travellers at remote places along the line. These are the Canadian, which runs from Toronto to Vancouver via Sioux Lookout and Edmonton, and the Sudbury to White River train. Arrangements should be made at least 48 hours in advance through your local Via Rail reservations office.

The fare will be based on the normal passenger fare between your point of departure and the next available station from your drop-off point, plus $35 for your canoe. For more information visit the Via Rail Web site at www.viarail.ca.

ONTARIO'S LONG-DISTANCE HIKING TRAILS

❧

From informal pathways to well-marked, mapped and maintained routes, there are thousands of kilometres of hiking trails in the province. Those listed below are among the best known, clearly marked and well-maintained.

Since they are often administered by volunteers, trail association offices—particularly those of the smaller associations—may change. A provincial umbrella organization that provides up-to-date information on its member trail associations is Hike Ontario, located at 1220 Sheppard Avenue East, North York M2K 2X1. Telephone (416) 426-7362.

When setting out on a trail it is often wise to remember the words of eminent naturalist E.T. Seton in *The Book of Woodcraft*: "I think it is a good rule in hiking, never to set out with the determination that you are going to show how hardy you are. ... Do not set out to make a record. Record breakers generally come to grief in the end."

BRUCE TRAIL

Stretching roughly 750 kilometres from Niagara Falls to Tobermory, the Bruce Trail follows the magnificent cliffs of the Niagara Escarpment. Scenery ranges from the lush fern-strewn forests of the Dundas Valley to the rugged grandeur of the Georgian Bay shoreline with its impossibly blue waters. The Bruce Trail Association publishes a detailed guidebook available in many outdoor

stores or through the association at Box 857, Hamilton L8N 3N9.
Telephone (905) 529-6821 or 1-800-665-4453.

ELGIN TRAIL
Heading north from the Lake Erie fishing town of Port Stanley,
the Elgin Trail winds through some beautiful Carolinian woodlands along Beaver Creek and Kettle Creek towards St. Thomas,
then west to Paynes Mills (a distance of roughly 35 kilometres).
For information contact the Elgin Hiking Trail Club at Box 250,
St. Thomas N5P 3T9.

ELORA CATARACT TRAILWAY
Easily accessible from Toronto, this 47-kilometre, multi-use trail
runs from the scenic village of Cataract in the east, where it connects with the Bruce Trail, to the dramatic Elora Gorge in the
west. Linking the Grand and the Credit Rivers, the trailway winds
through woodlots, rural communities and farmland. For information contact the Elora Cataract Trailway Association at Box 99,
Fergus N1M 2W7. Telephone (519) 843-3650.

GANARASKA TRAIL
From the historic town of Port Hope on Lake Ontario, the Ganar-
aska Trail heads north across the Oak Ridges Moraine through
Bobcaygeon in the Kawartha Lakes, and continues through wilder
terrain until it connects with the Bruce Trail near Georgian Bay.
For information contact the Ganaraska Trail Association, Box 19,
Orillia L3V 1R1.

GRAND VALLEY TRAIL
As it follows the course of the Grand River from Alton to the
shores of Lake Erie, this rural route offers opportunities for
inter-urban cycling and horseback riding. It includes the 32-kilo-
metre Hamilton to Brantford Rail-Trail that follows the abandoned roadbed of the Toronto Hamilton and Buffalo Railway.
Administered by the Grand River Conservation Authority and the

Hamilton Region Conservation Authority, the Rail-Trail forms part of the Trans Canada Trail System. For information contact the Grand River Conservation Authority at (519) 621-2761, the Brant Conservation Area at (519) 752-2040 or the Grand Valley Trails Association at 75 King Street South, Box 40068, RPO Waterloo Square, Waterloo N2J 4V1.

LAKE ONTARIO WATERFRONT TRAIL
An initiative of the Waterfront Regeneration Trust, this 325-kilometre trail connects communities, parklands and pathways along the north shore of Lake Ontario from Hamilton to Trenton. For information contact the Waterfront Regeneration Trust, 207 Queen's Quay West, Suite 580, Box 129, Toronto M5J 1A7.

OAK RIDGES TRAIL
This trail traverses the hills and valleys of the moraine north of Ontario's most populous area, from the Niagara Escarpment near Orangeville to Omemee. For information contact the Oak Ridges Trail Association, Box 28544, Aurora L4G 6S6.

RIDEAU TRAIL
From Kingston to Ottawa, the 400-kilometre Rideau Trail was blazed by the Duke of Richmond in 1819 as he searched for a military waterway route through the Canadian Shield. The Duke died en route, bitten by a rabid fox, but today hikers can enjoy the scenery with such genteel comforts as historic B&Bs along the route in the towns of Merrickville and Westport. The Ottawa branch of the Rideau Trail Club is very active and plans numerous excursions. Telephone (613) 730-2229. A pocket-sized copy of *The Rideau Trail Book* can be purchased at many outdoor stores or through the Rideau Trail Association, Box 15, Kingston K7L 4V6.

TRANS CANADA TRAIL
From Tuktoyaktuk to St. John's, builders of the Trans Canada Trail aimed to link thousands of communities in every province and

territory in the world's longest trail. For information contact Trans Canada Trail–Ontario, P.O. Box 3511 Station C, Ottawa K1Y 4H7. Telephone (613) 279-3341.

VOYAGEUR TRAIL

Serious stuff for dedicated outdoors enthusiasts, the Voyageur Trail lies across the northern part of the Great Lakes, from Manitoulin Island west toward Thunder Bay. The trail traverses the rugged landscape of the Lake Superior shoreline in Lake Superior Provincial Park and Pukaskwa National Park. For information contact Voyageur Trail Association, P.O. Box 20040, 150 Churchill Boulevard, Sault Ste. Marie P6A 6W3.

NATURE WATCHER'S CALENDAR

SPRING

March brings the first waves of migrating waterfowl to the north shores of Lake Erie and Lake Ontario. Long Point and Presqu'ile Provincial Parks are especially favourable places to see birds such as sandhill cranes, tundra swans, canvasback ducks and bufflehead ducks as they pass through en route to northern nesting grounds.

By the end of the month southern Ontario rivers swell with spring runoff. On a warm day yellow tufts of coltsfoot bloom along the Rouge River banks. Spring rains erode muddy banks, revealing roots, rocks and sometimes fossils. Each spring mudslide at Rock Glen uncovers a new wealth of Devonian era corals, shellfish and snails.

In April vernal ponds dot the woods, stirring peepers and other frogs into a nightly mating chorus. Loons have laid claim to their favourite northern lakes. This is the time, before the blackflies emerge in full force, to take a walk in the deep woods and look for the first flowers of spring: tiny white and pink spring beauties emerging from the leaf litter.

By early May moose are making their way to roadsides in Algonquin Park looking for salt dumped by winter road crews. Trilliums and hosts of other spring wildflowers carpet the forest floor and hurry into bloom before the trees shade out the sun's life-giving energy. Birding enthusiasts train their binoculars on colourful warblers migrating through Point Pelee National Park.

On the rocky bottoms of cool, clear lakes smallmouth bass defend their nests with fearless vigour.

SUMMER

In June the otherwise aquatic snapping turtles come ashore to dig their nests in sandy beaches or along gravelly roadsides. Pink and yellow lady's slipper orchids, some of the summer's showiest wildflowers, come into bloom along the Bruce Peninsula. By day hummingbirds hover over flowers and feeders, and as night falls, bats emerge to dine on a wealth of early summer insects. With iridescent wings sparkling in the sunlight, adult dragonflies emerge from their larvae. Their avid appetites soon put an end to the plague of blackflies.

The heat of July urges watery explorations. Paddle a canoe through the reedy channels of Wye Marsh where frogs bask on lily pads and turtles sun themselves in the duckweed. White pelicans fish near the islands in Lake of the Woods. The sand dunes of Pinery Provincial Park lure sunbathers and nature lovers who explore the oak savannah. Even in July Lake Superior remains frigid. Tiny arctic wildflowers bloom in the cool boreal woods on the lake's northern islands.

August is the month for wolf howls in Algonquin Park. Park staff guide visitors on evening excursions to call into the darkness in hopes of a return howl. In the south a rare remnant of grassland comes into full bloom at the Ojibway Prairie Provincial Nature Reserve. Tall grasses and towering flowers colour the landscape. In Bancroft the Rockhound Gemboree draws thousands of mineral collectors in search of rare specimens among abandoned mines.

By the end of August, many species of waterfowl are on the move. Look for great blue herons staging for their fall migration at Oshawa's Second Marsh.

AUTUMN

Sunny September days see masses of monarch butterflies congregating at points of land jutting south into Lake Erie and Lake

Ontario as they begin their long migration to Mexico. Mycologists delight in a clear day following a good rain, when conditions are at their prime for searching for perfect puffballs and tasty honey mushrooms. By mid-month the hawk migration is building with spectacular numbers. Raptors can be seen riding thermals along the Lake Erie shore.

During the last week of September and the first week of October fall colours in the Haliburton Highlands are often at their peak. A blaze of sugar maples makes for many scenic walks. Little brown bats return to their winter hibernacula at Bonnechere Caves. The beavers' tree-felling activities escalate as they build their winter stockpiles of branches and twigs. October is the perfect month for hiking a section of the Bruce Trail, looking for old-growth cedars along the escarpment.

In November tens of thousands of squawking gulls gather near Niagara Falls to fish the open, turbulent waters of the Niagara River.

WINTER

By December the birds of winter have arrived at backyard feeders. Chickadees will eat from visitors' hands along the Bird Feeder Trail in Lynde Shores Conservation Area.

On a cold January night the great horned owl calls for its mate, preparing to build its nest atop an old snag. Crusted snow and a shortage of rodents may drive great grey owls south where they silently wait and watch atop roadside fence posts for the slightest movement on the ground below. Snowy owls are driven south by weather conditions or food shortages. Look for them at Tommy Thompson Park.

By February deep snows have prompted white-tailed deer to gather into yards, where they tramp paths in the snow and seek shelter under the sloping branches of evergreens. Almost frozen, turtles sleep in the muddy bottoms of lakes and delicate salamanders survive the ice under forest soil insulated with rotting leaves, waiting for spring's return.

RESOURCES

FEDERATION OF ONTARIO NATURALISTS
Outings guided by expert naturalists provide opportunities for
observing nature. Working for Wilderness programs involve
volunteers in a variety of conservation work, including trail
building, habitat restoration and biological surveys. For
information contact the Federation of Ontario Naturalists at
355 Lesmill Road, Don Mills M3B 2W8. Telephone (416) 444-
8419 or 1-800-440-2366.

ONTARIO PARKS
For information on how to explore Ontario's 270 provincial
parks, check out Ontario Parks' Web site at www.mnr.gov.on.ca/
MNR/parks, or get a free copy of *Nearby and Natural*, the annual
guidebook, by contacting Travel Ontario at 1-800-ONTARIO.
Or contact the Ministry of Natural Resources at (416) 314-6557.

PARKS CANADA–Ontario Region
For information on National Parks in Ontario contact the Parks
Canada Ontario Regional Office, 111 Water Street East,
Cornwall K6H 6S2. Telephone (613) 938-5881.

TORONTO FIELD NATURALISTS
Through its member-led field trips and monthly newsletter,
this non-profit organization works to develop public interest
in natural history and to preserve natural heritage. Contact
Toronto Field Naturalists at 605-14 College Street, Toronto
M5G 1K2. Telephone (416) 968-6255.

CONSERVATION AUTHORITIES
AND ASSOCIATIONS

AUSABLE BAYFIELD
R.R. 3, Exeter N0M 1S5
Telephone: (519) 235-2610

CATARAQUI REGION
Box 160, 1641 Perth Road,
Glenburnie K0H 1S0
Telephone: (613) 546-4228

CATFISH CREEK
R.R. 5, Aylmer N5H 2R4
Telephone: (519) 773-9037

CENTRAL LAKE ONTARIO
100 Whiting Avenue,
Oshawa L1H 3T3
Telephone: (905) 579-0411

CONSERVATION LANDS
OF ONTARIO
400 Clyde Road, Box 729,
Cambridge N1R 5W6
Telephone: (519) 621-2761
or 1-888-376-2212

CREDIT VALLEY
1255 Derry Road West,
Meadowvale L5N 6R4
Telephone: (905) 670-1615
or 1-800-668-5557

CROWE VALLEY
70 Hughes Lane, Box 416,
Marmora K0K 2M0
Telephone: (613) 472-3137

ESSEX REGION
360 Fairview Avenue West,
Essex N8M 1Y6
Telephone: (519) 776-5209

GANARASKA REGION
Box 328,
Port Hope L1A 3W4
Telephone: (905) 885-8173

GRAND RIVER
400 Clyde Road,
Cambridge N1R 5W6
Telephone: (519) 621-2761

GREY SAUBLE
R.R. 4,
Owen Sound, N4K 5N6
Telephone: (519) 376-3076

HALTON REGION
2596 Britannia Road West,
R.R. 2, Milton L9T 2X6
Telephone: (905) 336-1158

HAMILTON REGION
838 Mineral Springs Road,
Box 7099, Ancaster L9G 3L3
Telephone: (905) 525-2181
or 1-888-319-4722

KAWARTHA REGION
277 Kenrei Park Road,
R.R. 1, Lindsay K9V 4R1
Telephone: (705) 328-2271

KETTLE CREEK
R.R. 8, St. Thomas N5P 3T3
Telephone: (519) 631-1270

LAKE SIMCOE REGION
Box 282,
120 Bayview Parkway,
Newmarket L3Y 4X1
Telephone: (905) 895-1281

LAKEHEAD REGION
Box 3476,
130 Conservation Road,
Thunder Bay P7B 5J9
Telephone: (807) 344-5857

LONG POINT REGION
R.R. 3, Simcoe N3Y 4K2
Telephone: (519) 428-4623

LOWER THAMES VALLEY
100 Thames Street,
Chatham N7L 2Y8
Telephone: (519) 354-7310

LOWER TRENT
441 Front Street,
Trenton K8V 6C1

MAITLAND VALLEY
Box 127, 93 Marietta Street,
Wroxeter N0G 2X0
Telephone: (519) 335-3557

MATTAGAMI REGION
100 Lakeshore Road,
Timmins P4N 8R5
Telephone: (705) 264-5309

MISSISSIPPI VALLEY
Box 268, Lanark K0G 1K0
Telephone: (613) 259-2421

MOIRA RIVER
c/o Quinte Conservation,
Box 698, Belleville K8N 5B3
Telephone: (613) 968-3434

NAPANEE REGION
c/o Quinte Conservation,
Box 698, Belleville K8N 5B3
Telephone: (613) 354-3312

NIAGARA PENINSULA
2358 Centre Street,
Allanburg L0S 1A0
Telephone: (905) 227-1013

NICKEL DISTRICT
West Tower, Civic Square,
200 Brady Street,
Sudbury P3E 5K3
Telephone: (705) 674-5249

NORTH BAY-MATTAWA
701 Oak Street East,
North Bay P1B 9T1
Telephone: (705) 474-5420

NOTTAWASAGA VALLEY
R.R. 1, Angus L0M 1B0
Telephone: (705) 424-1479

OTONABEE REGION
250 Milroy Drive,
Peterborough K9H 7M9
Telephone: (705) 745-5791

PRINCE EDWARD REGION
c/o Quinte Conservation
Box 968, Belleville K8N 5B3
Telephone: (613) 476-7408

RAISIN REGION
Box 429,
6589 Boundary Road,
Cornwall K6H 5T2
Telephone: (613) 938-3611

RIDEAU VALLEY
Box 599, 1128 Mill Street,
Manotick K4M 1A5
Telephone (613) 692-3571

SAUGEEN VALLEY
CENTRE
R.R. 1, Hanover N4N 3B8
Telephone: (519) 364-1255

SAULT STE. MARIE REGION
1100 Fifth Line East, R.R. 2,
Sault Ste. Marie P6A 5K7
Telephone: (705) 946-8530

SOUTH NATION
CONSERVATION
Box 69, 15 Union Street,
Berwick K0C 1G0
Telephone: (613) 984-2948

ST. CLAIR REGION
205 Mill Pond Crescent,
Strathroy N7G 3P9
Telephone: (519) 245-3710

TORONTO AND REGION
5 Shoreham Drive,
Downsview M3N 1S4
Telephone: (416) 661-6600

UPPER THAMES RIVER
1424 Clarke Road,
London N5V 5B9
Telephone: (519) 451-2800

BIBLIOGRAPHY AND
RECOMMENDED READING

Bennet, Doug, and Tim Tiner. *Up North: A Guide to Ontario's Wilderness from Blackflies to the Northern Lights*. Markham: Reed Books Canada, 1993.

Bennet, Doug, and Tim Tiner. *Up North Again: More of Ontario's Wilderness, from Ladybugs to the Pleiades*. Toronto: McClelland & Stewart, 1997. Enough fascinating trivia to start a board game enlivens these two clever volumes describing animals, plants, geology and meteorology in Canadian Shield cottage country.

Bentley, Cathy V., Brenda Chambers, and Karen Legasy. *Forest Plants of Central Ontario*. Edmonton: Lone Pine, 1996. Both colour photographs and black and white illustrations make this a great guide for identifying a full range of forest flora from trees to lichens. Handy portable format is easy to pack for hikes.

Boer, Arnold H., ed. *Ecology and Management of the Eastern Coyote*. Fredericton: Wildlife Research Unit, University of New Brunswick, 1992. Various papers describe how the expansion of the coyote's range into eastern North America has affected ecological relationships.

Canada. Ministry of the Environment. *Lead Sinkers and Jigs*, 1996.

Clark, Ella Elizabeth. *Indian Legends of Canada*. Toronto: McClelland and Stewart, 1961. A collection of myths, legends and stories from more than a dozen First Nations language groups across Canada.

Del Conte, Anna, Thomas Laessoe, and Gary Lincoff. *The Knopf Mushroom Book*. Toronto: Knopf Canada, 1996. Detailed, full-colour photographs and illustrations facilitate fungus identification. Good tips on collecting and cooking edible wild mushrooms.

Dennis, John V. *Beyond the Bird Feeder*. New York: Alfred A. Knopf, 1995. Fascinating accounts of bird behaviour from bathing to eluding enemies.

Doyle, James, ed. *Yankees in Canada*. Toronto: ECW Press, 1980. A collection of first-hand accounts of travellers in eighteenth- and nineteenth-century Canada.

Dykeman, Peter A., and Thomas S. Elias. *Edible Wild Plants: A North American Field Guide*. New York: Sterling Publishing, 1990. Colour photographs facilitate identification of wild edibles in this curious guide that offers both harvesting and culinary tips.

Givinish, Thomas J. "Ecology and Evolution of Carnivorous Plants." In *Plant-Animal Interactions,* edited by Warren Abrahamson. Toronto: McGraw-Hill, 1989.

Goodwin, Clive E. *A Bird-Finding Guide to Ontario*. Toronto: University of Toronto Press, 1995. An authoritative guide for serious birders.

Grady, Wayne. *Toronto the Wild: Field Notes of an Urban Naturalist*. Toronto: Macfarlane Walter & Ross, 1995. With considerable wit, Grady describes the tenacity of nature in the urban setting

as wildflowers spring up on empty lots, termite colonies
move into basements, bats roost in attics and coyotes roam
the Don Valley.

Hall, Roger, and Sandra Martin, ed. *Rupert Brooke in Canada*.
Toronto: Peter Martin Associates, 1978.

Jameson, Anna Brownell. *Winter Studies and Summer Rambles in
Canada: Selections*. Toronto: New Canadian Library, McClelland
and Stewart, 1965. First published 1838. In 1837, a gentle-
woman travels into the wilderness by canoe in this literary
travelogue rich in historical detail.

Johnson, Bob. *Familiar Amphibians and Reptiles of Ontario*.
Toronto: Natural Heritage/Natural History for the Toronto
Field Naturalists, 1989. With good pencil illustrations by Paul
Harpley, this guide by herpetologist Bob Johnson offers
many personal insights on observing toads, turtles, snakes and
salamanders.

Kieran, Sheila, ed. *The Waterfront Trail: Explore Yesterday, Today and
Tomorrow Along the Shores of Lake Ontario*. Toronto: The Waterfront
Regeneration Trust, 1995. Conceived with the intention of
inspiring public interest and support for the preservation of
Lake Ontario's remaining natural shoreline resources, this guide
directs readers to parks and conservation areas as well as places
of cultural and historic interest.

Kolenosky, George B. "Season of the Black Bear." *Ontario
Naturalist*, Summer (1978).

Kolenosky, George B., and Stewart M. Strathearn. "Black Bear."
Wild Furbearer Management and Conservation in North America.
Toronto: Ontario Trappers Association under Ontario Ministry
of Natural Resources, 1987.

Kolenosky, George B., Dennis Voigt, and R.O. Standfield. *Wolves and Coyotes in Ontario*. Toronto: Ontario Ministry of Natural Resources.

Lee, Thomas. *Ancient Forest Exploration Guide:White Bear Forest, Temagami, Ontario*. Toronto: Ancient Forest Exploration and Research, 1996. Brief, but well illustrated with black and white photos, this pocket guide explains the special ecology of old growth.

Montgomery, Sy. *Nature's Everyday Mysteries: A Field Guide to the World in Your Backyard*. Shelburne, Vermont: Chapters Publishing, 1993. Artfully written essays—most from the *Boston Globe*'s "Nature Journal"—cover subjects close to home, from spiders to skunks.

Novak, Milan John. *The Beaver in Ontario*. Toronto: Ministry of Natural Resources, 1976.

Parr Traill, Catharine. *The Backwoods of Canada*. Toronto: McClelland & Stewart, 1966. The vivid autobiographical account of an 1830s pioneer settler in Peterborough County. Both an avid naturalist and an astute observer of her surroundings, Parr Trail chronicles the landscape in realistic detail.

Parr Traill, Catharine. *The Canadian Settler's Guide*. Toronto: McClelland & Stewart, New Canadian Library, 1969. First published in 1855. Based on her experience in the backwoods, Catharine Parr Traill wrote this compendium of tips for would-be settlers, containing everything from recipes to furniture building.

Polk, James. *Wilderness Writers*. Toronto: Clarke Irwin & Company, Limited, 1972.

Rezendes, Paul. *Tracking and the Art of Seeing*. Charlotte, Vermont: Camden House Publishing, 1992. More than a great guide to animal tracks and signs, this very personal work shows readers how to find their place in relation to other creatures on this planet.

Seton, Ernest Thompson. *The Book of Woodcraft*. Berkeley: Creative Arts Book Company, 1988. Originally published by Doubleday, Page & Company in 1912. Activities for aspiring young woodsmen from the founder of the Boy Scouts.

Simcoe, Elizabeth. *Mrs. Simcoe's Diary*. Edited by Mary Quayle Innis. Toronto: Macmillan, 1965.

Smith, Dave. *Backcountry Bear Basics*. Vancouver: Greystone, 1997. In this slim but gripping volume Smith covers much of the contradictory advice offered on avoiding bear attacks and offers some strategies of his own. An important book to read *before* venturing into bear country.

Stokes, Donald W. *A Guide to Observing Insect Lives*. Toronto: Little, Brown and Company, 1983. Using extensive field experience Stokes offers some fascinating tips on watching many commonly seen insects, from ants to whirligigs. Even the most insect-phobic readers will gain new insights into bug behaviour. Other first-rate Stokes guides are offered on avian, amphibian and reptile behaviour.

Teasdale, Shirley. *Hiking Ontario's Heartland*. Toronto: Whitecap Books, 1993. A practical guide to some interesting hikes that can be done in an afternoon or a day.

Theberge, John B. "Ecological Classification, Status, and Management of the Gray Wolf, *Canis lupis*, in Canada." *The Canadian Field Naturalist* 105, no. 4 (October–December 1991): 459–63.

Theberge, John B., ed. *Legacy: The Natural History of Ontario*. Toronto: McClelland & Stewart, 1989. This authoritative and highly readable work offers many well-written essays on a wide range of flora, fauna and physical features across the province.

Wake, Winifred (Cairns) Wake, ed. *A Nature Guide to Ontario*. Toronto: University of Toronto Press, 1997. This comprehensive compendium lists conservation areas, parks and areas of natural interest throughout the province.

Westcott, Frank. *The Beaver: Nature's Master Builder*. Willowdale: Hounslow Press, 1989. A wealth of beaver trivia, from fur hats to Egyptian hieroglyphics, enriches this readable volume.

Wishner, Lawrence. *Eastern Chipmunks: Secrets of Their Solitary Lives*. Washington, D.C.: Smithsonian Institute Press, 1982.

INDEX

Acid rain, 121
Acorn weevil, 68
Albany River, 244
Algonquin Prov. Park, 14, 27, 60, 79–81,
        177–79, 182, 194, 195
American bittern, 150
American goldfinch, 23
American toad, 150, 210
Amherstburg, 11–12, 23, 24
Amherst Island, 85
Amphibians, 90, 210. *See also* Frogs;
        Salamanders; Toads
    field guide, 91
Animal tracks, 152
Animal watching. *See names of individual species*
Anishinabe Native Experience, 241–42
Apsley, 220
Archaeological sites, 34, 101–3, 109
Arctic arnica, 197
Arctic loon, 15, 71
Arctic tern, 19
Aspen, 216
Aspen Valley Wildlife Sanctuary, 190,
        191–92
Ausable River, 104
Autumn colours, 218–21

Backus Heritage Conservation Area,
        212–13, 214
Bald eagle, 17, 19, 22, 24, 103, 139,
        143–44, 198
Balsam fir, 196, 197, 209, 216, 237
Baltimore oriole, 18
Bancroft, 97–100, 219

Bank swallow, 156
Bannock bread, 233
Baptiste Lake, 135, 137
Barry's Bay, 140
Bass, 135–37, 148
Basswood, 168, 226
Bats, 23, 86–89
Battle Island, 236
Beaches, 19, 23, 24, 38, 55, 57, 63, 64, 67,
        70, 75, 81, 145, 233
Bearded seal, 232
Bears, 118, 188–91, 198, 219–20, 234
    books and pamphlets, 191
Beaver, 103, 168, 193–95, 219, 237
Beeches, 167, 214, 222, 226
Beluga whale, 232
Berry farms, 119
Bicycling, 38, 129, 132, 161, 162, 220, 250
Big bluestem grass, 51
Big Creek Marsh Nat. Wildlife Area, 23, 72
Big Grassy First Nation, 19, 20
Binoculars, 7
Birches, 216, 219, 239
Bird banding, 22, 25–28, 71, 72, 84
Bird feeders, 11, 12, 29, 30, 31, 32
Bird migrations, 11, 16, 21, 23, 36–37, 70, 71,
        73–74, 168, 170, 198, 234, 253, 254
Bird watching, 7, 8
    near Ajax, 226
    on Amherst Island, 85
    near Bowmanville, 21, 24
    near Brighton, 73–75
    near Combermere, 139
    near Dundalk, 146

near Dundas, 130
near Dunnville, 106
in Essex County, 11–12
near Gananoque, 9
near Grand Bend, 68
in Guelph, 82
near Hamilton, 112, 130, 165–67
in Kawarthas, 13–15
near Kleinburg, 30–32
at Long Point, 16, 70–72
near Mallorytown, 143–44
near Midland, 149, 150–52
near Milton, 33–34, 35, 84
near Moosonee, 234
in Niagara Falls, 5–8
near Oshawa, 168, 169, 170
near Peterborough, 103
at Point Pelee, 36–38
near Port Rowan, 213
near Port Stanley, 21–24
on St. Lawrence Islands, 143–44
near Temagami, 208
near Thunder Bay, 196, 198
in Toronto, 16, 156, 162–63
in Whitby, 29–30
in Windsor, 51
Bittern, American, 150
Black bear, 118, 188–91, 198, 219–20, 234
Blackburnian warbler, 26
Black-capped chickadee, 29–30, 31
Black cherry, 226
Black-crowned night heron, 162, 166, 170
Black duck, 139
Blackflies, 117–19
Black gum tree, 212, 213
Black-headed gull, 6
Black-legged kittiwake, 5
Black rat snake, 11, 141, 142, 144
Black's Park, 112
Black tern, 152
Bladderwort, 59
Blanding's turtle, 37, 60, 144, 167
Blind, tactile signage for the, 145
Bloodroot, 45, 46
Blue beech, 167

Blueberries, 118, 119, 143, 197, 245
Bluebird, eastern, 157
Blue dwarf lake iris, 56
Blue jay, 23, 31, 68
Blue Loon Adventures, 25, 27–28
Blue Mountain, 95
Blue-winged teal, 170
Blunt-leaved orchid, 197
Boat tours, 19, 138, 140, 142, 144, 202, 232, 234. See also Canoe trips
Bobby's Guide Service, 19
Bogs, 60, 147, 168, 197, 231, 243
Bolete mushroom, 41, 42–43
Bonaparte's gull, 5, 6
Bon Echo Prov. Park, 125
Bonnechere Caves, 86–88
Bonnechere Deer Yard, 183, 184
Bonnechere Prov. Park, 81
Brachiopods, 104–5
Brantford, 146
Brighton, 74
British soldier lichen, 120
Broad-winged hawk, 21–22
Broere's Fly-Fishing, 137
Bronte Creek, 212
Bruce Peninsula Nat. Park, 55–57, 112
Bruce Trail, 33, 111–13, 167, 249–50
    guidebook, 113
Bruce Trail Association, 113, 167
Buckeye butterfly, 37
Bufflehead, 156
Bullfrog, 138, 139–40
Bunchberry, 197
Burlington, 212
Burlington Bay, 152, 165
Butterfly watching
    near Brighton, 75
    in Dundas, 126
    near Grand Bend, 69
    in Niagara Falls, 8
    at Point Pelee, 37
    at Presqu'ile Prov. Park, 126–28
    in Windsor, 51
Butternut, 167
Byng Island Conservation Area, 147, 148

Cain Foray, 44
Caledon Hills, 112
Calypso orchid, 113
Cambridge, 146
Camelot Island, 144
Camping
    near Amherstburg, 24
    near Bancroft, 220
    near Belleville, 64, 66
    at Bonnechere Prov. Park, 81
    on Bruce Peninsula, 57
    near Collingwood, 96
    in Dunnville, 148
    near Elliot Lake, 217
    near Gananoque, 11
    near Grand Bend, 69
    on Lake of the Woods, 19
    at Long Point, 72
    near Mallorytown, 142
    near Peterborough, 103, 109
    near Point Pelee, 38
    near Port Rowan, 214
    near Rossport, 238
    on St. Lawrence Islands, 144, 145
    near Temagami, 207, 210
    near Thunder Bay, 199
    in Toronto, 155, 157
Camping, winter, 69, 220
Camp Jeegibik, 239–42
Canada anemone, 170
Canada goose, 160, 233
Canadian Chestnut Council, 131
Canadian Heritage Rivers, 146
Canadian Nature Federation, 211
Canadian Shield, 218
Canadian Wildlife Service, 72
Canoeing. See also Kayaking
    in Algonquin Prov. Park, 178, 179, 180
    near Bancroft, 219
    near Combermere, 140
    near Grand Bend, 69
    in Grand River marshes, 147
    near Midland, 149, 150, 152
    in Point Pelee Nat. Park, 38
    near Temagami, 208, 209, 210, 211

    near Thunder Bay, 27
    in Wabikimi Prov. Park, 243–46
Canoe rentals, 69, 140, 148, 208, 210, 219, 238
Canoe trips, guided, 27, 179–80, 211, 244, 246
Canvasback, 74
Cape May warbler, 26, 37
Cardinal, 32
Caribou, woodland, 121, 198, 237–38, 243, 245
Carnivorous plants, 58–60
Carolina wren, 38
Carolinian forest, 37, 69, 106, 147, 157, 167, 182, 212–14, 222, 250
Carp, 165, 166, 169
Caspian tern, 152, 156
Cassels Lake, 207
Cataract River, 112
Caterpillars, 127
Catfish, 147, 148
Cattails, 149, 150, 168
Caves, 86–88, 112
Cedar, 71, 111–12, 208, 209, 216, 240
Centipedes, 209
Central Ontario Railway trail, 99
Century Day, 36
Cerulean warbler, 37
Charles Sauriol Carolinian Forest, 213–14
Chester Marsh, 160
Chestnut, American, 130–31
Chestnut, sweet, 212
Chestnut-sided warbler, 25, 27
Chickadees, 29–30, 31, 152
Chinook salmon, 148
Chinquapin oak, 37, 106, 143, 147, 222
Chipmunk, 172–74, 222
Clintonia, 118
Cochrane, 231, 232, 234
Coho salmon, 168
Collingwood, 95, 108
Coltsfoot, 45–46, 156
Columbine, 56, 112
Combermere, 140
Commanda, 182, 184

Common hackberry, 106
Common loon, 13–15
Connecticut warbler, 36
Conroy's Marsh, 138–40
Conservation areas. *See also* Nature reserves;
    Parks; Wildlife areas
    Backus Heritage Conservation Area,
        212–13, 214
    Byng Island Conservation Area, 147, 148
    Crawford Lake Conservation Area, 33
    Dundas Valley Conservation Area, 132
    Holiday Beach Conservation Area, 23
    Kortright Centre for Conservation, 30–32
    Lynde Shores Conservation Area, 29–30, 32
    Mer Bleue Conservation Area, 60
    Rock Glen Conservation Area, 104–7
    Rockwood Conservation Area, 226
Conservation authorities and associations,
    257–59
Conservation Lands of Ontario, 148
Cooper's hawk, 130
Cootes Paradise, 112, 130, 165–67
Corals, 105, 106, 233
Cormorants, 19, 106, 163, 166, 198
Cottonwood poplar, 63, 160, 162
Corbett's Dam, 137
Coyote, 162, 163, 164, 169
Craigleith Prov. Park, 95–96
Crawford Lake Conservation Area, 33
Cree Cultural Centre, 232–33
Cree Way Wilderness Experiences, 235
Crinoids, 105, 233
Crossbill, 246
Cross-country skiing, 29, 31, 69, 152, 226
Crow, 30
Cruises. *See* Boat tours
Crystals, 97, 98
Currant bushes, 209
Curve Lake First Nation, 103, 187
Cypress Lake, 57

Darlington Prov. Park, 171
Deer, white-tailed, 68, 103, 106, 142, 155,
    178, 181–84, 198, 226
Deerberry, 142

Discovery North, 242
Dog-sledding trips, 211
Don River, 45
Don River Valley, 158–61
Don Valley Brickworks, 159, 161
Dorcas Bay, 55
Double-crested cormorant, 163
Downy woodpecker, 30, 226
Dragonflies, 23, 139, 140
Dream Island, 17
Drumlins, 108–9
Ducks, 36, 71, 73, 74, 139, 147, 152, 156,
    160, 165, 169, 170
Ducks Unlimited, 139
Duckweed, 149
Dundalk, 146
Dundas, 126
Dundas Valley, 129–32
Dundas Valley Conservation Area, 132
Dunes, 63, 64, 67
Dunnville, 147
Dunnville Fishway, 147
Durham Economic Development
    Department, 227
Durham Region Forest, 225–26, 227

Eagles. *See* Bald eagle; Golden eagle
Earthstar fungi, 226
Eastern bluebird, 157
Eastern fox snake, 37, 72
Eastern garter snake, 37
Edmund Fitzgerald, 237
Edward's Gardens, 172, 174
Eganville, 86
Eldorado, 97, 98
Elgin Trail, 250
Elliot Lake, 215, 239
Elora, 146, 147
Elora Cataract Trailway, 250
Elora Gorge, 146
Eramosa River, 226
Erratics, glacial, 216
Essex, 30
Essex County, 11–12, 30
Evening grosbeak, 30

Evening primrose, 160
Events
    Cain Foray, 44
    Lakeshore Lodge Weekend, 66
    Monarch Migration Festival, 126–27
    Ontario Hiking Day, 111
    powwows, 239
    Rockhound Gemboree, 97
    Rouge Park Day, 157
    Waterfowl Festival, 74, 75

Falconry, 21, 24
Falcons, 19, 22, 23, 24, 196
Federation of Ontario Naturalists, 60, 191
Fens, 231
Fergus, 146
Ferns, 112, 130, 150, 209, 223, 240
Field sparrow, 51
Finlayson Point Prov. Park, 207, 210
Firewood, 225
First Nations culture, 20, 35, 101, 102–3,
    109, 187, 232–33, 239–42
Fisher, 186, 198
Fishing, 137
    Baptiste Lake, 135
    Conroy's Marsh, 139
    Grand River, 147
    Holiday Beach Conservation Area, 23
    Lake Erie, 147
    Lake of the Woods, 19
    Rouge River, 157
Fish Point Prov. Nature Reserve, 37–38
Fish watching, 135–37, 147, 148
Five-lined skink, 37, 68, 123–25, 144
Flowerpot Island, 113
Flying squirrel, 68, 213
Forest canopy tour, 203
Forest fires, 209
Forests
    boreal, 196, 215–17, 243–46
    Carolinian, 37, 69, 106, 147, 157, 167,
        182, 212–14, 222, 250
    deciduous, 209–10, 211, 212, 215
    old-growth, 28, 111, 196–97, 207–11
Forks of the Credit Prov. Park, 112

Fossil Island, 233
Fossils, 95–96, 104–7, 112, 159, 233
Fox, 68, 156, 163, 198
Franklin's ground squirrel, 18
Franklin's gull, 5
Friends of Second Marsh, 171
Fringed gentian, 68
Frogs, 57, 90–92, 138, 139–40, 142, 149,
    150, 170, 244
    field guide, 91
Fruit flies, 10

Ganaraska River, 137
Ganaraska Trail, 250
Gardens, 9–11, 126, 167, 172, 174
Gardens at Landon Bay, The, 9–11
Garter snake, 113, 162
Geese, 36, 160, 233, 234
Geological features, 101, 108–9, 217. See
    also Fossils
Georgian Bay, 95, 112–13
Georgina Island, 143
Gizzard shad, 148
Glaciers, 108, 226
Glaucous gull, 6
Glen Rouge Park, 155
Golden Creek Bird Farm, 21, 24
Golden eagle, 22, 24, 103, 139
Goldeneye duck, 156
Golden Lake Reserve, 187
Goldenrod, 50, 52
Goldfinch, American, 23
Gooseberry, 209
Goshawk, 22
Grand River, 146–48
Grand Valley Trail, 148, 250–51
Grand Valley Trails Association, 148
Grasslands, 50–52
Great black-backed gull, 6
Great blue heron, 143, 147, 156, 170
Great egret, 146
Great grey owl, 84, 246
Great horned owl, 30, 82–83, 84
Green frog, 149, 150, 170
Green heron, 156, 166–67

Green-winged teal, 152
Greenwood Forest, 28
Grenadier Island, 142
Grey jay, 103, 246
Grosbeak, evening, 30
Grouse, 68
Gulls, 5–7, 19, 106, 162
Gum tree, black, 212, 213
Gyrfalcon, 24

Hackberry butterfly, 37
Hackberry, common, 106
Haliburton Forest, 202
Haliburton Forest Wolf Centre, 200–3
Haliburton Highlands, 203, 255
Hares, 57, 246
Harris hawk, 24
Harrow, 24
Hawk Cliff, 21, 22, 23
Hawks, 21–23, 24, 71, 130, 170, 208
Hawthorn, 168
Helenbar Lake, 216
Helleborine, 56
Hemlock, 143
Hepatica, 45
Hermitage ruin, 129, 132
Herons, 140, 143, 147, 156, 162,
    166–67, 170
Herring gull, 6, 162
Hickory, shagbark, 142–43, 147
Highland Creek, 212
High Park, 53, 54
High Park Citizens' Advisory Committee, 54
Hike Ontario, 111, 249
Hiking
    near Ajax, 226, 227
    in Algonquin Prov. Park, 195
    near Alton, 250
    near Arkona, 106
    near Bancroft, 98–99, 219–20
    near Belleville, 66
    near Brighton, 74–75
    on Bruce Peninsula, 57
    near Cataract, 250
    near Dundas, 129–32

    near Elliot Lake, 215–17
    near Grand Bend, 68–69
    along Grand River, 148
    near Hamilton, 166
    near Kingston, 251
    near Kleinburg, 31, 49
    at Long Point, 71, 72
    near Mallorytown, 142, 143
    near Meaford, 111
    near Midland, 150
    near Milton, 33, 35, 49
    near Moosonee, 232
    on Niagara Escarpment, 111–13
    near Niagara Falls, 222, 223
    near Oshawa, 169, 170
    near Ottawa, 251
    near Pembrooke, 209–10, 211
    near Peterborough, 103, 110
    at Point Pelee, 36
    near Port Hope, 250
    near Port Rowan, 214
    near Port Stanley, 250
    near Rockwood, 226
    on St. Lawrence Islands, 142, 144
    near Temagami, 208, 210, 211
    near Thunder Bay, 27, 196, 197
    in Toronto, 155, 156, 157, 160–61
    near West Guilford, 202
    in Whitby, 29
Hiking trails, long-distance, 249–52
Hill Island, 144
Hillside Nature Centre, 156
H.N. Crossley Nature Reserve, 60
Hoary puccoon, 63, 67
Hog-nose snake, 68
Holiday Beach Conservation Area, 11–12,
    23, 24
Honey mushroom, 41, 42
Hooded warbler, 38, 130
Horned lark, 36
Horsetail fern, 240
Hudsonian godwit, 234
Hummingbirds, 9–12, 23
Hummingbird Garden, 9
Hunting, 147, 148, 182

Indigo bunting, 51
Indigo dusky wing butterfly, 51
Insects, 10, 51, 68, 117–19, 197. *See also*
        Butterflies; Dragonflies
Interpretive centres. See Museums, etc.
Ironsides Island, 143
Ishpatina Ridge, 210
Island Hopper Charters, 142, 144

Jack-Fish Hammy's Guide Service, 19
Jack-in-the-pulpit, 170
Jack pine, 245
James Bay, 231, 232
Jameson, Anna Brownell, 7
J.C. Taylor Nature Centre, 82, 85
Jefferson salamander, 131
Jewelweed, 216
Juniper, 240

Kakabeka Falls, 95
Kasheese Studios, 187
Kawartha Kayaking, 13, 15
Kawartha Lakes, 13–15, 250
Kayaking, 13, 15, 69, 236, 238
Kayak rentals, 69, 238
Kenora, 17, 19
Kestrels, 22
Kettle Creek Inn, 23
Kettle Lakes Prov. Park, 109
Kingfisher, 160
Kingston, 141
Kingsville, 38
King Township, 42
Kirkwood Forest, 207
Kitchener, 146
Kleinburg, 30–32, 88, 90, 91
Kortright Centre for Conservation, 30–32,
        49, 88–89, 90–92

Labrador tea, 197
Lady Evelyn Outfitting, 211
Lady Evelyn-Smoothwater Prov. Park, 211
Lake Erie, 16, 21–24, 36–38, 70, 106, 126,
        147, 213
Lakefield, 15

Lake Huron, 55, 67, 95–96, 239
Lake Nipissing, 182
Lake of the Woods, 17–19
Lake of the Woods Prov. Park. See Ojibway
        Heritage Park
Lake Ontario, 63, 73–75, 126–28, 169, 171
Lake Ontario Waterfront Trail, 251
Lake Superior, 196, 197, 236–38
Lake Superior Prov. Park, 121
Lake Temagami, 207, 209
Lakeview Park, 171
Lambton County, 104
Landon Bay, 9–12
Large-leaf aster, 197
Lark, horned, 36
Lead poisoning, 150–51
Leamington, 37
Least bittern, 146
Leopard frog, 142
Leslie Street spit, 83, 127, 162–63, 164, 195
Lichens, 120–22, 196, 237, 245
Lighthouses, 74, 106, 164, 236
Little brown bat, 86–87
Lizards. *See* Five-lined skink
Logging, 182, 207, 216
London, 106
Long-eared owl, 168
Long Point, 70–72
Long Point Bird Observatory, 32, 71, 72
Long Point Prov. Park, 70, 71, 72, 127
Loons, 13–15, 19, 71, 219
Loring, 182
Loring Deer Yard, 183–84
Louisiana waterthrush, 213
Lupine, 68
Luther Marsh Wildlife Management Area,
        59, 60, 146, 148
Lynde Shores Conservation Area, 29–30, 32
Lynx, 246

Madawaska River, 138
Magnolia warbler, 26
Mallard, 139, 160, 165
Mallorytown, 142
Manitoulin Island, 113, 187, 239, 252

Maple Mountain, 210

Maples, 213, 215, 216, 219, 220, 225, 226

Map lichen, 121

Map turtle, 37, 156, 167

Marie Louise Lake, 198, 199

Mark S. Burnham Prov. Park, 109–10

Marram grass, 63

Marshes, 23, 29, 37, 59, 60, 72, 74,
    138–40, 144, 146–47, 148, 149–50,
    152, 156, 160, 165–67, 168–71, 234

Marsh marigold, 47

Marten, 198

Mayapple, 156

McLaughlin Bay Wildlife Reserve, 170–71

Meaford, 111

Meline, Al, 19

Mer Bleue Conservation Area, 60

Merganser, 156

Meromictic lakes, 34

Merrickville, 251

Milfoil, 177

Milkweed, 127

Milton, 33, 88, 89, 92

Minerals, 97–99

Mines, abandoned, 97, 98, 99, 198, 216

Ministry of Natural Resources, 217

Mink, 156

Mississagi Prov. Park, 215–17

Mohawk Island, 106

Monarch butterfly, 126–28

Monarch Migration Festival, 126

Mooneye, 148

Moorhen, 166

Moose, 177–79, 198, 201, 215–16, 246

Moose Factory, 232

Moose River, 231, 232

Moosonee, 231, 232, 234

Mosquitoes, 117–18

Mosses, 210, 216, 244, 245

Moth, papapeima, 51

Mountain-bike trails, 132, 220, 226

Mountsberg Wildlife Centre, 49, 84, 85, 88,
    89, 92

Mourning dove, 31

Mourning warbler, 38

Mouse, white-footed, 213, 246

Mud Creek, 159–60

Murphy's Point Prov. Park, 98–99, 100

Museums, nature centres, interpretive centres
    Backus Conservation Education Centre,
        214
    Bancroft mineral museum, 99
    Cootes Paradise nature centre, 167
    Crawford Lake Conservation Centre, 35
    Dundas Valley Trail Centre, 132
    Haliburton Forest Wolf Centre, 200–3
    Hillside Nature Centre, 156
    J.C. Taylor Nature Centre, 82, 85
    Kortright Centre for Conservation,
        30–32, 49, 88–89, 90–91
    Ojibway Nature Centre, 53–54
    Lighthouse Interpretive Centre, 75
    Pelee Island Heritage Centre, 38
    Point Pelee Visitor Centre, 37
    Presqu'ile nature centre, 128
    Todmorden Mills Museum, 161

Mushrooms, 41–44, 210, 216

Muskeg, 231

Musk turtle, 37

Muskoka, 24

Muskrat, 150

Mycological Society of Toronto, 41, 43–44

National Capital Commission, 60

Native peoples, 19, 20, 35, 68, 101, 102–3,
    109, 186–87, 232–33, 237, 239–42

Nature centres. See Museums, etc.

Nature programs, 81, 85, 88, 91, 92

Nature reserves. See also Conservation areas;
        Parks; Wildlife areas
    Fish Point Prov. Nature Reserve, 37–38
    H.N. Crossley Nature Reserve, 60
    Niagara Glen Nature Reserve, 222–24

Nature tours. See Ecotours

Niagara Escarpment, 33, 111–13

Niagara Escarpment Commission, 113

Niagara Falls, 5–8, 111, 222

Niagara Falls Canada Visitor and Convention
    Bureau, 8

Niagara Glen Nature Reserve, 222–24

Niagara Nature Tours, 222–23, 224
Niagara Parks Butterfly Conservatory, 8
Niagara Parks Commission, 8
Niagara River, 222, 223
North of Superior Tourism, 238
Northern harrier, 170
Northern hawk owl, 83
Northern parula, 121
Northern water snake, 156
Northland Paradise Lodge, 210

Oak Ridges Moraine, 156, 225–27,
    250, 251
Oak Ridges Trail, 251
Oaks, 37, 67, 68, 106, 130, 143, 147, 212,
    222, 226
Obabika River Prov. Park, 209, 211
Obatanga Prov. Park, 119
Ogoki River, 244
Ojibway Anishinabe Nation, 102
Ojibway Heritage Park, 18, 19–20
Ojibway Nature Centre, 54
Ojibway Park, 50–54
Old man's beard lichen, 121, 196, 237
Old Pine Lodge, 220–21
Oldsquaw, 74
Olympia marble-winged butterfly, 69
Ontario Herpetological Society, 91, 132
Ontario Hiking Day, 111
Ontario Northland, 234
Opossum, 106, 213
Orangeville, 148
Orchard oriole, 51, 166
Orchids, 55–56, 60, 113, 197, 208, 245
Orioles, 18, 51, 166, 213
Oshawa, 168
Osprey, 11, 19, 22, 138, 144, 208, 216, 233
Ottawa, 60
Ottawa Valley, 209
Ottawa Valley Tourist Association, 211
Otter, 60, 152
Outfitters, 179, 211, 246
Owl prowls, 85
Owls, 27, 30, 82–85, 168, 208, 246, 255
Oyster mushroom, 42

Paddleboats, 69
Painted turtle, 37, 149, 167
Papapeima moth, 51
Parks, 15. See also Conservation areas;
    Nature reserves; Wildlife areas
  Algonquin Prov. Park, 14, 27, 60, 79–81,
      177–79, 182, 194, 195
  Black's Park, 112
  Bon Echo Prov. Park, 125
  Bonnechere Prov. Park, 81
  Bruce Peninsula Nat. Park, 55–57, 112
  Craigleith Prov. Park, 95–96
  Darlington Prov. Park, 171
  Finlayson Point Prov. Park, 207, 210
  Forks of the Credit Prov. Park, 112
  Gardens at Landon Bay, The, 9
  High Park, 53, 54
  Kettle Lakes Prov. Park, 109
  Lady Evelyn-Smoothwater Prov. Park, 211
  Lake Superior Prov. Park, 121, 252
  Lakeview Park, 171
  Long Point Prov. Park, 70, 71, 72, 127
  Mark S. Burnham Prov. Park, 109–10
  Mississagi Prov. Park, 215–17
  Murphy's Point Prov. Park, 98–99, 100
  Obabika River Prov. Park, 209, 211
  Obatanga Prov. Park, 119
  Ojibway Heritage Park, 18
  Ojibway Park, 50–54
  Petroglyphs Prov. Park, 101–3
  Pinery Prov. Park, 67–69, 125
  Point Pelee Nat. Park, 36–38, 125
  Polar Bear Prov. Park, 235
  Presqu'ile Prov. Park, 73–75, 126
  Rock Point Prov. Park, 106, 107
  Rouge Park, 155–57
  St. Lawrence Islands Nat. Park, 141–45
  Sandbanks Prov. Park, 63–65, 66
  Serena Gundy Park, 48
  Serpent Mounds Park, 108–9
  Silent Lake Prov. Park, 219–21
  Sleeping Giant Prov. Park, 28, 191,
      196–99
  Solace Prov. Park, 211
  Tidewater Prov. Park, 232

Tommy Thompson Park, 83, 162–63, 164, 195
Wabikimi Prov. Park, 243–46
Wheatley Prov. Park, 38
Windy Lake Prov. Park, 119
Paw-paw, 37, 212
Pelee Island, 37–38
Pelee Island Winery, 37
Pelicans, 17–18, 19
Pembrooke, 209
Peregrine falcon, 19, 22, 24, 196
Peterborough, 103
Peterborough County, 108
Peterborough Crown Game Reserve, 103, 181–82, 183
Petroglyphs, 101–2
Petroglyphs Prov. Park, 101–3
Pheasant, 68, 106
Pickerel Lake, 198
Picnic areas, 96, 107, 132, 145, 148, 169, 216
Pictographs, 237
Pileated woodpecker, 143, 208, 213
Pine needle tea, 241
Pinery Prov. Park, 67–69, 125
Pines, 142, 143, 196–97, 207, 208, 209, 215, 216, 225, 239, 245
Pine sisken, 246
Piney Wood Hills, 196–97
Pink lady's slipper, 56, 197
Pink moccasin flower, 56
Pitcher plant, 57, 58–59, 60
Pitch pine, 142, 143
Plants. See also Wildflowers; names of individual species
    arctic, 197, 237
    carnivorous, 57, 58–60
    field guides, 122
    recipes using, 2, 219, 241
Platyceras, 105
Plovers, 170
Point Pelee Nat. Park, 36–38, 125, 127
Poison ivy, 215, 216, 224
Polar Bear Express, 231–32, 234
Polar Bear Prov. Park, 235
Ponds, 195, 219, 253

Pontoon boat rental, 140
Poplar, cottonwood, 63, 160, 162
Porcupine, 177, 185–87, 192
Portage Store, 180
Port Carling, 60
Port Hope, 137
Port Rowan, 72, 214
Port Stanley, 250
Powwows, 239
Pow-Wow Wilderness Trips, 179
Prairie falcon, 24
Prairie fringed orchid, 56
Prairie warbler, 68
Presqu'ile Prov. Park, 73–75, 126
Prickly pear cactus, 37
Prince Edward County, 63
Project Feederwatch, 32
Prothonotary warbler, 36, 37, 38
Puffball mushroom, 41, 210, 216
Pukaskwa Nat. Park, 237, 252
Pukaskwa pits, 237
Purple-fringed orchid, 60, 208
Pyrola, 197

Rabbits, 18, 226
Rainbow trout, 148, 155, 156–57, 168
Rainy Lake, 18, 19
Rainy River, 18
Ramshead lady's slipper, 56
Rat snake, black, 11, 141, 142, 144
Rattlesnake plantain orchid, 56, 208
Raven, 79, 103
Redback salamander, 131
Redhead, 74
Red-headed woodpecker, 51
Red knot, 234
Red-necked grebe, 28
Red-shouldered hawk, 22
Red-spotted salamander, 144
Red-tailed hawk, 22, 24
Red-throated loon, 15
Red-winged blackbird, 147, 165
Reindeer lichens, 121
Restouille, 182
Rice Lake, 108

Rideau Trail, 251
Ring-billed gull, 6, 162
Ringneck, 152
Robin, 121
Rock Glen Conservation Area, 104–7
Rockhound Gemboree, 97
Rock hounding, 97–100
Rocklyn Creek Management Area, 111–12
Rock Point Prov. Park, 106, 107
Rock polypody fern, 130
Rock tripe lichen, 121–22
Rockwood Conservation Area, 226
Rossport, 236, 238
Rossport Islands, 236, 238
Rouge Park, 155–57
Rouge River, 155, 156
Rough-legged hawk, 22
Royal Botanical Gardens, 165, 167
Ruby-throated hummingbird, 9–12, 23
Rue anemone, 143
Ruffed grouse, 226

St. Lawrence Islands Nat. Park, 141–45
St. Lawrence River, 85, 141
St. Thomas, 23
Salamanders, 129, 131, 144, 209, 210
Salmon, 148, 168
Sandbanks Prov. Park, 63–65, 66
Sandhill crane, 71
Sandpipers, 170
Sarsaparilla, 197
Sassafras, 37, 71, 129, 213
Savannahs, 51, 53, 67–68
Saw-whet owl, 84, 168
Sawyer beetle, 197
Scarborough Bluffs, 16, 65
Scarlet tanager, 18
Scouring rush, 150
Sea kayaking. See Kayaking
Seal, bearded, 232
Second Marsh, 168–70, 171
Serena Gundy Park, 48
Serpent Mounds Park, 108–9
Serpent River Band, 239–41
Seton, Ernest Thompson, 158

Shagbark hickory, 142–43, 147
Sharp-shinned hawk, 22
Shaw Woods, 209–10, 211
Ship Sands Island, 234
Showy lady's slipper, 56, 170
Silent Lake, 103, 220
Silent Lake Prov. Park, 219–21
Silver Islet, 198–99
Simcoe, Elizabeth, 15
Skink, five-lined, 37, 68, 123–25, 144
Skunk, 192
Skunk cabbage, 130
Slate Islands, 237–38
Sleeping Giant Prov. Park, 28, 191, 196–99
Smoothwater Outfitters, 211
Snakes, field guide, 91
Snake watching
    on Flowerpot Island, 113
    near Grand Bend, 68
    on Hill Island, 144
    at Landon Bay, 11
    at Long Point, 72
    at Point Pelee, 37
    in Toronto, 156, 162
Snapping turtle, 37, 64–66, 140
Snow goose, 233
Snowshoeing, 69, 152
Snowy owl, 83, 84–85, 255
Solace Prov. Park, 211
Southern cloudy wing butterfly, 51
Sparrow Lake, 24
Sparrows, 26, 51
Spotted turtle, 37
Spring beauty, 45, 46–47
Spring peeper, 90–91
Spring water, 227
Spruce, 208, 209, 244
Squirrels, 68, 213, 215, 222
Starflower, 197
Stony Lake, 13, 15
Striped coralroot, 55–56
Stump puffball, 210
Sturgeon, 148
Sumac, staghorn, 218, 219, 223, 240
Sundew, 59

Sunset Country Travel Association, 19
Superior Ecoventures, 236, 238
Swallow, bank, 156
Swallowtail butterfly, 37
Swamps, 168, 213, 245
Swamp white oak, 212
Swans, 36, 71, 149, 150–52, 169
Swimming, 24, 38, 55, 81, 145, 244
Sycamore, 156, 212

Tamarack, 71, 231
Task Force to Bring Back the Don, 160, 161
Temagami, 207–10
Temagami Island, 209
Terns, 19, 152, 156, 162
Thessalon, 207
Thimbleberry, 197
Thousand Islands, 11, 141–44
Three Sisters Islands, 18
Thunder Bay, 25–28, 95, 196
Thunder Cape Bird Observatory, 198
Tidewater Prov. Park, 232
Timmins, 109
Toads, 150, 210
Tobermory, 113
Tobermory Chamber of Commerce, 57
Tobogganing, 69
Todmorden Mills, 161
Tommy Thompson Park, 83, 127, 162–63,
    164, 195
Toronto, 16, 45–49, 53, 65, 83, 127, 161,
    162–63, 164, 172, 195, 212
Toronto Field Naturalists, 48
Tours. See Boat tours; Canoe trips
Traill, Catharine Parr, 46
Trails, long-distance hiking, 249–52
Train trips, 227, 231–34
Trans Canada Trail System, 251–52
Trillium, 45, 47, 156
Trilobites, 95–96, 105
Trout, 23, 147, 148
Trout lily, 45, 46, 156
Trumpeter swan, 149, 150–52
Tufted titmouse, 51
Tulip tree, 37, 69, 71, 213, 214, 222, 223

Tundra swan, 36, 71
Turkey vulture, 33–34, 111
Turkey, wild, 144
Turtle watching
    near Combermere, 140
    near Hamilton, 167
    at Landon Bay, 11
    at Long Point, 72
    near Midland, 149
    near Ottawa, 60
    at Point Pelee, 37
    in Prince Edward County, 64
    on St. Lawrence Islands, 144
    in Toronto, 156
Twinflower, 197, 237, 243
Two Bay Enterprises, 234

Underwater observation, 136
University of Guelph, 82, 85
Urquhart Butterfly Garden, 126

Violets, 47–48, 156
Vireos, 213
Virginia creeper, 223
Voyageur Trail, 252

Wabikimi Prov. Park, 243–46
Walking fern, 130
Walleye, 244
Wanapitei, Camp, 211
Warblers, 25–27, 28, 36–37, 38, 68, 121,
    130, 143, 155, 162, 169, 246
Waterfalls, 5, 95, 106, 111, 222
Waterfowl Festival, 74
Waterfront Regeneration Trust, 171
Weasels, 186, 198
Western meadowlark, 18
Westport, 251
Wetlands, 168
    Algonquin Prov. Park, 60, 177
    Big Creek Marsh Nat. Wildlife Area, 23, 72
    Chester Marsh, 160
    Conroy's Marsh, 138–40
    Cootes Paradise, 112, 165–67
    Hill Island Marsh, 144

H.N. Crossley Nature Reserve, 60
Lower Rouge Marsh, 156
Luther Marsh Wildlife Management Area,
    59, 60, 146–47, 148
Lynde Shores Conservation Area, 29, 32
Mer Bleue Conservation Area, 60
Petroglyphs Prov. Park, 103
Point Pelee Nat. Park, 37
Sleeping Giant Prov. Park, 197
Wye Marsh, 149–52
Whale, beluga, 232
Wheatley Prov. Park, 38
Wheelchair accessible destinations, 35, 54,
    69, 145, 169
Whetung Gallery, 187
Whimbrel, 234
Whitby, 29–30
White Bear Forest, 207–8
White-breasted nuthatch, 30
Whitefish Lake, 28
White-tailed jackrabbit, 18
White-throated sparrow, 26
Widgeon, 152
Wildflowers, 45–49, 51, 53, 55–57, 63,
    68, 113, 130, 142, 156, 170, 197,
    222, 245
    field guides, 48, 57
Wild ginger, 45, 223
Wildlife areas. See also Conservation areas;
    Nature reserves; Parks
    Big Creek Marsh Nat. Wildlife Area, 72
    Luther Marsh Wildlife Management Area,
        59, 60, 146–47
    McLaughlin Bay Wildlife Reserve, 170–71
    Rocklyn Creek Management Area, 111–12
    Wye Marsh Wildlife Centre, 149–52
Wildlife sanctuaries, 190, 191–92

Wildlife viewing, guidelines for, 2
Wild plants, recipes using, 2, 219, 241
Wild rose, 63, 233
Wild turkey, 144
Wild Waters Wilderness Tours, 244, 246
Willow, 170
Wilmot Orchards, 21, 119
Wilson's phalarope, 147
Windsor, 50–52
Windsor, Essex County and Pelee Island
    Convention and Visitors Bureau, 24
Windy Lake Prov. Park, 119
Winery tours, 37
Winter camping, 69, 220
Wintergreen, 245
Witch hazel, 130
Wolf howls, 79–81, 203
Wolves, 27, 79–80, 192, 198, 200–3
Wood duck, 152, 155, 166
Woodpeckers, 30, 51, 68, 143, 208, 213, 226
Wren, Carolina, 38
Wye Marsh Wildlife Centre, 149–52

Yarrow, 240
Yellow-bellied sapsucker, 213
Yellow-breasted chat, 38, 51
Yellow-headed blackbird, 18, 71
Yellow lady's slipper, 45, 56
Yellowleg, 170
Yellow mandarin lily, 130
Yellow oak. See Chinquapin oak
Yellow-spotted salamander, 144
York–Durham Heritage Railway, 227
York River, 138
Yurt, 220

Zebra mussels, 73